Virginia
Fishing
Guide

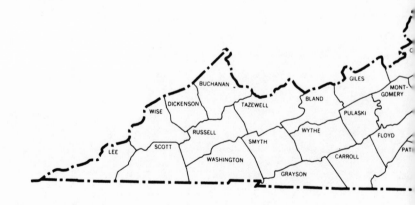

BOB GOOCH

Virginia
Fishing Guide

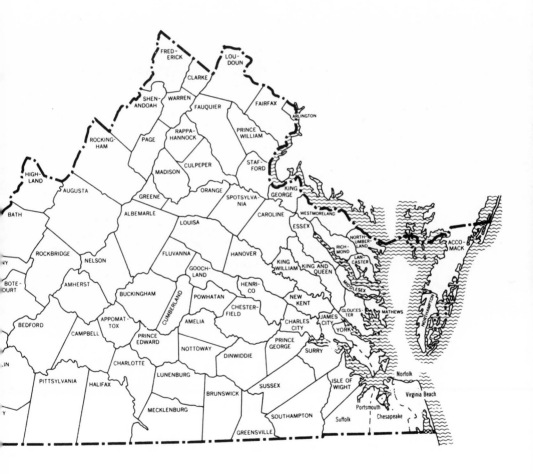

University Press of Virginia———Charlottesville

THE UNIVERSITY PRESS OF VIRGINIA
Copyright © 1988 by the Rector and Visitors
of the University of Virginia

First published 1988

Library of Congress Cataloging-in-Publication Data

Gooch, Bob, 1919–
    Virginia fishing guide.

    Includes index.
    1. Fishing—Virginia—Guide-books. I. Title.
SH557.G66   1988   799.1′09755   87–18906
ISBN 0–8139–1141–9 (pbk.)

Printed in the United States of America

CONTENTS

ACKNOWLEDGMENTS

My special thanks go to the professional staffs of the Department of Game and Inland Fisheries, the Virginia Institute of Marine Science, and the Virginia Marine Resources Commission. Specifically, I want to mention Executive Director Richard H. Cross, Jr., Deputy Executive Director John P. Randolph, Fish Division Chief Jack M. Hoffman, Assistant Chief William E. Neal, Supervising Fishery Biologists J. W. Kauffman, M. D. Norman, D. K. Whitehurst, and R. E. Wollitz, and Fishery Biologists L. O. Mohn, C. A. Sledd, P. P. Smith, and E. L. Steinkoenig—all of the Department of Game and Inland Fisheries. My thanks also go to Jon A. Lucy, Marine Recreation Specialist of the Virginia Institute of Marine Science, and to Robert D. Craft, Finance Officer of the Virginia Marine Resources Commission.

The advice and counsel of these professional fishery managers proved invaluable.

Virginia
Fishing
Guide

INTRODUCTION

The river we now call the James was a rich striped-bass fishery when Captain John Smith ventured ashore on Jamestown Island almost four centuries ago. Herring and shad also made their annual spawning runs up the mighty river, creating a bonanza from which the Indians reaped a tasty harvest. Down the river a few miles was a big estuary now known as the Chesapeake Bay, with its bluefish, cobia, croakers, flounders, gray trout, spot, and other fish of the briny waters. Inland waters produced such native fish as brook trout, catfish, largemouth bass, rock bass, and walleyes. The walleye, however, was not then known to the natives of what is now eastern Virginia.

The region was rich in rivers and streams in Captain John Smith's day, but lakes and ponds were virtually nonexistent.

There was what we now know as Lake Drummond in the deep swamp and to the west in the high mountains was a sparkling body of water we now call Mountain Lake. There were beaver ponds, of course, and possibly a few small mountain lakes plus a few freshwater ponds along the coast, but nothing of significance.

Eventually, millponds added a rich dimension to fishing, and shallow ice ponds, from which the early settlers filled their ice-houses, provided new habitat for the colorful little sunfish. Chain pickerel and crappie became abundant in the millponds. It was not, however, until the twentieth century that the farm pond and the proliferation of flood-control and hydroelectric lakes added thousands of acres of new fishing water for the Virginia angler.

Soon after the turn of the century modern fishery management began to slowly evolve. Private interests had already brought a few fish from the Old World, popular ones such as the brown trout and questionable ones such as the German carp. Eventually, rainbow trout were introduced from the western United States, and smallmouth bass were moved across the mountains to fast-flowing rivers such as the upper James and the Shenandoah.

Modern fishery management came on strong after World War II, and today Virginia anglers enjoy such introduced species as muskies and northern pike. Walleyes have joined the smallmouth bass in eastern waters, and landlocked striped bass have become one of the true trophies of Virginia's fresh waters. The postwar years also saw the development of the modern offshore fishing yacht and the discovery of a rich saltwater fishery off the Virginia coast where the waters of the Gulf Stream and the Labrador Current mix along the outer edge of the continental shelf. That means such blue-water battlers as bonito, dolphin, marlin, and wahoo.

Fishing was never better in Virginia than it is today.

Fishery management at the professional level anglers have come to expect today has made major strides over the last few decades. Officially, however, it began in 1875, when the Commission of Fisheries was established. That body's early efforts were apparently more or less limited to recommendations as to the stocking of streams, the building of fish ladders, and the like. It had no law enforcement responsibilities. What enforcement there was apparently was carried out at the local level by county wardens. It is interesting to note that the early commission seemed to be as much or even more involved with freshwater fishing as it was with saltwater, its only area of responsibility today.

Two decades after its birth the name of the commission was changed to Board of Fisheries, but then in 1907 it again became the Commission of Fisheries.

Modern fishery management got its start in 1916, when the old Department of Game and Inland Fisheries came into being under the Commission of Fisheries. The department's responsibilities included the management of wildlife as well as fish resources.

Ten years later, following a period of much debate, the department was divorced from the Commission of Fisheries, and the Commission of Game and Inland Fisheries was established. At that point, freshwater and saltwater fishery management was separated, with the Commission of Fisheries assuming responsibility for the briny waters and the new Commission of Game and Inland Fisheries limiting its efforts to freshwater fish.

Ever since the Commission of Game and Inland Fisheries was established on July 1, 1926, responsibility for it has been delegated to a body of commissioners appointed by the governor. It is an independently financed agency, its only income being from the sale of hunting and fishing licenses and from excise taxes raised at the federal level under the Dingle-Johnson, Pittman-Robertson, and Wallop-Breaux acts. The federal taxes are levied on the sale of boating, fishing, and hunting equipment, and the revenues so generated are distributed among the states. In recent years the commission has been given the responsibility for the management of nongame species, a program financed solely by donations from interested private citizens. As of July 1, 1987, the name of the Commission of Game and In-land Fisheries was changed back to the Department of Game and Inland Fisheries, its present name.

The Commission of Fisheries, on the other hand, was, and still is, financed from the general fund. Subsequent to the sepa-ration of the two agencies, the name of the Commission of Fish-eries was changed to the Marine Resources Commission, and today it is involved primarily with the enforcement of commer-cial fishing regulations.

Though the old Commission of Fisheries apparently carried on very limited research and fishery management in its early days, serious management of saltwater or marine fish did not begin until 1930, when the General Assembly directed the state health commissioner and the fisheries commissioner to join forces and establish a marine fisheries laboratory. Subsequently, a small laboratory was established in Newport News, but it was abandoned in 1932 because of the lack of funds.

While there was some research at the federal level between 1932 and 1940, the 1940 session of the General Assembly—at the urging of the Commission of Fisheries and the biology de-partment of the College of William and Mary—authorized the two institutions to develop the Virginia Fisheries Laboratory. Laboratories were established at the college, in Yorktown, and later at Gloucester Point. The Virginia Fisheries Laboratory later assumed its present name of Virginia Institute of Marine Science (VIMS), and today the VIMS is the School of Marine Science of The College of William and Mary.

Currently, the Marine Resources Commission is charged with the enforcement of saltwater fishing regulations, while the Virginia Institute of Marine Science is responsible for research and management recommendations. Both are financed from the general fund.

Anglers themselves, as individuals and through their orga-nizations such as Trout Unlimited, the Virginia Angler's Club, the Virginia B.A.S.S. Federation, the Virginia chapter of the Izaak Walton League, the Virginia Wildlife Federation, and others, have made substantial contributions to modern fishery management. Secure in their roles as private citizens, they are often able to exert pressure for needed changes when professional fishery managers cannot.

By law, fish are the property of the state or federal government. The authority of the state ends 3 miles offshore, and the federal government, through the Atlantic States Marine Resources Commission, assumes jurisdiction from that point to 200 miles out. Beyond the 200-mile limit the ocean waters become international.

Fish become the property of the angler once they are caught by legal means. Generally, this means being taken on a fishing rod, reel, and line. Although a landing net used as an aid in landing hooked fish and, in some instances, dipnetting are legal, netting is generally limited to commercial fishing. In some waters gigging, grabbing, seining, snagging, and snaring are permitted, but such methods are limited. The current *Virginia Fishing Regulations* should be consulted before engaging in such methods. Trot lines or set poles to take nongame fish are generally legal, and carp and gar may be taken with the bow and arrow. The emphasis here will be on the traditional methods of fishing with rod and reel or cane pole.

Generally, an angler needs one or more fishing licenses or permits. Exceptions include residents under sixteen years of age or sixty-five and over, landowners and their families when fishing waters on their own property, tenants if they have the written permission of the landowner, guests fishing individually owned private ponds, and nonresidents under twelve years of age.

Depending upon the kind of fishing the angler is interested in, he may need one or more of the following licenses:

County or city resident to fish in county or city of residence
State resident to fish only
Nonresident to fish only
Resident or nonresident to fish for five consecutive days in private waters or in public waters not stocked with trout
State and country resident to fish in designated trout waters—required in addition to regular fishing license
Nonresident to fish in designated trout waters—required in addition to regular nonresident fishing license

National forest permit to fish, hunt, and trap in national forests—required in addition to other licenses

County dip net to take herring, mullet, and shad

With the exception of county dip-net permits, all licenses and permits are sold through clerks of circuit courts in most counties, or through license agencies such as tackle shops and sporting-goods stores. County dip-net permits are usually available through clerks of circuit courts in the counties in which they are required.

A license is not required for fishing the salt waters of Virginia, though there is strong sentiment for such a license to produce funds for saltwater fishery management.

Reciprocal agreements between the Department of Game and Inland Fisheries and the appropriate agencies in Maryland and North Carolina enable properly licensed Virginia anglers to fish the *fresh* waters of the Potomac River and the entire waters of Buggs Island and Gaston lakes that straddle the Virginia–North Carolina line. The Potomac River is owned by the state of Maryland, and a Maryland saltwater license is required for fishing the *salt* waters of the river.

Fishing regulations in Virginia are not complex. Generally there are no closed seasons. Exceptions include the trout season, which is closed from an hour after sunset on February 1 to the third Saturday in March, and the season on striped bass in the Chesapeake Bay and its tributaries, which is closed from December 1 through May 31. There are also special seasons on certain trout waters, and the *Virginia Fishing Regulations* should be consulted before fishing these waters. The special Shenandoah National Park trout season, for example, closes October 15.

Bass, muskies, northern pike, pickerel, striped bass, trout, and walleye are generally subject to creel and size limits. Here again, the *Virginia Fishing Regulations* should be consulted.

Except for a size limit on flounder and a closed season, creel limit, and size limit on striped bass, there are very few regulations on saltwater fishing in Virginia.

Chain pickerel, landlocked striped bass, muskellunge, northern pike, trout, walleye, white bass, and various members of the big sunfish family including bluegills, crappie, largemouth bass, rock bass, smallmouth bass, and spotted bass are considered game fish in Virginia. All other freshwater fish are considered nongame fish. There is, however, no such classification of salt-water fish.

Since fishing guides are not licensed in Virginia, there is no central listing of them, but the newcomer to angling can learn much from a good guide or boat captain. Those most active in the field are listed in Appendix H. They offer an excellent intro-duction to fishing in Virginia.

Rivers and Streams, a Valuable Resource

Virginia's intricate system of rivers and streams is one of her most valuable recreational resources, not only for fishing, but also for boating, canoeing, hunting, swimming, and other outdoor activities. How much they are used and for what kinds of fishing depends much upon their size, but just about every stream from the tiny trickles high in the Allegheny Mountains to the broad tidal rivers such as the Rappahannock and York offer fishing of some kind. At the highest elevations the catch may be a brightly colored little brookie, but the broad waters at the mouth of the James River might turn up a giant striped bass of thirty pounds or more. Both freshwater and saltwater species fin the state's rivers and streams.

Most of Virginia's streams form well within the state; they then flow to just about every other point of the compass. The famous Shenandoah, for example, flows north to the Potomac River, while not far away the Cowpasture and Jackson gather their waters to flow south to form the headwaters of the historic James. The James flows east to the Chesapeake Bay. Farther east the Blackwater, Meherrin, and Nottoway rivers spring from the fertile soil of Southside Virginia to flow south into North Carolina to form the Chowan River and eventually empty into Albemarle Sound. The picturesque Southwest Virginia rivers, however, flow generally west—the Clinch, Powell, and Holston rivers into Tennessee, the Pound northwest to join the Russell Fork and then west into Kentucky, and the New River north into West Virginia, where it eventually joins the Kanawha River to head due west through the Mountain State. The Roanoke, though it forms west of the city of Roanoke, cuts a southwesterly course across Southside Virginia to flow into North Carolina and eventually into Albemarle Sound.

Rivers forming along the eastern slopes of the Allegheny Mountains eventually enter the Atlantic Ocean by way of the Chesapeake Bay or North Carolina's Albemarle Sound, but those to the southwest are a part of the Mississippi River drainage system, flowing generally west to eventually enter the Gulf of Mexico by way of the Mississippi River.

Whether a stream is a public waterway or the property of the riparian landowners is often a moot question. Unfortunately, its status in this regard determines whether it is available to the angling public.

Generally, streams that have been used for public transportation at some point in our history are considered public waters. So are those that flow through public land such as national or state forests. In some cases the extent of continued public use is the criterion.

The streams discussed in this chapter are, in the opinion of the Department of Game and Inland Fisheries, public waters—

Rivers and Streams

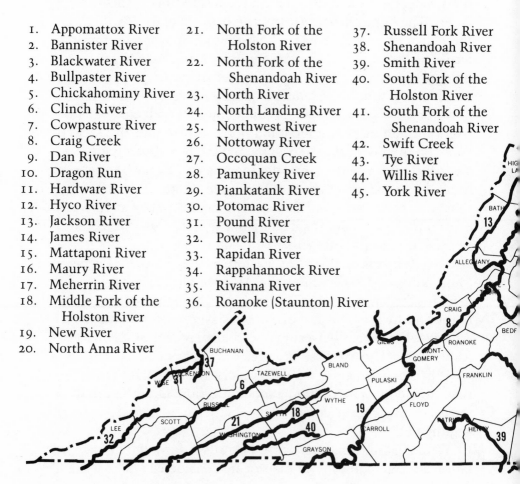

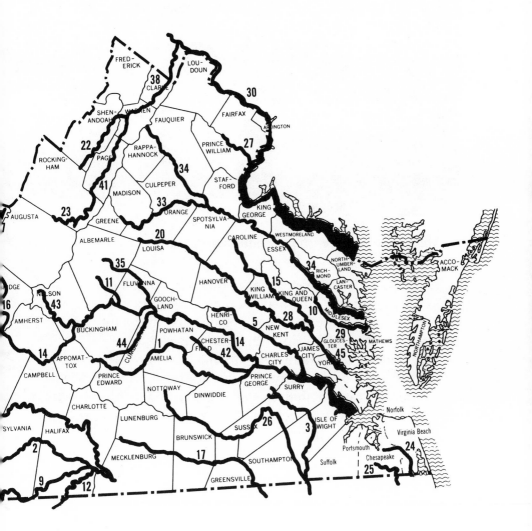

Bass fishermen on the Shenandoah River.

at least in part. The Department points out, however, that their list is not considered conclusive. Other streams may also be public. The list is on the conservative side, and many fine fishing waters are not listed, because their status is cloudy.

Just about every county in Virginia has some stretches of public streams, but generally their tributaries are considered private. Many of those tributaries offer some fine fishing, fishing well worth the effort of seeking out the landowners and getting permission to fish.

More detail on the major public streams follows.

Appomattox River

The Appomattox River is a major tributary of the James River, but it is a slower stream, more likely to hold such popular fish as chain pickerel and largemouth bass than the smallmouth bass the upper James River is noted for. It is one of the few eastern streams that offers fishing for spotted or Kentucky bass. It enters the James River at Hopewell. Lake Chesdin, west of Petersburg, is a major impoundment on the river.

LOCATION: Formed by tiny streams in eastern Appomattox and western Prince Edward counties, it flows into Cumberland to form the boundaries between Amelia and Cumberland counties, Amelia and Chesterfield counties, Chesterfield and Dinwiddie counties, and Chesterfield and Prince George counties.

WATER: The current generally moves slowly, though there are a few mild riffles in its upper stretches. There is some white water at the fall line between Lake Chesdin and the mouth of the river, and the river just upstream from its confluence with the James is tidal.

CAMPING: There are developed campgrounds in Bear Creek State Park in Cumberland County, Holiday Lake State Park in Appomattox and Buckingham counties, and Pocahontas State Park in Chesterfield County.

ACCESS: The Department of Game and Inland Fisheries maintains a boat-launching ramp on Lake Chesdin, but otherwise there is only informal access such as public-road crossings and farm or logging roads, where the permission of the landowner is required.

FISH: Catfish, chain pickerel, crappie, eel, fallfish, gar, herring, largemouth and spotted bass, shad, striped bass, sucker, sunfish, walleye, white perch, and yellow perch.

TRIBUTARIES: Buffalo and Bush rivers; Briery, Cellar, Deep, Flat, Namozine, Nibbs, Sandy, Swift, and West creeks.

PUBLIC HIGHWAYS: U.S. Highway 15 in Prince Edward County to its mouth.

Bannister River

A major tributary of the Dan River, the Bannister is known mostly for its rough fish such as catfish, eels, and suckers. It forms the northern boundary of the White Oak Mountain Wildlife Management Area in Pittsylvania County.

LOCATION: Pittsylvania and Halifax counties.

WATER: The current is moderately fast, with mild riffles and numerous pools of slow water.

CAMPING: Camping in self-contained units is permitted in the White Oak Mountain Wildlife Management Area.

ACCESS: There is no formal access, but the wildlife management area can be used to launch canoes or small boats.

FISH: Carp, catfish, eels, sunfish, and a few largemouth bass.

TRIBUTARIES: Cherrystone, Elkhorn, Georges, Polecat, Sandy, Stinking, and Terrible creeks.

PUBLIC WATER: Only that stretch of the river adjacent to the White Oak Mountain Wildlife Management Area is public.

Blackwater River

The Blackwater is a typical cypress and tupelo-gum bordered river of the southeast, with dark acidic waters that give it its name. It is slow flowing and picturesque. Upriver the stream is completely covered by the forest canopy, but downstream it widens considerably. Runs of shad and other anadromous fish usually end at Franklin. There is a small dam just above Franklin.

LOCATION: The river forms in Prince George County, and it forms part of the boundary between Surry and Sussex counties, between Isle of Wight and Southampton counties, and between Southampton County and the city of Suffolk.

WATER: The water is acid stained and very slow flowing.

CAMPING: There are no public camping facilities.

ACCESS: The Department of Game and Inland Fisheries maintains boat-launching ramps at Blackwater Bridge in Southampton County and at Joyners Bridge in Isle of Wight County.

TRIBUTARIES: Cypress, Mill, Otterdam, Seacock, Second, and Warwick swamps.

FISH: Bowfin, catfish, chain pickerel, crappie, gar, herring, largemouth bass, redfin pickerel, shad, and sunfish.

Bullpasture River

The Bullpasture is a fast mountain stream and a major tributary of the Cowpasture River. It flows into the Cowpasture at Williamsville. Well known as one of the top trout streams in Virginia, it also offers fishing for rock bass and smallmouth bass.

LOCATION: The Bullpasture rises in West Virginia and flows through Bath and Highland counties.

WATER: The river is a fast mountain stream that is best fished by wading, though a canoe can be used on its lower stretches. Downstream, however, there are some rapids rated classes 3, 4, and 5.

CAMPING: There is primitive camping in self-contained vehicles in the Highland Wildlife Management Area.

ACCESS: There is no formal access, but canoes can be launched in the national forest and the wildlife management area.

FISH: Brook, brown, and rainbow trout, chain pickerel, smallmouth bass, suckers, and sunfish.

TRIBUTARIES: Crab and Davis Runs.

PUBLIC WATER: Only that section of stream in the George Washington National Forest and the Highland Wildlife Management Area is public.

Chickahominy River

The Chickahominy is an acid-stained, cypress-bordered stream that forms in Henrico County just north of Richmond to become a short, but major, tributary of the James River. It enters the James a few miles upstream from the Chippokes Plantation State Park. The Chickahominy Lake impounds its lower stretches.

LOCATION: Near its headwaters the river forms part of the boundary between Hanover and Henrico counties, between Henrico and New Kent counties, between Charles City and New Kent counties, and between Charles City and James City counties.

CAMPING: Camping is allowed only in self-contained vehicles in the Chickahominy Wildlife Management Area.

ACCESS: The Department of Game and Inland Fisheries maintains a boat-launching ramp on Morris Creek in Charles City County.

FISH: Bowfin, catfish, chain pickerel, crappie, gar, herring, largemouth bass, shad, striped bass, sunfish, white perch, and yellow perch.

TRIBUTARIES: Beaverdam, Gordon, Grassy Swamp, Lickinghole, Little, Morris, Schimino, and Yarmouth creeks; Collin River; Toe Ink Swamp; and Rumley Marsh.

PUBLIC WATER: U.S. Highway 60 to the mouth of the river.

Clinch River

The Clinch is one of the major rivers in Southwest Virginia, and like others there, it flows southwest into Tennessee and eventually into the Mississippi River. It is one of the few Virginia streams to offer sauger fishing, and it has also produced at least one state-record muskie.

LOCATION: The river forms in Tazewell County and flows through Russell and Scott counties, forming part of the boundary between Russell and Wise counties.

WATER: The stream is generally deep and wide, with a good mixture of fast water and long, deep pools.

CAMPING: There is primitive camping in the Jefferson National Forest, and there is a developed campground in the Clinch Mountain Wildlife Management Area.

ACCESS: The Department of Game and Inland Fisheries maintains boat-launching ramps at Blackford Bridge, Carterton, Cleveland Park, Clinch Port, Nashes Ford, and Puckett's Hole in Russell County; at Craft Mill, Dungannon, and State Line in Scott County; and at St. Paul in Wise County.

FISH: Catfish, crappie, largemouth bass, muskie, sauger, smallmouth bass, sunfish, walleye, and white bass.

TRIBUTARIES: Big, Big Cedar, Chaney, Copper, Cove, Indian, Lewis, Lick, Mill, Mudlick, Pine, Stock, Valley, and Weaver creeks; Bull, Guest, and Little rivers; Drakes, Meade, and Pounding Mill branches; and South Fork.

PUBLIC WATER: From Carbo in Russell County to the Tennessee line.

Cowpasture River

The Cowpasture gathers its waters in Bath and Highland counties and flows south to join forces with the Jackson River and form the headwaters of the James River at Iron Gate. It is one of the largest rivers in the state to be considered private water, except where it flows through public land, a classification that is constantly being challenged.

LOCATION: Allegheny and Bath counties.

WATER: The Cowpasture is a fast mountain stream with numerous long, quiet pools. There is some classes 2 and 3 water near its headwaters and again downstream near its confluence with the Jackson River.

CAMPING: There is primitive camping in the George Washington National Forest and a developed campground in Douthat State Park.

ACCESS: There is no public access except at public road crossings and on the lands of the national forest.

FISH: Catfish, chain pickerel, muskie, smallmouth bass, suckers, and sunfish.

TRIBUTARIES: Mill, Simpson, and South Fork Pad creeks; Dry and Spring runs; Bullpasture River; and Shaw Fork.

PUBLIC WATER: From U.S. Highway 60 bridge to Iron Gate.

Craig Creek

Craig Creek is a reasonably fast mountain stream that forms in the Brush Mountain region of Montgomery County to flow north and enter the James River near Eagle Rock.

LOCATION: Botetourt, Craig, and Montgomery counties.

WATER: Craig Creek is a fast, mountain stream with much classes 1 and 2 water, but also many long, deep pools.

CAMPING: There is primitive camping in the Jefferson National Forest.

ACCESS: There is no formal public access, but some of the stream is in the national forest, where canoes or light boats can be launched.

FISH: Chain pickerel, smallmouth bass, suckers, sunfish, and trout.

TRIBUTARIES: Barbours, Johns, Meadow, Mill, and Trout creeks; Lick Branch; and Broad Run.

PUBLIC WATER: That part of the stream that flows through the Jefferson National Forest is public water.

Dan River

The Dan River is one of the major feeder streams for Buggs Island Lake, and it is best known for its spawning runs of land-locked striped bass.

LOCATION: Henry, Pittsylvania, and Halifax counties

WATER: The Dan is a reasonably fast stream near its headwaters, but it calms down considerably in the lower stretches prior to entering Buggs Island Lake.

CAMPING: The nearest developed campground is in the Staunton River State Park near the headwaters of Buggs Island Lake.

ACCESS: The Department of Game and Inland Fisheries maintains boat-launching ramps at City Farm in Danville and at Hyco and South Boston in Halifax County.

FISH: Carp, catfish, eel, striped bass, suckers, sunfish, and white bass.

TRIBUTARIES: Ballous, Big Toby, Birch, Brandon, Cane, Double, Lawsons, McGuffs, Sandy, Storys, and Winns creeks; Mountain, North Mayo, Sandy, Smith, and South Mayo rivers.

PUBLIC WATER: From Danville to Halifax County line.

Dragon Run

Dragon Run is a short stream in the coastal plains and is noted for its wilderness setting. It offers good pickerel fishing, and canoeists like to explore its placid waters. It flows into the Piankatank River.

LOCATION: Dragon Run forms the boundary between King and Queen and Middlesex counties and between Middlesex and Gloucester counties.

WATER: The Dragon flows slowly and offers plenty of quiet water for fishing.

CAMPING: There are no public campgrounds.

ACCESS: There is no formal public access other than public road crossings. The permission of the landowner is needed to use farm or private roads.

FISH: Catfish, chain pickerel, largemouth bass, striped bass, sunfish, white perch, and yellow perch.

TRIBUTARIES: Briery, Church, Exol, and Holmes swamps.

PUBLIC WATERS: From U.S. Highway 17 in Middlesex County to the mouth of the stream.

Hardware River

The Hardware River is a small stream forming in the Blue Ridge foothills of Albermarle County and flowing through Fluvanna County to enter the James River.

LOCATION: Albermarle and Fluvanna counties.

WATER: The Hardware is a moderately fast stream most suitable for wading. It offers mild riffles and many long, quiet pools.

CAMPING: Camping in self-contained vehicles is allowed in the Hardware River Wildlife Management Area.

ACCESS: The Department of Game and Inland Fisheries boat-launching ramp on the James River in the Hardware Wildlife Management Area provides access to the river.

FISH: Catfish, chain pickerel, largemouth bass, smallmouth bass, suckers, and sunfish.

TRIBUTARIES: The North and South forks of the Hardware River.

PUBLIC WATER: Only that section of the stream within the Hardware River Wildlife Management Area is considered public.

Hyco River

The Hyco is a short river that forms in North Carolina to flow into Buggs Island Lake.

LOCATION: Halifax County.

WATER: The Virginia section of the Hyco River is slow flowing.

CAMPING: There is a developed campground in the Staunton River State Park near the headwaters of Buggs Island Lake.

ACCESS: The Department of Game and Inland Fisheries maintains a boat-launching ramp at Hyco in Halifax County.

TRIBUTARIES: Big Bluewing and Coleman creeks.

FISH: Carp, catfish, chain pickerel, crappie, largemouth bass, striped bass, suckers, sunfish, and white bass.

PUBLIC WATER: That portion of the stream that is flooded by Buggs Island Lake is public.

Jackson River

The Jackson River is the twin of the Cowpasture, and together they form the headwaters of the James River. The river also forms Lake Moomaw, and the ownership of its waters downstream from the dam have been the subject of much controversary. The potential for an excellent tailwaters trout fishery here has been blunted by the landowners' contention that the river is privately owned, though it has been declared navigable.

LOCATION: Highland, Bath, and Allegheny counties.

WATER: The Jackson is a fast mountain stream, but offering many stretches of long, quiet pools where the fishing is good for bass, pickerel, and sunfish. Much of the fast water is classified as classes 2 and 3.

CAMPING: There is primitive camping in the George Washington National Forest, and there are developed campgrounds on Lake Moomaw.

ACCESS: There are public boat-launching ramps on Lake Moomaw and several undeveloped sites on the river below the lake.

FISH: Catfish, chain pickerel, smallmouth bass, suckers, sunfish, and trout.

TRIBUTARIES: Back, Dunlap, Jackson, Little Back, Ogle, Potts, and Wilson creeks; Bolar, Harmon, Muddy, and Pounding Mill runs.

PUBLIC WATERS: Westvaco Dam at Covington to the mouth of the stream at Iron Gate, stretches of the stream in the Gathright Wildlife Management Area, and in the George Washington National Forest. Downstream from Lake Moomaw the stream has been declared navigable, but its status remains in doubt.

James River

The James River is known as Virginia's finest smallmouth bass stream, and it is also one of the top muskie streams. Below the fall line in Richmond it offers excellent fishing for largemouth bass and crappie. Shad and herring make spawning runs in the spring, and as the water becomes briny just before it enters the Chesapeake Bay, it offers fishing for croakers, spot, and other popular saltwater fish.

LOCATION: Forming at Iron Gate, the James flows through Botetourt County, a section of Rockbridge, and forms the boundary between Amherst and Bedford counties, Amherst and Campbell counties, Amherst and Appomattox counties, Appomattox and Nelson counties, Buckingham and Nelson counties, Buckingham and Albemarle counties, Buckingham and Fluvanna counties, Cumberland and Fluvanna counties, Cumberland and Goochland counties, Goochland and Powhatan counties, and Chesterfield and Henrico counties—both above and below Richmond. Continuing downstream, it forms the boundary between Charles City and Chesterfield counties, Charles City and Prince George counties, Charles City and Surry counties, James City and Surry counties, and Isle of Wight County and the city of Newport News.

WATER: West of Richmond the James River is a fast stream with plenty of white water, but also long stretches of quiet water. Many of the rapids are classed as 2 or 3, and near its headwaters there is at least one class-4 rapids. There are also a number of low dams on the river, some of which have been breached. From Richmond to its mouth, the James is a broad tidal stream.

CAMPING: There is primitive camping in the George Washington and Jefferson national forests and on Smith Island, owned by Westvaco. Camping in self-contained vehicles is permitted in the Hardware River and James River wildlife management areas.

ACCESS: The James is one of the most accessible rivers in Virginia, with the Department of Game and Inland Fisheries maintaining boat-launching ramps at Beaumont, Bent Creek, Buchanan, Cartersville, Columbia, Deep Bottom, Denbigh, Dutch Gap, Glasgow, Hardware River, Horseshoe Bend, Howardsville, Huguenot Bridge, Lawnes Creek, Midway, Monocan Park, Morris Creek, Poney Pasture Park, Scottsville, Springwood, Tyler's Beach, Watkins, West View, and Wingina.

FISH: Black drum, bluefish, bowfin, carp, catfish, chain pickerel, crappie, croaker, eel, flounder, gar, gray trout, herring, largemouth bass, muskie, shad, smallmouth bass, striped bass, suckers, sunfish, walleye, white perch, and yellow perch.

TRIBUTARIES: Bear Garden, Beaver, Beaverdam, Bent, Buffalo, Byrd, Catawba, Cedar, Chippoakes, Craig, David, Deep, Falling, Fine, Gray's, Harris, Hopper, Hughes, Hunting, Ivy, Janes, Lawnes, Looney Mill, Mill, Mohawk, North, Possum, Tuckahoe, Turkey Island, and Wreck Island creeks; Appomattox, Chickahominy, Cowpasture, Hardware, Jackson, Maury, Pagan, Pedlar, Rivanna, Rockfish, Slate, Tye, Willis, and Warwick rivers.

PUBLIC WATER: From Iron Gate in Allegheny County to its mouth.

Mattaponi River

The Mattaponi and Pamunkey rivers, like the Cowpasture and Jackson rivers in the west, are twins that join their waters at West Point to form the York, a broad tidal river. The Mattaponi is a relatively short river, subject to the tides in its lower stretches.

LOCATION: The Mattaponi forms in Caroline County, but then flows southeast to form the boundary between King and Queen and King William counties. It also forms part of the boundary between Caroline and King and Queen counties. Its headwaters are appropriately formed by the Mat, Po, and Ni rivers, which gather their waters in Spotsylvania County but join forces in Caroline County.

WATER: The Mattaponi is a relatively fast-flowing stream, broad and deep, and with little or no riffles.

CAMPING: Camping in self-contained vehicles is allowed on the Fort A. P. Hill Military Reservation.

ACCESS: The Department of Game and Inland Fisheries maintains boat-launching ramps at Aylett, Melrose, Waterfence, and West Point.

FISH: Catfish, chain pickerel, largemouth bass, shad, striped bass, sunfish, white perch, and yellow perch.

TRIBUTARIES: Buckyard, Burnt Mill, Chapel Hill, Corbin, Courthouse, Herring, Maracossic, Market, Polecat, and Reedy creeks, Bull Swamp, and Gravel, Matta, Ni, Po, and South rivers.

PUBLIC WATER: From U.S. Highway 360 bridge to the mouth of the stream.

Maury River

The Maury is a fast mountain stream and a major tributary of the James River, offering much the same kind of fishing. It is a short stream, entering the James River at Glasglow.

LOCATION: Rockbridge County.

WATER: The Maury, an extremely fast stream at its source, calms considerably before it enters the James. The Goshen Pass section offers possibly the most exciting rapids in Virginia. A few are classed 4 to 5 and others 2 to 3.

CAMPING: There is primitive camping in the George Washington National Forest, and camping in self-contained units is permitted in the Little North Mountain–Goshen Wildlife Management Area.

ACCESS: There are no formal access points, but canoes or light boats can be launched in the Little North Mountain–Goshen Wildlife Management Area.

FISH: Carp, catfish, smallmouth bass, suckers, sunfish, and trout.

TRIBUTARIES: Buffalo, Hays, Irish, and Miller creeks; Bratton Run; and South River.

PUBLIC WATER: From Lexington to the mouth of the river and that section flowing through the Little North Mountain–Goshen Wildlife Management Area.

Meherrin River

The name of the Meherrin River was no doubt in some way derived from the hordes of herring that migrate up a number of Virginia rivers. It is one of the Southside Virginia streams that flow into North Carolina and eventually into Albemarle Sound. It is also home to Roanoke bass, a close relative of the rock bass so popular in western Virginia. The fish is a member of the big sunfish family.

LOCATION: While its origin is in Lunenburg County, the Middle and South forks of the Meherrin join forces on the Mecklenburg-Lunenburg county line to form the main stem and the boundary between the two counties. The North Fork enters the river a few miles downstream. The river crosses Brunswick and Greensville counties and serves as the boundary between Greensville and Southampton counties before entering North Carolina.

WATER: This is a slow, quiet river typical of those found in southeastern Virginia.

CAMPING: There are no public campgrounds.

ACCESS: Generally there is no public access, though a public boat-launching ramp on the Emporia Reservoir can be used to reach the river upstream from the small impoundment. Anglers use public road crossings and private roads where they can get permission.

FISH: Catfish, chain pickerel, herring, largemouth bass, shad, smallmouth bass, suckers, and sunfish.

TRIBUTARIES: Crooked, Flat Rock Fontaine, Genito, Great, Kettlestick, Mason, Mountain, Rattlesnake, Roses, Smith, Stony, Tarrara, Taylor, and Three creeks; Mill Swamp; and the North, South, and Middle forks of the Meherrin.

PUBLIC WATER: From Virginia Primary Route 49 in Lunenburg County to the North Carolina line.

Middle Fork of the Holston River

The Middle Fork of the Holston River forms near Rural Retreat in Wythe County and joins the South Fork to become one of the major feeder streams of South Holston Lake.

LOCATION: Wythe, Smyth, and Washington counties.

WATER: A reasonably fast mountain stream with many long, quiet pools.

CAMPING: There is primitive camping in the Jefferson National Forest, and there is a developed campground in Hungry Mother State Park.

ACCESS: There is no formal public access, but there are many public road crossings and private access where the permission of the landowner can be obtained. Upper stretches, though on private property, are designated trout waters open to public fishing.

FISH: Catfish, crappie, largemouth bass, smallmouth bass, suckers, sunfish, trout, and white bass.

TRIBUTARIES: Carlock, Staleys, and Walker creeks.

PUBLIC WATER: From Chilhowie to South Holston Lake.

New River

───────

The New River is possibly the oldest river in Virginia. It is unique in that it flows north in a region where most of the major rivers flow east or west. It rises in North Carolina and flows through Virginia to enter West Virginia. It is also the major feeder stream of Claytor Lake.

LOCATION: Grayson, Carroll, Wythe, Pulaski, and Giles counties; the river also forms part of the boundary between Pulaski and Montgomery counties.

WATER: While it has some stretches of fast water, much of the river is quiet, though the current moves at a good rate.

CAMPING: There is primitive camping in the Jefferson National Forest, and there is a developed campground in Claytor Lake State Park.

ACCESS: The Department of Game and Inland Fisheries maintains boat-launching ramps at Allisonia, Baywood Bridle Creek, Claytor Dam, Claytor Lake State Park, Dublin, Fries, Glen Lyn, Independence, Ivanhoe, Mouth of Wilson, Narrows, Oldtown, Riverside and White Thorne.

FISH: Catfish, crappie, largemouth bass, muskie, smallmouth bass, spotted bass, suckers, sunfish, walleye, and white bass.

TRIBUTARIES: Back, Big Island, Brush, Chestnut, Cripple, Crooked, Elk, Fox, Little Reed Island, Meadow, Mill, Peach Bottom, Reed, Shorts, Stony, Toms, Turkey Fork, Walker, and Wolf creeks; Dry, Slate, Staunton, and Wilson branches; and Little River.

PUBLIC WATER: The entire Virginia section of the river is public.

North Anna River

───────

The North Anna River, forming in Orange County, is the major feeder stream for Lake Anna. It flows into the Pamunkey River.

LOCATION: Rising in Orange County, the North Anna forms part of the boundary between Louisa and Orange counties, Louisa and Spotsylvania counties, Hanover and Spotsylvania counties, and Caroline and Hanover counties.

WATER: North Anna is a reasonably fast-flowing stream with mild riffles and many stretches of quiet water.

CAMPING: There are no developed campgrounds.

ACCESS: Except for public road crossings and private roads, the only access is the boat-launching ramp in Lake Anna State Park.

FISH: Catfish, chain pickerel, crappie, fallfish, largemouth bass, herring, shad, suckers, sunfish, white perch, and yellow perch.

TRIBUTARIES: Christopher, Clear, Duckinghole, Foremost, Gold Mine, Hickory, Northeast, and Pamunkey creeks; Pigeon and Ridge runs; and Little and Taylors Creek rivers.

PUBLIC WATER: Only that part of the river in Lake Anna.

North Fork of the Holston River

The North Fork is one of three forks of the Holston River. Because of mercury pollution from an old plant in Saltville, eating fish taken from the river is prohibited, but catch-and-release fishing is permitted.

LOCATION: Wythe, Smyth, and Washington counties.

WATER: The North Fork is a reasonably fast mountain and valley stream with some fast water, but a good deal of quiet water in long pools.

CAMPING: There is primitive camping in the Jefferson National Forest, and there are developed campgrounds in Hungry Mother State Park and in Washington County Park on South Holston Lake.

ACCESS: There is no formal access, but anglers use public road crossings and private access where permission can be obtained.

FISH: Catfish, crappie, largemouth bass, smallmouth bass, suckers, sunfish, trout, and white bass.

TRIBUTARIES: Big Laurel, Big Tumbling, Cove, Garrett, Greendale, Lick, and Possum creeks; and Wolf Run.

PUBLIC WATER: Only that in Clinch Mountain Wildlife Management Area.

North Fork of the Shenandoah River

The North and South Forks of the Shenandoah and the main stem make up the Shenandoah River system, well known for its smallmouth-bass fishing.

LOCATION: Rockingham, Shenandoah, and Warren counties.

WATER: The North Fork is a fast mountain stream with long stretches of relatively quiet water. The upstream section offers a good bit of white water, and downstream there are some class 2 and 3 rapids.

CAMPING: There is primitive camping in the George Washington National Forest, and there are developed campgrounds in the Shenandoah National Park.

ACCESS: The Department of Game and Inland Fisheries maintains boat-launching ramps at Chapman, Meems Bottom, and Riverton.

FISH: Carp, catfish, crappie, fallfish, largemouth bass, smallmouth bass, suckers, sunfish, and trout.

TRIBUTARIES: Cedar, Linville, Mill, Passage, Smith, and Stoney creeks; Crooked, Mill, and Sheep runs; Dry and Shoemaker rivers; and Meadow Brook.

PUBLIC WATER: From Timberville to Riverton and that part of the river in the George Washington National Forest.

North Landing River

The North Landing River doubles as the Intracoastal Waterway, connecting the Chesapeake Bay and Currituck Sound.

LOCATION: The cities of Chesapeake Bay and Virginia Beach.

WATER: While the river doubles as a waterway, it is a picturesque river, slow flowing, broad, crooked, and marshy.

CAMPING: There is a developed campground in Seashore State Park.

ACCESS: The Department of Game and Inland Fisheries maintains a boat-launching ramp at Great Bridge.

FISH: Catfish, chain pickerel, crappie, largemouth bass, sunfish, and white perch.

TRIBUTARIES: Several marshy creeks.

PUBLIC WATER: The entire river.

North River

The North River is one of the three major streams that form the headwaters of the South Fork of the Shenandoah River. They join forces at Port Republic, where the South Fork begins. The North River forms on the eastern slope of Shenandoah Mountain.

LOCATION: Augusta and Rockingham counties.

WATER: A fast stream in the mountains with plenty of white water and some class-4 rapids, the river slows to a more placid pace once it enters the Shenandoah Valley.

CAMPING: There is primitive camping in the George Washington National Forest.

ACCESS: There is no formal access, but the national forest provides access upstream, and downstream anglers use public road crossings or private access if they can get permission to do so.

FISH: Carp, catfish, crappie, largemouth bass, smallmouth bass, suckers, sunfish, and trout.

TRIBUTARIES: Dry, Little, and Middle rivers.

PUBLIC WATER: From the Bridgewater Dam to the mouth of the river and that section in the national forest.

Northwest River

The Northwest River, probably so named because it drains from the northwest, forms in the Great Dismal Swamp, and enters Currituck Sound in North Carolina. It is a short stream in a swampy setting characterized by cypress and tupelo gum. The waters are dark and acidic, and very narrow upstream. Downstream, it broadens considerably and there are several islands.

LOCATION: City of Chesapeake.

WATER: The water is dark and acidic, and it flows slowly.

CAMPING: There are no developed campgrounds other than tent camping in the Great Dismal Swamp National Wildlife Refuge.

ACCESS: There is no formal public access, but public roads bridge the river.

FISH: Bowfin, catfish, crappie, gar, largemouth bass, sunfish, and white perch.

TRIBUTARIES: There are no major tributaries, but a few marsh creeks.

PUBLIC WATER: The entire river is public.

Nottoway River

The Nottoway River, named for the Nottoway Indians who once lived along its shore, is one of the most popular fishing streams in the southeastern part of Virginia. It forms in Nottoway County, joins the Blackwater to create the Chowan just below the North Carolina line, and eventually enter Albemarle Sound.

LOCATION: The river leaves Nottoway County to form the boundary between that county and Brunswick County and between Nottoway and

Lunenburg counties. It also forms the boundary between Brunswick and Dinwiddie counties and Greensville and Dinwiddie counties and part of the boundary between Greensville and Sussex counties.

WATER: There is good white-water canoeing at the fall line, and the river is relatively fast near its headwaters. Downstream it flattens out and becomes calm, with many quiet stretches.

CAMPING: There is primitive camping in Prince Edward–Gallion State Forest and developed campgrounds in Goodwin Lake and Prince Edward state parks. Camping in self-contained vehicles is permitted in the Fort Pickett Military Reservation.

ACCESS: The Department of Game and Inland Fisheries maintains boat-launching ramps at Carey's, Hercules, Peters Bridge, and General Vaughan Bridge.

FISH: Bowfin, carp, catfish, chain pickerel, crappie, gar, largemouth bass, redfin pickerel, Roanoke bass, shad, smallmouth bass, suckers, sunfish, walleye, and white perch.

TRIBUTARIES: Beaverpond, Big Hounds, Birching, Buckskin, Crooked, Hunting Quarter, Popular Swamp, Raccoon, Rowanty, Sappony, Spring, Stony, Sturgeon, Three, Tommeheton, Turkey Egg, and Waqua creeks; Hurricane and Long branches; and Assamoosiac, Jones Hole, Nottoway, and Southwest swamps.

PUBLIC WATER: From Virginia Primary Highway 63 in Nottoway County to the North Carolina line.

Occoquan Creek

Occoquan Creek is a short stream that empties into the Potomac River. It is also a major feeder stream of Occoquan Lake.

LOCATION: The creek forms the boundary between Fairfax and Prince William counties.

WATER: There are a number of dams on Occoquan Creek, but there is some class-1 water upstream, and below Occoquan Lake there is some class 2 to 4 water at the fall line. The stream becomes tidal just before it enters the Potomac River.

CAMPING: There is a developed campground in Prince William Forest Park.

ACCESS: There are no formal public-access points, but anglers use public road crossings and private access where they can secure permission.

FISH: Bowfin, carp, catfish, crappie, gar, largemouth bass, striped bass, suckers, sunfish, white perch, and yellow perch.

TRIBUTARIES: Broad, Bull, Cedar, Kettle, Sandy, Stillwell, and Wolf runs.

PUBLIC WATER: From Virginia Primary Highway 123 to the mouth of the stream.

Pamunkey River

The Pamunkey is the twin of the Mattaponi River, and together they form the headwaters of the tidal York River. Its headwaters are formed by the confluence of the North and South Anna rivers near the Caroline-Hanover county line.

LOCATION: Together with the North Anna River, the Pamunkey forms the boundary between Caroline and Hanover counties; downstream it forms the boundaries between Hanover and King William counties and King William and New Kent counties.

WATER: A winding, slow stream with few riffles, it is relatively deep. It becomes tidal near its mouth.

CAMPING: There are no public campgrounds.

ACCESS: The Department of Game and Inland Fisheries maintains boat-launching ramps at Lester Manor and West Point.

FISH: Catfish, chain pickerel, crappie, fallfish, largemouth bass, shad, striped bass, suckers, sunfish, white perch, and yellow perch.

TRIBUTARIES: Black, Campbell, Cohoke, Crump, Harrison, Jacks, Matadequin, Totopotomy, and Webb creeks; Judy and St. Peters swamps; South Branch; and the North and South Anna rivers.

PUBLIC WATER: From the U.S. Highway 360 bridge to the mouth of the stream.

Piankatank River

The Piankatank River is the tidal extension of Dragon Run, a small estuary and a very short river that flows into the Chesapeake Bay.

LOCATION: The river forms part of the boundary between Gloucester and Middlesex counties and the entire boundary between Mathews and Middlesex counties.

WATER: A tidal estuary.

CAMPING: There are no public campgrounds.

ACCESS: The Department of Game and Inland Fisheries maintains a boat-launching ramp at Deep Point.

FISH: Catfish, chain pickerel, crappie, croaker, gar, gray trout, largemouth bass, spot, striped bass, sunfish, and white perch.

TRIBUTARIES: Carvers Creek and Dragon Run.

PUBLIC WATER: The entire river.

Potomac River

The Potomac River actually belongs to Maryland, but thanks to a reciprocal agreement between the Virginia Commission of Game and Inland Fisheries and the Maryland Department of Natural Resources, licensed Virginia anglers can fish the freshwater section of the river. They need a Maryland saltwater license to fish the salt water, however.

LOCATION: Loudoun, Fairfax, Prince William, Stafford, King George, Westmoreland, and Northumberland counties.

WATER: West of Washington, D.C., the river is a fast stream with plenty of wadable water and a mixture of rapids, riffles, and long, quiet pools. Some of the white water is too difficult for all but the most experienced canoeists. From Washington downstream the Potomac is a broad tidal stream.

CAMPING: There are developed campgrounds in Prince William Forest Park and Westmoreland State Park.

ACCESS: The Department of Game and Inland Fisheries maintains boat-launching ramps at Bonum's Creek, Colonial Beach, and McKimmey. There is also a public launching ramp in Westmoreland State Park.

FISH: Bluefish, bowfin, carp, catfish, chain pickerel, crappie, croakers, gray trout, largemouth bass, smallmouth bass, spot, striped bass, suckers, sunfish, white perch, and yellow perch.

TRIBUTARIES: Accokee, Accotink, Aquia, Bonum, Catoctin, Chopawamsic, Choptank, Dutchman, Goose, Hull, Jackson, Lodge, Lower Machodoc, Mattox, Mill, Monroe, Nomini, Occoquan, Podes, Pohick, Potomac, Powell's, Presley, Quantico, Rosier, and Run creeks; Broad, Difficult, and Piney runs; Hampton Hall and Long branches; Blackwater Swamp; and Mountain Stream.

PUBLIC WATER: The entire stream.

Pound River

The Pound River gathers its waters near the Kentucky border and flows north to form the John W. Flannagan Lake; it then joins the Russell Fork River to flow west into Kentucky.

LOCATION: Wise and Dickenson counties.

WATER: A fast mountain stream in its headwaters, it becomes calmer in its lower stretches.

CAMPING: There is primitive camping in the Jefferson National Forest, and there are developed campgrounds in Breaks Interstate Park and on both the John W. Flannagan Lake and the North Fork of the Pound Lake.

ACCESS: There is informal access from the Jefferson National Forest and public boat-launching ramps on the John W. Flannagan Lake and the North Fork of the Pound Lake.

FISH: Catfish, crappie, muskie, sauger, smallmouth bass, spotted bass, suckers, sunfish, trout, walleye, white bass, and trout.

TRIBUTARIES: Indian and Pine Pine creeks; Cranesnest River and the North Fork of the Pound River; Cane Branch; and George's Fork.

PUBLIC WATER: That stretch of the river in the Jefferson National Forest.

Powell River

The Powell River forms in the rugged mountains of Wise County on the Kentucky border and flows southwest into Tennessee.

LOCATION: Wise and Lee counties.

WATER: A fast mountain stream in its headwaters, the Powell becomes calmer downstream but still maintains a good current.

CAMPING: There is primitive camping in the Jefferson National Forest.

ACCESS: No formal access, but the Jefferson National Forest lands can be used to launch canoes or small boats. Public road crossings can be used, and there is private access if permission is obtained.

FISH: Carp, catfish, crappie, largemouth bass, muskie, sauger, smallmouth bass, suckers, sunfish, trout, walleye, and white bass.

TRIBUTARIES: Bear, Hardy's, Jones, Martin's, Mud Lick, and Wallen creeks; Rocky and Roaring forks; and North, Middle, and South forks of the Powell River.

PUBLIC WATER: Only that portion of the stream in the Jefferson National Forest.

Rapidan River

The Rapidan River may be best known as the stream President Hoover sought for trout fishing and relief from his depression-plagued White House. That section of the river in the Shenandoah National Park is a well-known catch-and-release trout stream. It is a delightful stream from its headwaters to its confluence with the larger Rappahannock River.

LOCATION: Rising in Madison County, it forms the boundary between Madison and Orange counties, Orange and Culpeper counties, and Culpeper and Spotsylvania counties.

WATER: A fast trout stream at its headwaters, the river flows swiftly most of its course, with alternating stretches of rapids and riffles and long pools.

CAMPING: There are developed campgrounds in the Shenandoah National Park, and camping in self-contained vehicles is allowed in the Rapidan Wildlife Management Area.

ACCESS: The Department of Game and Inland Fisheries maintains boat-launching ramps at Elys Ford and at Germanna Ford.

FISH: Carp, catfish, chain pickerel, crappie, fallfish, largemouth bass, smallmouth bass, suckers, sunfish, and trout.

TRIBUTARIES: Blue, Brook, Flat, Mine, Mountain, Potato, Russell, and Summerduck runs; Conway, Robinson, and South rivers; and Cedar Creek.

PUBLIC WATER: That portion of stream in the Shenandoah National Park and from Raccoon Ford to its confluence with the Rappahannock River.

Rappahannock River

The Rappahannock River, rising in the Blue Ridge foothills and flowing into the Chesapeake Bay, is one of Virginia's most popular canoeing streams. Its Kellys Ford rapids are well known to white-water enthusiasts.

LOCATION: Gathering its waters in Fauquier and Rappahannock counties, it serves as the boundary between those two counties, between Culpeper and Fauquier counties, Culpeper and Stafford counties, Stafford and Spotsylvania counties, Stafford and Caroline counties, Caroline and King George counties, King George and Essex counties, Westmoreland and Essex counties, between Richmond and Essex counties, and between Lancaster and Middlesex counties.

WATER: With fast mountain water in its headwaters, some class 3 and 4 water downstream, many long quiet stretches, and tidewater from Fredericksburg to the Chesapeake Bay, it is a river of many moods.

CAMPING: Camping in self-contained vehicles is allowed in the C. F. Phelps Wildlife Management Area.

ACCESS: The Department of Game and Inland Fisheries maintains boat-launching ramps at Carter's Wharf, Fredericksburg, Hoskins Creek, Kellys Ford, Mill Creek, Mill Stone, Motts Run, Saluda, Simonson, and Totuskey.

FISH: Bluefish, carp, catfish, chain pickerel, crappie, croaker, fallfish, flounder, gray trout, herring, largemouth bass, shad, smallmouth bass, spot, striped bass, suckers, sunfish, white perch, and yellow perch.

TRIBUTARIES: Brockenbrough, Elmwood, Goldenswale, Hoskins, Middle, Mill, Mount, Occupacia, Peedee, and Piscataway creeks; Hazel, Jordan, Rapidan, and Thornton rivers; and Carter, Deep, Falls, Great, Hazel, Motts, Mountain, Negro, Popcastle, Rock, Ruffians, South, and White Oak runs.

PUBLIC WATER: From U.S. Highway 211 in Fauquier County to the Chesapeake Bay.

Rivanna River

The Rivanna River is a major tributary of the James, and it offers much the same kind of fishing.

LOCATION: Albemarle and Fluvanna counties.

WATER: A moderately fast stream with plenty of long, deep pools.

CAMPING: There are no public campgrounds.

ACCESS: The Department of Game and Inland Fisheries maintains boat-launching ramps at Columbia, Crofton, Milton, and Palmyra.

FISH: Carp, catfish, chain pickerel, crappie, fallfish, gar, largemouth bass, smallmouth bass, suckers, and sunfish.

TRIBUTARIES: Ballingers, Buck Island, Judy, Mechunk, and Raccoon creeks; and the North and South forks of the Rivanna River.

PUBLIC WATER: From the Greene County line to the river's mouth.

Roanoke River

The Roanoke River is many things to many people. Slowed by numerous dams of various sizes, it forms in the mountainous country west of Roanoke, flows southeast to North Carolina, and eventually empties into Albemarle Sound. En route it forms Smith Mountain Lake, Leesville Lake, Buggs Island Lake, Gaston Lake, and, in North Carolina, Roanoke Rapids lake. It is probably best known in Virginia for its spawning runs of land-locked striped bass out out of Buggs Island Lake.

LOCATION: Flowing through Bedford and Franklin counties, it forms the boundary between Bedford and Franklin counties, Bedford and Pittsylvania counties, Campbell and Pittsylvania counties, Campbell and Halifax counties, and Charlotte and Halifax counties, and then flows into Mecklenburg County.

WATER: A fast mountain trout stream at its headwaters, the Roanoke (called Staunton by some anglers) gradually slows to a minimum of current as it enters Buggs Island Lake.

CAMPING: There is primitive camping in the Jefferson National Forest, and there are developed campgrounds in Smith Mountain and Staunton River state parks.

ACCESS: The Department of Game and Inland Fisheries maintains boat-launching ramps at Anthony Ford, Brookneal, City Farm, Clover, Hales Ford, Hardy Ford, Leesville Dam, Long Island, Myers Creek, Penhook, Scruggs, South Boston, and Watkins Bridge.

FISH: Carp, catfish, crappie, gar, largemouth bass, Roanoke bass, smallmouth bass, striped bass, suckers, sunfish, trout, walleye, and white bass.

TRIBUTARIES: Back, Buckskin, Catawba, Cow, Cub, Difficult, Ellis, Georges, Gillis, Goose, Hunting, Lynville, Prater, Roanoke, and Twittys creeks; Dry Run; Wallace Branch; and Big Chestnut, Blackwater, Falling, Otter, Pigg, and North and South forks of the Roanoke and the Seneca rivers.

PUBLIC WATER: From Smith Mountain Lake to the North Carolina Line.

Russell Fork River

The Russell Fork River belongs mostly to Kentucky, but it rises in mountainous Dickenson County to flow west into the neighboring state.

LOCATION: Dickenson County.

WATER: A rapidly flowing mountain stream in the Virginia section.

CAMPING: There are developed campgrounds on John W. Flannagan Lake and in Breaks Interstate Park, and there is primitive camping in the Jefferson National Forest.

ACCESS: No formal access, but boats can be launched in the national forest.

FISH: Carp, catfish, sauger, smallmouth bass, spotted bass, suckers, sunfish, trout, walleye, and white bass.

TRIBUTARIES: Burts Lick, Fox, Frying Pan, Hurricane, and Indian creeks; War Fork; and the Pound River.

PUBLIC WATER: Only that section of the stream in the Jefferson National Forest and in Breaks Interstate Park.

Shenandoah River

The main stem of the Shenandoah River forms at Riverton and flows through West Virginia to enter the Potomac River at Harpers Ferry.

LOCATION: Warren and Clarke counties.

WATER: A fast valley stream with a good mixture of rapids and riffles and long, quiet stretches.

CAMPING: There is primitive camping in the George Washington National Forest.

ACCESS: The Department of Game and Inland Fisheries maintains boat-launching ramps at Berry's, Castleman's Ferry, Lockes, Morgan's Ford, and Riverton.

FISH: Carp, catfish, crappie, largemouth bass, smallmouth bass, suckers, and sunfish.

TRIBUTARIES: The North and South Forks of the Shenandoah River; Dog and Crooked runs.

PUBLIC WATER: From Riverton to the West Virginia line.

Smith River

The Smith River, forming in the Blue Ridge Mountains of Patrick County, forms Philpott Lake, and it is best known for its tailwaters brown-trout fishing. The river below the lake could well offer the best trout fishing in Virginia.

LOCATION: Patrick and Henry counties.

WATER: Generally a fast mountain stream that meanders dramatically downstream from Philpott Lake.

CAMPING: There are developed campgrounds in Fairy Stone State Park and on Philpott Lake.

ACCESS: U.S. Army Corps of Engineers boat-launching ramps on Philpott Lake offer limited access to the stream.

FISH: Crappie, largemouth bass, smallmouth bass, suckers, sunfish, trout, and walleye.

TRIBUTARIES: Burgess, Cobbs, Fall, Marrowbone, Rangeley, Reed, Rock Castle, Runnett Bag, Shooting, Turkeycock, and Widgeon creeks.

PUBLIC WATER: From Philpott Lake to the city of Danville.

South Fork of the Holston River

The South Fork of the Holston River is one of the major feeder streams for South Holston Lake and one of the three forks of the Holston River.

LOCATION: Smyth and Washington counties.

WATER: Beginning as a fast mountain stream, the river maintains a good current as a valley stream with long, quiet stretches between rapids and riffles.

CAMPING: There are developed campgrounds on South Holston Lake, and there is primitive camping in the Jefferson National Forest.

ACCESS: There is no formal access, but canoes can be launched in the Jefferson National Forest. Anglers use public road crossings and private land where they can get permission.

FISH: Catfish, crappie, smallmouth bass, suckers, sunfish, trout, and white bass.

TRIBUTARIES: Comers, Dicky, Houndshell, Raccoon, Roland's, St. Clair, Stoeffel, and White Rock creeks; Straight Branch.

PUBLIC WATER: From Alvarado to the Tennessee line.

The South Fork of the Shenandoah River

Historically, this is perhaps Virginia's most famous smallmouth-bass stream. It and the North Fork join at Riverton to form the main stem of the Shenandoah, which enters the Potomac River at Harpers Ferry.

LOCATION: Rockingham, Page, and Warren counties.

WATER: For the most part, this is a fast-paced valley stream with alternating stretches of fast and quiet water. There are some low dams and some classes 2 and 3 rapids.

CAMPING: There are developed campgrounds in the Shenandoah National Park, and primitive camping is permitted in the George Washington National Forest.

ACCESS: The Department of Game and Inland Fisheries maintains boat-launching ramps at Bentonville, Fosters, Front Royal, Grove Hill, Karo,

Massanutten, Newport, Riverton, Simpson's Landing, and White House.

FISH: Catfish, carp, crappie, largemouth bass, smallmouth bass, suckers, and sunfish.

TRIBUTARIES: Gooney, Naked, and Passage creeks; Boone's, Cub, and Spring runs; and the Middle, North, and South rivers.

PUBLIC WATER: From Port Republic to Riverton.

Swift Creek

Swift Creek is the major feeder stream for Swift Creek Lake in Chesterfield County.

LOCATION: Powhatan and Chesterfield counties.

WATER: Generally a very slow stream, but some class-2 rapids.

CAMPING: There are developed campgrounds in Pocahontas State Park, and there is primitive camping in Pocahontas State Forest.

ACCESS: There are no boat-launching ramps, but boats can be launched from lands of state park and state forest.

FISH: Carp, catfish, chain pickerel, crappie, largemouth bass, suckers, sunfish, and yellow perch.

TRIBUTARIES: Deep, Dry, Licking, Little Tomahawk, and Tomahawk creeks; First, Second, and Third branches; and Spring Run.

PUBLIC WATER: That stretch of the stream flowing through the Pocahontas State Park and Pocahontas State Forest.

Tye River

The Tye River is a major tributary of the James River; an excellent trout stream at its headwaters, it has fine smallmouth bass and redbreast sunfish downstream.

LOCATION: Primarily in Nelson County, but it forms part of the boundary between Amherst and Nelson counties.

WATER: The Tye is a fast mountain stream throughout its length, but there is a fair amount of quiet water between the rapids and riffles.

CAMPING: There is primitive camping in the George Washington National Forest.

ACCESS: There are no public boat-launching areas, but anglers use public road crossings and private land where they can get permission.

FISH: Carp, catfish, gar, smallmouth bass, suckers, sunfish, and trout.

TRIBUTARIES: Buffalo, North Fork of the Tye, and Piney rivers.

PUBLIC WATER: That stretch of the stream that flows through the national forest.

Willis River

The Willis is a slow Southside Virginia stream that offers a unique kind of public fishing. It rises in the Appomattox-Buckingham State Forest not far from the headwaters of the Slate River, a major tributary of the James River, as is the Willis River.

LOCATION: Buckingham and Cumberland counties.

WATER: A very slow stream in the southern Piedmont.

CAMPING: There are developed campgrounds in Bear Creek State Park and in Holiday Lake State Park, and there is primitive camping in the Appomattox-Buckingham and Cumberland state forests.

ACCESS: There is no formal boat access, but the lands of the two state forests and the state parks can be used to launch boats.

FISH: Carp, catfish, chain pickerel, crappie, gar, largemouth bass, suckers, and sunfish.

TRIBUTARIES: Randolph Creek.

PUBLIC WATER: From U.S. Highway 15 in Buckingham County to the mouth of the river.

York River

The York River is a long tidal estuary formed by the Mattaponi and Pamunkey rivers. It is primarily a stream for saltwater fishing.

LOCATION: The river forms the boundary between King and Queen and New Kent counties, King and Queen and James City counties, Gloucester and James City counties, and Gloucester and York counties.

WATER: A tidal river subject to tides.

CAMPING: There are no public campgrounds.

ACCESS: The Department of Game and Inland Fisheries maintains boat-launching ramps at Croaker, Gloucester Point, Tanyard, and West Point.

FISH: Bluefish, croaker, flounder, gray trout, striped bass, and white perch.

TRIBUTARIES: Mattaponi and Pamunkey rivers; Adam, Bland, Carter, Cedar Bush, Poropotank, Skimino, Timberneck, and Ware creeks.

PUBLIC WATER: The entire river.

The Big Lakes and Reservoirs _____

Virginia was not spared the reservoir-building hysteria that swept America during the 1950s and 1960s. The John H. Kerr Reservoir, better known as Buggs Island Lake in Virginia, was begun in 1946 and completed in 1951 and added 50,000 acres of big-water fishing in the Old Dominion. Others followed, and before the dam building had slowed with the creation of Lake Moomaw in 1979, over 150,000 acres of brand new fishing water had been added.

Many of these projects were controversial. Few were without at least token opposition, but collectively their impact on fishing in the state has been dramatic. The lure of big water, big fish, and big boats attracted many newcomers to fishing, and a new breed of anglers had suddenly arrived.

These large lakes offered a kind of fishing that was unknown to most Virginia anglers prior to World War II. With their coming, old anglers had to learn new tricks such as reading flat water, deep trolling, the use of depth and fish finders, and safe boatsmanship.

That the impoundments have meant much to fishing in Virginia is beyond debate. For one thing they can absorb many more anglers, thereby easing the demands on the smaller, more vulnerable waters. They have also provided a rich new habitat for a wide variety of fish, and have furnished Department of Game and Inland Fisheries biologists with bright new waters to explore and manage.

Included in this chapter is Back Bay, 25,000 acres of brackish, shallow water in the city of Virginia Beach. It is not an impoundment, and its shallow waters remove it from the typical deepwater impoundment. Its slight salinity is man imposed by pumping salt water in from the ocean. It is big water, however, and unlike any other in the state.

Most of the reservoirs are large, 5,000 acres or more, but included here also are a few in the 400- to 500-acre range. They are typical of the larger impoundments in many ways. Among them are Beaverdam Creek Reservoir in Loudoun County, Lee Hall in the city of Newport News, Ni Reservoir in Spotsylvania County, and the Rivanna Reservoir in Albemarle.

Buggs Island is by far the largest of the large lakes, over twice the size of Lake Gaston and Smith Mountain Lake, its closest competitors.

Over the past few decades most of these new waters have all developed their own personalities, things that make them stand out in the minds of anglers not only in Virginia but elsewhere also. Buggs Island is probably best known for its landlocked striped bass, and is the lake where this new kind of fishing got its start in Virginia. Lake Gaston has produced several state-record largemouth bass, and Claytor Lake hangs onto the histor-

Big Lakes and Reservoirs

1. Lake Anna
2. Back Bay
3. Beaverdam Creek Reservoir
4. Buggs Island Lake
   (John H. Kerr Reservoir)
5. Burnt Mills Lake
6. Lake Cahoon
7. Carvins Cove Lake
8. Lake Chesdin
9. Chickahominy Lake
10. Claytor Lake
11. Diascund Lake
12. Lake Drummond
13. John W. Flannagan Lake
14. Gaston Lake
15. Lee Hall Lake
16. Leesville Lake
17. Little Creek Lake
18. Little Creek Reservoir

19. Lunga Reservoir
20. Lake Manassas
21. Lake Meade
22. Lake Moomaw
23. Ni River Lake
24. Occoquan Lake
25. Philpott Lake
26. Lake Prince
27. Rivanna Reservoir
28. Smith Mountain Lake
29. South Holston Lake
30. Swift Creek Lake
31. Western Branch Lake
32. Lake Whitehurst

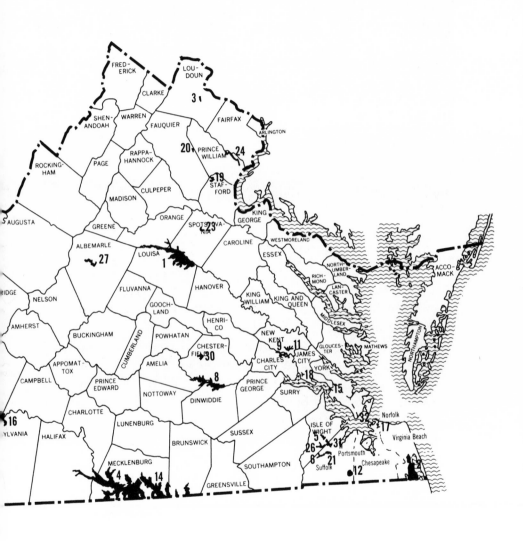

Anglers head out on South Holston Lake.

ical state-record smallmouth bass. Philpott developed an early reputation for deep-water trout fishing, and Chickahominy is known for its lunker chain pickerel.

Buggs Island, Gaston, and South Holston are border lakes that Virginia anglers share with North Carolina and Tennessee.

A desire to create new fishing waters, however, was not the need that fostered these big lakes. Flood control, municipal water supply, and the generation of electricity were the economic and social needs used to justify most of them, needs often questioned by those who opposed the projects.

These waters are here to stay, however, hopefully to continue to serve the needs that hatched them, and to provide good fishing for the anglers of Virginia. Here is a closer look at them.

Lake Anna

Lake Anna is one of Virginia's newest impoundments, and one of the most popular. It is owned by Virginia Power Company, created as a cooling source for its nuclear power plant in Louisa County. It developed an early reputation for its excellent largemouth-bass fishing, but it is also coming on as a landlocked striper lake. It is also noted for its crappie fishing.

LOCATION: Louisa, Orange, and Spotsylvania counties.

SIZE: The lake and three cooling ponds total 13,000 acres, but the lake alone is 9,600 acres. The cooling ponds are not open to the public, nor are they managed for fishing.

FISH: Carp, catfish, chain pickerel, crappie, largemouth bass, striped bass, sunfish, yellow perch, walleye, and white perch.

CAMPING: There are no public campgrounds.

ACCESS: U.S. Highway 522 from north and south and Virginia Primary Highway 208 from east and west.

FEEDER STREAMS: North Anna River; Beverly, Douglas, Foremost, Pamunkey, Pigeon, and Terrys runs; and Boggs, Christopher, Coleman, Contrary, Duckinghoe, Dukes, Elk, Freshwater, Gold Mine, Hackneys, Harlows, Harris, Holladay Mill, Levy, Marshall, Millpond, Mitchell, Moody, Northeast, Plentiful, Rock, Rockland, Scerks, Sedges, and Tomahawk creeks.

BOAT-LAUNCHING AREA: The Virginia Division of Parks maintains a boat-launching area in Lake Anna State Park, and there is also a Department of Game and Inland Fisheries launching ramp.

WATER: When compared to most large impoundments or reservoirs, the lake is relatively shallow. The river channel at the dam, however, is in excess of fifty feet deep, and even up the lake the channel may be fifty feet deep or more. Many acres of the headwaters are ten feet or less in depth, however, and much of the shoreline water is under ten feet.

Back Bay

At 25,000 acres, Back Bay is the second largest body of fresh water in Virginia. While it eventually enters the Atlantic Ocean, it does so seventy miles to the south through North Carolina's Oregon Inlet. The only salt water that enters it is pumped in by the City of Virginia Beach. Back Bay is not subject to lunar tidal action, but there are wind tides of up to three feet. Anglers know Back Bay best for its shallow-water largemouth bass fishing and its abundant crappie populations.

LOCATION: Entirely within the City of Virginia Beach.

SIZE: 25,000 acres.

FISH: Catfish, crappie, largemouth bass, sunfish, white perch, and yellow perch.

CAMPING: Camping is permitted in False Cape State Park, but only primitive facilities are available.

ACCESS: The major access is Virginia Secondary Route 615, Princess Anne Road, which runs north and south along the western side of the bay.

FEEDER STREAMS: Ward's Ditch, and Beggars Bridge, Devil, Hell Point, Nawney, and Tabernicle creeks.

BOAT-LAUNCHING AREA: The Department of Game and Inland Fisheries maintains launching ramps at Back Bay on Mill Landing Road and at the Trojan Waterfowl Management Area.

WATER: A very shallow body of water bordered by extensive marshes on the west and barren pine forests and sand dunes on the east. The average depth is only three to four feet, and much of the water can be waded. The maximum depth is ten feet.

Beaverdam Creek Reservoir

At approximately 400 acres, this is one of the smaller water-supply reservoirs open to the fishing public. It is owned by the city of Fairfax, but is located in Loudoun County. Only electric outboard motors are allowed.

LOCATION: Loudoun County.

SIZE: 400 acres.

FISH: Catfish, crappie, largemouth bass, and sunfish.

CAMPING: There are no public campgrounds.

ACCESS: Virginia Secondary Routes 861 and 659 west of Ashburn lead to the lake.

FEEDER STREAMS: Beaverdam Creek.

BOAT-LAUNCHING AREA: There is a primitive boat-launching ramp off of Route 659 at Mount Hope Church.

WATER: The lake is reasonably deep, with a moderately sloping shoreline.

Buggs Island Lake

Known officially as the John H. Kerr Reservoir, this big lake on the Virginia–North Carolina line is called Buggs Island Lake by Virginia anglers. Primarily a flood-control project built and managed by the U.S. Army Corps of Engineers, it is also used to produce hydroelectric energy. Its 800-mile shoreline offers almost unlimited fishing opportunities. It is Virginia's largest lake.

LOCATION: Charlotte, Halifax, and Mecklenburg counties.

SIZE: 50,000 acres.

FISH: Carp, catfish, chain pickerel, crappie, largemouth bass, striped bass, sunfish, walleye, and white bass.

CAMPING: There are developed campgrounds in both the Occonneechee and Staunton River state parks, and camping is permitted in the U.S. Army Corps of Engineers public use areas.

ACCESS: U.S. Highway 15 from the north and south and U.S. Highway 58 from the east and west.

FEEDER STREAMS: Dan, Hyco, and Roanoke (Staunton) rivers; and Aarons, Bluestone, Buffalo, Butchers, Eastland, Grassy, and Island creeks.

BOAT-LAUNCHING AREA: Either the Department of Game and Inland Fisheries, the Division of Parks, or the U.S. Army Corps of Engineers, maintain boat-launching ramps at Bluestone Creek, Eastland, Grassy Creek, Hyco, Island Creek, Ivy Hill, Longwood, Northland, Occonneeche State Park, South Boston, and Staunton River State Park.

WATER: Much of the water is deep, with that near the dam being over ninety feet. Many of the creek and river channels are also fifty feet deep or more. There are a number of inundated creeks and old roadbeds. The shallow water is generally limited to the shoreline.

Burnt Mills Lake

This is one of the well-known Suffolk Lakes, so named because they cluster around the city of Suffolk. The Burnt Mills dam is located on the Isle of Wight County–city of Suffolk line, however, and most of the lake is in the county. It is owned by the city of Norfolk and serves as part of the city's water-supply system. A permit from the city is required to fish it. Burnt Mills Lake is noted for its big bluegills.

LOCATION: Island of Wight County and city of Suffolk.

SIZE: 600 acres.

FISH: Bowfin, catfish, chain pickerel, crappie, largemouth bass, sunfish, and yellow perch.

CAMPING: There are no public campgrounds.

ACCESS: Virginia Secondary Route 603, approximately ten miles east of Windsor on U.S. Highway 460.

FEEDER STREAMS: Great Swamp Drainage.

BOAT-LAUNCHING AREA: There is an undeveloped dirt boat-launching ramp off of Secondary Route 603 near Everetts.

WATER: For a flat-country lake Burnt Mills is deep, with a maximum depth of approximately fifty feet.

Lake Cahoon

Cahoon is one of the famous Suffolk Lakes, but it is owned by the city of Portsmouth. It is a flat, coastal-plain lake that forms a part of the city's water-supply system. Permits, available at Cahoon-Meade fishing station, are needed to fish the lake.

LOCATION: City of Suffolk.

SIZE: 510 acres.

FISH: Catfish, chain pickerel, crappie, largemouth bass, and sunfish.

CAMPING: There are no public campgrounds.

ACCESS: Access to the lake is at the Cahoon-Meade fishing station located off of Virginia Secondary Route 604 west of Suffolk.

FEEDER STREAMS: Cahoon Creek and Eley Swamp.

BOAT-LAUNCHING AREA: There is a concrete boat-launching ramp at the fishing station.

WATER: This is a reasonably shallow coastal-plain lake with a maximum depth of thirty-two feet. Many coves provide good fishing.

Carvins Cove Lake

Carvins Cove is a deep mountain lake owned by the city of Roanoke as part of its water-supply system. Permits from the city are required for fishing the lake, but they can be purchased on an annual or a daily basis.

LOCATION: Botetourt and Roanoke counties.

SIZE: 630 acres.

CAMPING: There is primitive camping in the nearby Jefferson National Forest.

ACCESS: Virginia Secondary Routes 601 and 711, approximately five miles north of Roanoke.

FISH: Catfish, chain pickerel, crappie, largemouth bass, sunfish, and walleye.

FEEDER STREAMS: Carvins Creek.

BOAT-LAUNCHING AREA: The city of Roanoke maintains a public launching ramp.

WATER: This is a deep mountain lake fed by cold mountain streams. The water is very clear, but structure is limited.

Lake Chesdin

Lake Chesdin on the Appomattox River is owned and maintained by the Appomattox River Authority. It is possibly best known for its fine crappie fishing.

LOCATION: Located primarily in Chesterfield County, the lake forms the boundary between Chesterfield and Amelia counties and Chesterfield and Dinwiddie counties.

SIZE: 3,060 acres.

FISH: Catfish, chain pickerel, crappie, hybrid striped bass, largemouth bass, sunfish, and walleye.

CAMPING: There are no public campgrounds.

ACCESS: Virginia Secondary Routes 602, 628, and 636 off of Primary Highway 36, and Secondary Routes 601, 708, 611, and 623 off of Primary Highway 226, all west of Petersburg.

FEEDER STREAMS: Appomattox River; Gunn Run; and Ashton, Herring, Namozine, Tinsbury, Whipponock, and Winterpock creeks.

BOAT-LAUNCHING AREA: The Department of Game and Inland Fisheries maintains a boat-launching ramp near the dam on the south side of the lake.

WATER: Chesdin is a reasonably deep flat-country lake and is long and narrow.

Chickahominy Lake

A part of the water-supply system of the city of Newport News, Chickahominy Lake is one of the most popular fishing lakes in Virginia.

LOCATION: It forms the boundary between Charles City and New Kent counties.

SIZE: 1,500 acres.

FISH: Bowfin, catfish, chain pickerel, crappie, gar, largemouth bass, northern pike, sunfish, and white perch.

CAMPING: There are no public campgrounds.

ACCESS: Virginia Secondary Routes 627, 647, and 650 off U.S. Highway 60.

FEEDER STREAMS: Chickahominy River; Black Stump and Yarmouth creeks; and Big and Tonyham swamps.

BOAT-LAUNCHING AREA: There are no public boat-launching ramps, but several commercial ones.

WATER: This is a shallow coastal-plain lake bordered with marshes. Its water is acid-stained, but fertile.

Claytor Lake

Claytor is an Appalachian Power Company lake on the New River, and one of the major big lakes in Southwest Virginia. It is noted for its flathead catfish, smallmouth bass, and spring runs of white bass.

LOCATION: Pulaski County.

SIZE: 4,485 acres.

FISH: Carp, catfish, crappie, largemouth bass, muskie, smallmouth bass, spotted bass, striped bass, sunfish, walleye, white bass, and yellow perch.

ACCESS: Interstate Highway 81 provides access from the east and west, and Virginia Primary Highways 99 and 100 and Secondary Routes 660, 661, 663, 671, and 672 from the north and south.

FEEDER STREAMS: New River; Pine Run; and Macks and Peak Creeks.

BOAT-LAUNCHING AREA: The Department of Game and Inland Fisheries maintains boat-launching ramps at Dublin and in Claytor Lake State Park. The Division of Parks also maintains a boat-launching ramp in Claytor Lake State Park.

WATER: Claytor is a deep valley lake with a limited amount of shallow water.

Diascund Lake

Owned by the city of Newport News as part of its water-supply system, Diascund Lake is very popular among anglers in the Richmond metropolitan area. It is closed during the winter months, however.

LOCATION: Located primarily in New Kent County, it forms part of the boundary between James City and New Kent counties.

SIZE: 1,700 acres.

FISH: Bowfin, carp, catfish, chain pickerel, crappie, largemouth bass, sunfish, and white perch.

CAMPING: There are no public campgrounds.

ACCESS: Virginia Secondary Route 603 off of U.S. Highway 60 from the south or off of Interstate 64 from the north.

FEEDER STREAMS: Beaverdam and Diascund creeks.

BOAT-LAUNCHING AREA: Only rental boats can be used on the lake.

WATER: This is a reasonably deep coastal-plain lake with a timbered shore-line.

Lake Drummond

Lake Drummond, in the Great Dismal Swamp National Wildlife Refuge, is one of only two major natural lakes in Virginia, the other being Mountain Lake in Giles County.

LOCATION: Primarily in the city of Chesapeake, but it brushes the city of Suffolk.

SIZE: 3,000 acres.

FISH: Catfish, crappie, sunfish, and yellow perch.

CAMPING: There is a developed campground adjacent to the Feeder Ditch, the major access to the lake.

ACCESS: The major access is by boat through the Feeder Ditch accessible from U.S. Highway 17 from the east.

FEEDER STREAMS: Springs in the lake. The water actually flows out of the lake.

BOAT-LAUNCHING AREA: The Department of Game and Inland Fisheries maintains a boat-launching ramp on the Dismal Swamp Canal. It is accessible from U.S. Highway 17.

WATER: The water is reasonably shallow and very acidic. The more popular fish such as chain pickerel and largemouth bass do not survive there. A swamp wilderness borders the lake.

John A. Flannagan Lake

This is a U.S. Army Corps of Engineers flood-control lake on the Pound River.

LOCATION: Dickenson County.

SIZE: 1,143 acres.

FISH: Catfish, crappie, largemouth bass, spotted bass, sunfish, and walleye.

CAMPING: There is primitive camping in the Jefferson National Forest, and there are developed campgrounds on the lands of the U.S. Army Corps of Engineers.

ACCESS: Virginia Primary Highways 63 and 80 from the north and south and 83 from the east. From these major highways Secondary Routes 611, 615, 619, 683, 686, and 714 lead to the lake.

FEEDER STREAMS: Cranesnest and Pound rivers; and Cane, Lower Twin, and Upper Twin branches.

BOAT-LAUNCHING AREA: There are four U.S. Army Corps of Engineers boat-launching ramps at the lake.

WATER: A deep mountain lake with steep shorelines that pitch into the water.

Gaston Lake

Gaston Lake is owned by the Virginia Power Company for the production of hydroelectric energy. It is immediately downstream from Buggs Island Lake and on the Virginia–North Carolina line. It is probably best known for its lunker largemouth bass, having yielded several state records.

LOCATION: Brunswick and Mecklenburg counties.

SIZE: 20,300 acres.

FISH: Catfish, chain pickerel, crappie, largemouth bass, striped bass, sunfish, walleye, white bass, and white perch.

CAMPING: There are no public campgrounds.

ACCESS: Interstate Highway 85 and U.S. Highway 1 cross the lake, and Secondary Routes 611, 615, 617, 618, 619, 626, 237, 644, 650, 660, 665, 666, 670, 717, 1214, and 1344 provide access off of U.S. Highway 58 from the north.

FEEDER STREAMS: Roanoke River; and Allen, Blue Mud, Cotton, Dockery, Flat, Great, Hagood, Little Poplar, Lizard, Middle, Miles, Mill, Parham, Pea Hill, Pigeonwood, Poplar, Reedy, Sixpound, Smith, and Songbird creeks.

BOAT-LAUNCHING AREA: The Department of Game and Inland Fisheries maintains boat-launching ramps at Pea Hill, Poplar Creek, and Steel Bridge.

WATER: This is a deep lake in a major river valley, but it offers a good amount of shallow water. There is very little fluctuation in the water level.

Lee Hall Lake

Lee Hall Lake is part of the water-supply system of the city of Newport News and possibly best known for its chain pickerel fishing. Northern pike, released there by the Commission of Game and Inland Fisheries, also grow rapidly and furnish some exciting fishing. Only electric outboard motors are permitted on the lake.

LOCATION: City of Newport News.

SIZE: 400 acres, but only that above the railroad, approximately 230 acres, is open to the public.

FISH: Catfish, chain pickerel, crappie, largemouth bass, northern pike, sunfish, white perch, and yellow perch.

CAMPING: The city of Newport News maintains a developed campground.

ACCESS: Interstate Highway 64 and Virginia Primary Highway 143 cross the lake, but access is from the east off of U.S. Highway 17.

FEEDER STREAMS: Warwick River.

BOAT-LAUNCHING AREA: The city of Newport News maintains boat-launching ramps.

WATER: This is a shallow coastal-plain lake with a wooded shoreline. A dense growth of pondweed in the upper part of the lake provides good habitat for pickerel and pike.

Leesville Lake

Leesville is the lower lake in the Smith Mountain–Leesville lake pumped-storage complex of the Appalachian Power Company. After being used to generate power at the Smith Mountain Dam, the water is pumped back into the upper lake from Leesville Lake. Leesville is probably best known for its striped bass fishing.

LOCATION: The lake forms part of the boundary between Bedford and Pittsylvania counties and between Campbell and Pittsylvania counties.

SIZE: 4,000 acres.

FISH: Carp, catfish, crappie, largemouth bass, smallmouth bass, striped bass, sunfish, and white bass.

CAMPING: There is a developed campground in Smith Mountain Lake State Park.

ACCESS: Virginia Secondary Route 642 west off of U.S. Highway 29 at Gretna, Routes 630 and 631 off of Primary Highway 43 at Leesville, and Secondary Routes 609 or 642 from the south off of Primary Highway 40 provide access.

FEEDER STREAMS: Roanoke River; Clay, Long, and Meadow branches; and Mill, Myers, Pigg, Roer, Stony, Tanker, and Terrapin creeks.

BOAT-LAUNCHING AREA: The Department of Game and Inland Fisheries maintains boat-launching ramps at Leesville Dam and Myers Creek.

WATER: This is a reasonably deep mountain lake, long and narrow, with much of the lake in the old riverbed.

Little Creek Lake

Little Creek Lake is part of the water-supply system of the city of Norfolk. Fishing and boating permits are required, and they are available from the city. Outboard motors are limited to ten horsepower or less.

LOCATION: City of Virginia Beach.

SIZE: 709 acres.

FISH: Catfish, chain pickerel, crappie, hybrid striped bass, largemouth bass, sunfish, walleye, white perch, and yellow perch.

CAMPING: There are no public campgrounds.

ACCESS: Access is off of U.S. Highway 13 three miles south of the Chesapeake Bay Bridge-Tunnel.

FEEDER STREAMS: Several swamps.

BOAT-LAUNCHING AREA: The city of Norfolk maintains a boat-launching ramp.

WATER: This is a shallow coastal-plain lake.

Little Creek Reservoir

This is a new reservoir in the city of Newport News water-supply system.

LOCATION: James City County.

SIZE: 860 acres.

FISH: Catfish, chain pickerel, crappie, sunfish, white perch, and yellow perch.

CAMPING: There is no public campground.

ACCESS: Accessible off of Interstate 64 or U.S. Highway 60.

FEEDER STREAMS: Several small swamps.

BOAT-LAUNCHING AREA: The city of Newport News maintains a boat-launching ramp.

WATER: A reasonably shallow coastal-plain lake.

Lunga Reservoir

Lunga Reservoir is the largest of a number of small lakes and ponds on the Quantico Marine Corps Base. It is usually closed during the winter months, but rental boats and motors are available during the summer months.

LOCATION: Stafford County.

SIZE: 670 acres.

FISH: Catfish, chain pickerel, crappie, largemouth bass, white perch, and yellow perch.

CAMPING: There is no public campground.

ACCESS: The lake is reached by Virginia Secondary Route 641 west off of Interstate 95 or off of U.S. Highway 1.

FEEDER STREAMS: Beaver Dam and Flat runs; Cannon Creek; and South Branch.

BOAT-LAUNCHING AREA: The U.S. Marine Corps maintains a boat-launching ramp.

WATER: A fairly deep lake with a wooded shoreline.

Lake Manassas

Lake Manassas, owned by the city of Manassas, is the major source of water for the city. The lake is noted for its crappie and walleye fishing. Only electric outboard motors are allowed.

LOCATION: Prince William County.

SIZE: 800 acres.

FISH: Catfish, crappie, largemouth bass, sunfish, and walleye.

CAMPING: There is no public campground.

ACCESS: Access is off of Virginia Secondary Route 604 from Primary Highway 215 near Greenwich.

FEEDER STREAMS: Broad and South runs.

BOAT-LAUNCHING AREA: There is a public boat-launching ramp off of Route 604 at Greenwich. Rental boats are available.

WATER: The maximum depth is 50 feet, and the shoreline slopes moderately.

Lake Meade

Lake Meade is one of the Suffolk Lakes and a part of the water-supply system of the city of Portsmouth. A permit from the city is needed to fish it. The lake contains a good deal of swamp drainage, an ideal habitat for flier and warmouth, members of the sunfish family.

LOCATION: City of Suffolk.

SIZE: 512 acres.

FISH: Catfish, chain pickerel, crappie, largemouth bass, striped bass, sunfish, white perch, and yellow perch.

CAMPING: There are no public campgrounds.

ACCESS: Virginia Secondary Route 604 off of U.S. Highway 58 west of Suffolk metropolitan area and Secondary Route 638 off of U.S. Highway 460 north of the metropolitan area. Secondary Routes 604 and 634 off of U.S. Highway 460 also provide access.

FEEDER STREAMS: Cahoon Creek and Eley Swamp.

BOAT-LAUNCHING AREA: Boat rentals and concrete launching ramps are available at the Lake Kilby filtration plant and the Cahoon-Meade fishing stations.

WATER: Meade is a reasonably deep coastal-plain lake.

Lake Moomaw

Moomaw is a U.S. Army Corps of Engineers flood-control lake on the Jackson River. Supervision of the recreational facilities, however, is by the George Washington National Forest.

LOCATION: Alleghany and Bath counties.

SIZE: 2,530 acres.

FISH: Catfish, chain pickerel, crappie, largemouth bass, smallmouth bass, sunfish, and trout.

CAMPING: There are developed national forest campgrounds on the shore of the lake.

ACCESS: Virginia Secondary Route 687 south off of Primary Highway 39, and Secondary Route 600 north off of Interstate 64 or U.S. Highway 60.

FEEDER STREAMS: Back Creek and Jackson River.

BOAT-LAUNCHING AREA: The U.S. Forest Service maintains a boat-launching ramp on the west side of the lake near the dam.

WATER: Moomaw is a mountain lake fed by cold mountain streams. It is generally deep, but there is some shallow water.

Ni River Lake

This is a small water-supply reservoir on the Ni River in Spotsylvania County and owned by the county. It is open from early April through the middle of October. A county permit, daily or seasonal, is needed to fish it.

LOCATION: Spotsylvania County.

SIZE: 417 acres.

FISH: Catfish, chain pickerel, crappie, hybrid striped bass, largemouth bass, sunfish, and tiger muskie.

CAMPING: There are no public camping facilities.

ACCESS: The lake is accessible off of Virginia Secondary Route 627.

FEEDER STREAMS: Ni River.

BOAT-LAUNCHING AREA: There is a public boat-launching ramp, and rental boats are available. Only electric outboard motors are allowed.

WATER: This is a small, reasonably deep water-supply lake.

Occoquan Lake

Occoquan Lake is part of the water-supply system of the county of Fairfax. It is noted for its northern-pike fishing. Outboard motors are limited to ten horsepower.

LOCATION: It forms part of the boundary between Fairfax and Prince William counties.

SIZE: 2,100 acres.

FISH: Catfish, chain pickerel, crappie, hybrid striped bass, largemouth bass, northern pike, smallmouth bass, striped bass, sunfish, white bass, and white perch.

CAMPING: There are no public camping facilities.

ACCESS: U.S. Highway 1 and Interstate 95 cross the Occoquan River just below the dam, and Virginia Primary Highways 123 and 253 and Secondary Route 641 provide access from the north. Also accessible at Fountainhead Regional Park Marina from Secondary Route 647 and at Bull Run Marina from Secondary Route 612.

FEEDER STREAMS: Bull, Cabin, Hooes, Sandy, and Stillwell runs; and Occoquan and Wolf creeks.

BOAT-LAUNCHING AREA: Rental boats and launching ramps at two marinas.

WATER: This a long, narrow lake, mostly in the riverbed. The shoreline is steep.

Philpott Lake

Philpott is a flood-control and hydroelectric U.S. Army Corps of Engineers lake on the Smith River. It is located along the eastern slopes of the Blue Ridge Mountains.

LOCATION: The lake forms part of the boundary between Franklin and Henry counties, and part of that between Franklin and Patrick counties.

SIZE: 2,800 acres.

FISH: Catfish, crappie, largemouth bass, smallmouth bass, sunfish, trout, and walleye.

CAMPING: There are developed campgrounds in Fairy Stone State Park and on the lands of the U.S. Army Corps of Engineers.

ACCESS: Secondary Routes 605, 623, 776, 778, 780, 785, 787, 903, 907, and 934 off of Primary Highway 40 from the north and west, and Routes 346, 623, 624, 713, 822, and 838 off of Primary Highway 57 from the south.

FEEDER STREAMS: Smith River; Beards, Bowers, Goblintown, Nicholas, Otter, Poppy and Runnett Bag creeks; and Cow, Green, Ryan, and Spring branches.

BOAT-LAUNCHING AREA: The U.S. Army Corps of Engineers maintains boat-launching ramps at Bowens Creek, Goose Point, Horseshoe Point, Jamison Mill, Mines Branch, Philpott Park and Overlook, Runnett Bag, Ryans Branch, and Salthouse Branch.

WATER: This s a deep mountain lake with sharply pitching shorelines.

Lake Prince

Prince, a very beautiful lake, is one of the Suffolk Lakes, a cluster of coastal-plain lakes in the city of Suffolk. It is part of the water-supply system of the city of Norfolk, and a city permit is needed to fish it. It provides good fishing all year, with good winter fishing for chain pickerel and striped bass.

LOCATION: City of Suffolk.

SIZE: 777 acres.

FISH: Catfish, chain pickerel, crappie, largemouth bass, striped bass, and sunfish.

CAMPING: There is no public campground.

ACCESS: From Secondary Routes 604, 611, 633, and 690 north off of U.S. 460, and Secondary Routes 601, 603, 604, and 606 east off of Primary Highways 10 and 32.

FEEDER STREAMS: Ennis Pond and Carbell Swamp drainages.

BOAT-LAUNCHING AREA: There is a boat-launching ramp at Lake Prince fishing station on Route 604, two miles north of U.S. Highway 460, and rental boats are available.

WATER: A relatively deep coastal-plain lake, with a maximum depth of forty feet. Many long, narrow coves extend out from the main body of the lake.

Rivanna Reservoir

The Rivanna Reservoir is a segment of the water-supply system of the city of Charlottesville and is located on the South Fork of the Rivanna River. It is noted for its crappie fishing.

LOCATION: Albemarle County.

SIZE: 450 acres.

FISH: Catfish, crappie, largemouth bass, smallmouth bass, sunfish, and walleye.

CAMPING: There are no public camping facilities.

ACCESS: Secondary Routes 631, 643, 659, 660, 661, 676, and 743 off of U.S. Highway 29, north of Charlottesville.

FEEDER STREAMS: Mechums and Moormans rivers; the South Fork of the Rivanna River; and Ivy Branch.

BOAT-LAUNCHING AREA: There is a public boat-launching ramp at the end of Route 649, near the dam.

WATER: This is a long, reasonably deep mountain lake, mostly within the riverbed.

Smith Mountain Lake

Smith Mountain, a pumped-storage hydroelectric impoundment on the Roanoke River, is one of Virginia's most popular fishing lakes. It is owned by the Appalachian Power Company. Noted for its striped-bass fishing, it has also given up a couple of state-record muskies and some big crappie. The variety of fishing it offers is rich. It is one of Virginia's largest lakes.

LOCATION: The lake forms part of the boundary between Bedford and Franklin counties, Bedford and Pittsylvania counties, and Franklin and Pittsylvania counties.

SIZE: 20,000 acres.

FISH: Catfish, crappie, largemouth bass, muskie, smallmouth bass, striped bass, sunfish, walleye, white bass, and yellow perch.

CAMPING: There is a developed campground in Smith Mountain State Park.

ACCESS: Primary Highway 40 west off of U.S. Highway 29 at Gretna, and north to the lake on Secondary Routes 605, 626, 751, 777, 799, and 834. Primary Highway 122 between Bedford and Rocky Mount crosses the lake, and Secondary Routes 608, 616, and 670 lead east to the lake. Secondary Route 626 off of Primary Highway 43 between Altavista and Bedford also leads south to the lake.

FEEDER STREAMS: Blackwater and Roanoke rivers; Merriman Run, and Beckys, Betty, Foul, Gille, Grimes, Hales, Indian, Jumping, Lynville, Poplar Camp, Standiford, Stony, and Walton creeks; and the West Fork of Beaverdam Creek.

BOAT-LAUNCHING AREA: The Department of Game and Inland Fisheries maintains boat-launching ramps at Anthony Ford, Hales Ford, Hardy Ford, Penhook, and Scruggs.

WATER: A reasonably deep mountain lake, with plenty of shallow water.

South Holston Lake

South Holston is a Tennessee Valley Authority lake on the Virginia-Tennessee border and is enjoyed by anglers from Tennessee as well as by those from Virginia. Unfortunately, Virginia and Tennessee do not have a reciprocal agreement with respect to this lake as do Virginia and North Carolina on Buggs Island and Gaston lakes. Virginia anglers need a Tennessee license to fish the Tennessee portion of the lake, but fortunately, much of the lake is in Virginia.

LOCATION: Washington County.

SIZE: 7,580 acres.

FISH: Carp, catfish, crappie, largemouth bass, smallmouth bass, sunfish, trout, walleye, and white bass.

CAMPING: There is a developed campground in Washington County Park on the shores of the lake.

ACCESS: Virginia Primary Highway 75 and Secondary Route 670 south off of Interstate 81 and U.S. Highway 11. Secondary Routes 663, 664, 669, 670, 672, and 676 lead to the north side of the lake, and from the south there are Routes 664, 670, 674, and 835.

FEEDER STREAMS: Middle and South forks of the Holston River; Dry Run; Mays Branch; and Cox Mill and Spring creeks.

BOAT-LAUNCHING AREA: There is a public boat-launching ramp in Washington County Park, and the Department of Game and Inland Fisheries maintains a ramp at Avens.

Swift Creek Lake

Swift Creek Lake is part of the water-supply system of the county of Chesterfield. Gasoline motors are prohibited, and bank fishing is limited to the highway. The lake is generally referred to as Brandermill, and because public access is limited, it is not managed by the Department of Game and Inland Fisheries.

LOCATION: Chesterfield County.

SIZE: 1,800 acres.

FISH: Catfish, chain pickerel, crappie, largemouth bass, and sunfish.

CAMPING: There are no camping facilities.

ACCESS: Secondary Routes 604, 652, 667, and 668 off of U.S. Highway 360 lead to the lake.

FEEDER STREAMS: Deep, Dry, Tomahawk, and Swift creeks.

BOAT-LAUNCHING: There are no public launching ramps other than improvised ones.

WATER: A reasonably deep water-supply lake.

Western Branch Lake

Western Branch is one of the Suffolk Lakes located in the city of Suffolk, but actually belonging to the city of Norfolk. It is part of Norfolk's water-supply system, and a city permit is needed to fish it. The lake sprang into prominence in the 1960s as a hot spot for chain pickerel. Today, however, it is better known for its largemouth bass and striper fishing and its crappie, redbreasted sunfish, and warmouth. The lake is called The Branch by local anglers.

LOCATION: City of Suffolk.

SIZE: 1,579 acres.

FISH: Catfish, chain pickerel, crappie, largemouth bass, muskie, striped bass, sunfish, and walleye.

CAMPING: There are no public camping facilities.

ACCESS: Secondary Routes 601, 603, 605, 622, 634, and 695 off of Primary Highways 10 and 32, and Routes 604 and 682 off of U.S. Highway 460.

FEEDER STREAMS: Western Branch of the Nansemond River.

BOAT-LAUNCHING AREA: There is a gravel boat-launching ramp just off of Route 603 near Everetts and a Department of Game and Inland Fisheries launching ramp just off of the Girl Scout Road below Lake Prince Dam.

WATER: Western Branch, with maximum depths of 51 feet, is a rather deep lake for the coastal plain country.

Lake Whitehurst

Lake Whitehurst is part of the water-supply system for the city of Norfolk, and a city permit is required to fish it. Though known for a long time as a good largemouth-bass lake, for years it offered little more. A Department of Game and Inland Fisheries management plan, however, has expanded the fishery greatly. Today the lake offers a rich variety of fishing.

LOCATION: City of Norfolk.

SIZE: 458 acres.

FISH: Catfish, chain pickerel, crappie, hybrid striped bass, largemouth bass, striped bass, sunfish, walleye, white perch, and yellow perch.

CAMPING: There are no public camping facilities.

ACCESS: Access is off of U.S. Highway 13, approximately three miles south of the Chesapeake Bay Bridge-Tunnel.

FEEDER STREAMS: Small swamps.

BOAT-LAUNCHING AREA: There is a boat-launching ramp, and rental boats and electric motors are also available.

WATER: Generally shallow, but with some depths of forty feet over borrow pits.

Trout Waters

Some of the best trout fishing in the South can be found in Virginia's cold mountain streams. A few lakes also hold trout, but most angling effort is directed toward over 160 designated trout streams where fishing is supported by hatchery-reared fish. There are also several hundred native trout streams where brook trout enjoy natural reproduction.

While many of the better streams are found high in the mountains, there are also some good limestone streams in Southwest Virginia and in the Shenandoah Valley. Many of the mountain streams are too infertile to provide much food. As a consequence native brook trout, though they reproduce in such waters, do not often grow to appreciable size. In the better streams, however, they may reach ten to twelve inches.

Stream degradation and fishing pressure are the major problems faced by biologists charged with managing the state's trout-fishing waters.

The brook is the only trout native to Virginia waters, the rainbow having been introduced from the western United States and the brown from Europe.

Many of the designated trout streams are marginal waters that are stocked heavily with trout prior to opening day in March and at frequent intervals during April, May, and June. While the food in many of these streams is adequate to carry good trout populations, stream flow becomes a problem during the summer. Additionally, the water temperatures in some of the lower-elevation streams become too high for trout.

The native brookie is fairly easy to catch, and the populations will decline rapidly under too much fishing pressure. As a consequence the best fishing is usually found in the more remote streams.

Despite these few problems, Virginia anglers enjoy good trout fishing during a long season that generally opens at noon on the third Saturday in March and continues through the first of February.

Virginia anglers enjoy a wide range of possibilities that together provide them with good fishing throughout the long season. The possibilities can be classified five ways—the put-and-take fishing in designated trout waters, fee-fishing waters, fish-for-fun waters, the special trout waters, and native brook-trout streams. These options will be discussed separately.

PUT-AND-TAKE TROUT STREAMS

The over 160 trout streams that are stocked heavily prior to and during the early months of the trout season support the bulk of the trout fishing in Virginia. Trout for these waters are reared in the hatcheries of the Department of Game and Inland Fisheries

A trout angler works the Bullpasture River.

and released in the streams and a few lakes only after they have grown to legal size. Most are in the ten- to twelve-inch range, and some are larger. A few breeders, from which eggs have been stripped for the hatcheries, are also released to provide the opportunity for a trophy fish. Some of these fish top three pounds.

Designated trout waters are marked with "trout waters" signs. To fish them the angler needs a trout license in addition to the basic fishing license. The revenue generated by the trout licenses is used to operate the hatcheries and distribute the trout. Many of these streams are on private lands, and their status as public fishing water is always subject to change. Many, however, have been open for public fishing for years. The department, of course, does not stock private water not open to the public.

The list that follows includes the major designated trout streams. It may vary slightly from year to year.

ARARAT RIVER: In Patrick County, and stocked with brooks, browns, and rainbows.

BACK CREEK: Flows through Highland and Bath counties, and stocked with brooks and rainbows. Part of the stream is in the George Washington National Forest.

BACK CREEK: In Augusta County, and stocked with rainbows. Included are the main stem and the South Fork. Part of the stream is in the George Washington National Forest.

BACK CREEK: In Frederick County, and stocked with rainbows.

BARBOURS CREEK: In Craig County, and stocked with brooks and rainbows. Included are the main stem and the North Fork.

BIG BRUMLEY CREEK: In Washington County, and stocked with brooks and rainbows.

BIG CEDAR CREEK: In Russell County, and stocked with brooks, browns, and rainbows.

BIG FOX CREEK: In Grayson County, and stocked with browns and rainbows.

BIG IVY CREEK: In Patrick County, and stocked with brooks and rainbows.

BIG LAUREL CREEK: In Smyth County, and stocked with brooks and rainbows.

BIG PAULS CREEK: In Carroll County, and stocked with brooks.

BIG REED ISLAND CREEK: In Carroll County, and stocked with brooks, browns, and rainbows.

BIG STONEY CREEK: In Giles County, and stocked with brooks, browns, and rainbows.

BIG STONEY CREEK: In Scott County, and stocked with brooks and rainbows.

BIG STONEY CREEK: In Shenandoah County, and stocked with brooks, browns, and rainbows.

BIG TUMBLING CREEK: In Washington County, and stocked with brooks and rainbows. Part of the stream is a fee-fishing stream.

BIG WILSON CREEK: In Grayson County, and stocked with brooks and rainbows.

BOONE'S RUN: In Rockingham County, and stocked with brooks. Part of the stream is in the George Washington National Forest.

BRIERY BRANCH: In Rockingham County, and stocked with rainbows.

BROWN'S CREEK: In Amherst County, and stocked with brooks. Part of the stream is in the George Washington National Forest.

BULLPASTURE RIVER: In Highland and Bath counties, and stocked with brooks, browns, and rainbows.

BURKES FORK: In Carroll and Floyd counties, and stocked with brooks, browns, and rainbows.

BURNS CREEK: In Wise County, and stocked with rainbows. Part of the stream is in the Jefferson National Forest.

CEDAR CREEK: In Shenandoah and Frederick counties, and stocked with brooks, browns, and rainbows.

CLEAR CREEK: In Wise County, and stocked with rainbows. Part of the stream is in the Jefferson National Forest.

COMER'S CREEK: In Smyth County, and stocked with rainbows. Part of the stream is in the Jefferson National Forest.

COVE CREEK: In Craig County, and stocked with brooks.

COVE CREEK: In Tazewell County, and stocked with brooks and rainbows.

CRAIGS CREEK: In Montgomery County, and stocked with browns and rainbows. Part of the stream is in the Jefferson National Forest.

CRESSY CREEK: In Smyth County, and stocked with rainbows. Part of the stream is in the Jefferson National Forest.

CROOKED CREEK: In Carroll County, and stocked with brooks and rainbows. Part of the stream is fee-fishing water.

DAN RIVER: In Patrick County, and stocked with brooks, browns, and rainbows.

DAVIS MILL CREEK: In Amherst County, and stocked with brooks. Part of the stream is in the George Washington National Forest.

DICKEY'S CREEK: In Smyth County, and stocked with rainbows. Part of the stream is in the Jefferson National Forest.

DISMAL CREEK: In Giles County, and stocked with brooks. Part of the stream is in the Jefferson National Forest.

DISMAL RIVER: In Buchanan County, and stocked with brooks and rainbows.

DRY RIVER: In Rockingham County, and stocked with brooks and rainbows.

EAST FORK OF STONEY CREEK: In Wythe County, and stocked with rainbows. Part of the stream is in the Jefferson National Forest.

ELK CREEK: In Grayson County, and stocked with browns and rainbows.

FALLS HOLLOW: In Augusta County, and stocked with brooks. Part of the stream is in the George Washington National Forest. The stream is also known as Buffalo Branch.

FRYING PAN CREEK: In Dickenson County, and stocked with rainbows.

GARTH RUN: In Madison County, and stocked with brooks, browns, and rainbows.

GERMAN RUN: In Rockingham County, and stocked with browns and rainbows.

GLADE CREEK: In Roanoke County, and stocked with browns and rainbows.

GOOSE CREEK: In Floyd County, and stocked with browns and rainbows.

GREEN COVE CREEK: In Washington County, and stocked with brooks and rainbows. A section of the stream is subject to special regulations.

GULLION FORK CREEK: In Wythe County, and stocked with rainbows. Part of the stream is in the Jefferson National Forest.

HELTON CREEK: In Grayson County, and stocked with rainbows.

HOGUE CREEK: In Frederick County, and stocked with brooks, browns, and rainbows.

HONE QUARRY RUN: In Rockingham County, and stocked with rainbows. Part of the stream is in the George Washington National Forest.

HOWELL CREEK: In Floyd County, and stocked with brooks and rainbows.

HUGHES RIVER: In Madison County, and stocked with brooks and rainbows.

HUNTING CREEK: In Bedford County, and stocked with brooks. Part of the stream is in the Jefferson National Forest.

HURRICANE CREEK: In Smyth County, and stocked with rainbows. Part of the stream is in the Jefferson National Forest.

IRISH CREEK: In Rockbridge County, and stocked with brooks and rainbows.

JACKSON RIVER: In Highland and Bath counties, and stocked with brooks, browns, and rainbows. Part of the stream is in the George Washington National Forest.

JENNINGS CREEK: In Botetourt County, and stocked with brooks and rainbows.

JERRY'S RUN: In Alleghany County, and stocked with rainbows. Part of the stream is in the George Washington National Forest.

LAUREL CREEK: In Tazewell County, and stocked with brooks and rainbows. Part of the stream is fee-fishing water.

LAUREL FORK CREEK: In Bland County, and stocked with rainbows.

LAUREL FORK CREEK: In Carroll County, and stocked with brooks.

LAUREL FORK CREEK: In Floyd County, and stocked with brooks.

LICK CREEK: In Bland County, and stocked with rainbows. Part of the stream is in the Jefferson National Forest.

LITTLE INDIAN CREEK: In Floyd County, and stocked with rainbows.

LITTLE IRISH CREEK: In Amherst County, and stocked with brooks. Part of the stream is in the George Washington National Forest.

LITTLE REED ISLAND CREEK: In Carroll County, and stocked with browns and rainbows.

LITTLE RIVER: In Floyd County, and stocked with brooks, browns, and rainbows. Included are the main stem and the West Fork.

LITTLE PASSAGE CREEK: In Shenandoah County, and stocked with rainbows. Part of the stream is in the George Washington National Forest.

LITTLE STONY CREEK: In Scott County, and stocked with brooks and rainbows.

LITTLE TUMBLING CREEK: In Tazewell County, and stocked with brooks and rainbows.

LOVILLS CREEK: In Carroll County, and stocked with rainbows.

LYNCH RIVER: In Greene County, and stocked with rainbows.

MCFALLS CREEK: In Botetourt County, and stocked with rainbows. Part of the stream is in the Jefferson National Forest.

MAGGADEE CREEK: In Franklin County, and stocked with brooks, browns, and rainbows.

MARTIN'S CREEK: In Lee County, and stocked with brooks, browns, and rainbows.

MAURY RIVER: In Rockbridge County, and stocked with browns and rainbows.

MAYO RIVER: In Patrick County, and stocked with brooks, browns, and rainbows. Includes North and South forks.

MEADOW CREEK: In Floyd County, and stocked with rainbows.

MIDDLE CREEK: In Botetourt County, and stocked with rainbows. Part of the stream is in the Jefferson National Forest.

MIDDLE FORK OF HOLSTON RIVER: In Smyth County, and stocked with browns and rainbows.

MIDDLE FORK OF POWELL RIVER: In Wise County, and stocked with brooks and rainbows.

MIDDLE FOX CREEK: In Grayson County, and stocked with brooks and rainbows.

MILL CREEK: In Shenandoah County, and stocked with brooks and rainbows.

MIRA FORK CREEK: In Floyd County, and stocked with brooks.

MOORMANS RIVER: In Albemarle County, and stocked with brooks and rainbows. Included are the North and South forks.

MOUNTAIN FORK: In Wise County, and stocked with rainbows. Part of the stream is in the Jefferson National Forest.

NORTH CREEK: In Botetourt County, and stocked with rainbows. Part of the stream is in the Jefferson National Forest, and another part is subject to special regulations.

NORTH RIVER: In Augusta County, and stocked with brooks and rainbows. Part of the stream is in the George Washington National Forest.

PADDY RUN: In Shenandoah and Frederick counties, and stocked with browns and rainbows. Part of the stream is in the George Washington National Forest.

PADS CREEK: In Bath County, and stocked with rainbows. Part of the stream is in the George Washington National Forest.

PASSAGE CREEK: In Shenandoah County, and stocked with brooks, browns, and rainbows.

PEACH BOTTOM CREEK: In Grayson County, and stocked with brooks and rainbows.

PEAK CREEK: In Pulaski County, and stocked with browns and rainbows, but in the West Fork only.

PEDLAR RIVER: In Amherst County, and stocked with brooks, browns, and rainbows.

PETERS MILL CREEK: In Shenandoah County, and stocked with rainbows. Part of the stream is in the George Washington National Forest.

PINEY RIVER: In Amherst County, and stocked with brooks. Included are the South Fork and the main stem.

POORHOUSE CREEK: In Patrick County, and stocked with brooks.

POTTS CREEK: In Craig County, and stocked with brooks, browns, and rainbows.

POUND RIVER: In Dickenson County, and stocked with browns and rainbows.

POUNDING MILL CREEK: In Alleghany County, and stocked with rainbows. Part of the stream is in the George Washington National Forest.

POVERTY CREEK: In Montgomery County, and stocked with rainbows. Part of the stream is in the Jefferson National Forest.

POWELL RIVER: In Lee County, and stocked with browns and rainbows, but in the North Fork only.

RAMSEY'S DRAFT: In Augusta County, and stocked with brooks. Part of the stream is in the George Washington National Forest.

ROANOKE RIVER: In the cities of Roanoke and Salem, and stocked with browns and rainbows.

ROANOKE RIVER: In Montgomery County, and stocked with browns and rainbows, but in the South Fork only.

ROARING FORK: In Tazewell County, and stocked with brooks and rainbows.

ROARING RUN: In Botetourt County, and stocked with browns and rainbows.

ROBINSON RIVER: In Madison County, and stocked with brooks, browns, and rainbows.

ROCK CASTLE CREEK: In Patrick County, and stocked with brooks and rainbows.

ROSE RIVER: In Madison County, and stocked with brooks and rainbows.

ROUND MEADOW CREEK: In Patrick County, and stocked with brooks and rainbows.

RUNNETT BAG CREEK: In Franklin County, and stocked with browns and rainbows.

RUSH FORK CREEK: In Floyd County, and stocked with brooks.

RUSSELL FORK RIVER: In Dickenson County, and stocked with browns and rainbows.

SHENANDOAH RIVER: In Rockingham County, and stocked with brooks, browns, and rainbows, but in the North Fork only.

SHOEMAKER RIVER: In Rockingham County, and stocked with rainbows. Part of the stream is in the George Washington National Forest.

SKIDMORE FORK: In Rockingham County, and stocked with brooks. Part of the stream is in the George Washington National Forest.

SMITH CREEK: In Alleghany County, and stocked with brooks. Much of the stream is in the George Washington National Forest and part is also subject to special regulations.

SMITH RIVER: In Henry County, and stocked with brooks, browns, and rainbows. A section of the stream is subject to special regulations.

SNAKE CREEK: In Carroll County, and stocked with browns and rainbows. A section of the stream is subject to special regulations.

SOUTH FORK OF THE HOLSTON RIVER: In Smyth County, and stocked with brooks, browns, and rainbows. Part of the stream is in the Jefferson National Forest.

SOUTH FORK OF POTOMAC RIVER: In Highland County, and stocked with brooks, browns, and rainbows.

SOUTH RIVER: In Greene County, and stocked with brooks, browns, and rainbows.

SOUTH RIVER: In Rockbridge County, and stocked with browns and rainbows.

SPRING RUN: In Bath County, and stocked with brooks, browns, and rainbows.

STALEY'S CREEK: In Smyth County, and stocked with brooks, browns, and rainbows.

STEWARTS CREEK: In Carroll County, and stocked with brooks.

STOCK COUNTY: In Scott County, and stocked with rainbows.

STRAIGHT BRANCH: In Washington County, and stocked with rainbows. Part of the stream is in the Jefferson National Forest.

SWIFT RUN: In Greene County, and stocked with browns and rainbows.

TENNESSEE LAUREL: In Washington County, and stocked with browns and rainbows. There is good wild-trout fishing in the upper reaches of the stream.

TINKER CREEK: In Roanoke County, and stocked with browns and rainbows.

TYE RIVER: In Nelson County, and stocked with brooks, browns, and rainbows. Included are the North Fork and the main stem.

VALLEY CREEK: In Washington County, and stocked with rainbows.

WEST FORK OF DRY RUN: In Wythe County, and stocked with brooks. Part of the stream is in the Jefferson National Forest.

WEST FORK OF REED CREEK: In Wythe County, and stocked with rainbows. Part of the stream is in the Jefferson National Forest.

WHITETOP LAUREL: In Washington County, and stocked with brooks, browns, and rainbows. A section of the stream is subject to special regulations.

WILKINS CREEK: In Frederick County, and stocked with brooks, browns, and rainbows.

WILSON CREEK: In Bath County, and stocked with brooks. Part of the stream is in the George Washington National Forest, and that within the boundaries of Douthat State Park is fee-fishing water.

WOLF CREEK: In Bland County, and stocked with browns and rainbows.

WOLF CREEK: In Tazewell County, and stocked with browns and rainbows.

Also included in the put-and-take system of trout waters are a number of lakes and ponds. They include Bark Camp Lake in Wise County, Beartree Lake in Washington, Braley Pond in Augusta, Briery Lake in Rockingham, Clearbrook Lake in Frederick, Clifton Forge Lake in Alleghany, Dry Run Lake in Rockingham, Elkhorn Lake in Augusta, Gullion Fork Pond in Wythe, Hales Lake in Grayson, Hearthstone Lake in Augusta, Hone Quarry lake in Rockingham, lower Sherando Lake in Augusta, Silver Lake in Rockingham, Skidmore Lake in Rockingham, Tomahawk Pond in Shenandoah, Sugar Hollow Lake in Albemarle, and upper Sherando lake in Augusta County.

Beartree Lake and Gullion Fork Pond are in the Jefferson National Forest, and Braley Pond, Briery Lake, Clifton Forge Lake, Elkhorn Lake, Hearthstone Lake, Hone Quarry Lake, lower Sherando Lake, Tomahawk Pond, and upper Sherando Lake are in the George Washington National Forest.

Most of the lakes and ponds are stocked with rainbows, but a few also receive some brooks and browns.

FEE-FISHING WATERS

Fee-fishing waters are a refinement of the put-and-take concept. They are stocked more frequently, usually weekly, and more often if the fishing pressure warrants it. Anglers pay a daily fee, for which they can take a limit of trout. The fee-fishing season runs from the March opening of the trout season through Labor Day. During this period anglers must pay the daily fee and also possess a basic state fishing license. The usual trout license is not required. After Labor Day, however, these waters revert to designated trout waters, and a trout license is required.

There are a trio of fee-fishing complexes in Virginia, two of which include a lake as well as a stream.

The Upper Reaches of Big Tumbling Creek and Laurel Bed Lake and Creek

Big Tumbling Creek forms in the Clinch Mountain Wildlife Management Area in Smyth County and flows through Washington County to join the North Fork of the Holston River. Laurel Bed Lake, a 300-acre high-elevation lake, is formed by Laurel Bed Creek, which joins Brier Cove Creek to form Big Tumbling Creek. Laurel Bed Creek forms in Russell County, but flows mostly through the wildlife management area. Laurel Bed Lake is in the wildlife management area.

There is a boat-launching ramp on the lake and a developed campground in the wildlife management area.

The lake and the streams are reached by Secondary Routes 613 and 647 out of Saltville.

The wildlife management area spreads into Russell, Smyth, and Tazewell counties, with Laurel Bed Lake in Russell counties Laurel Bed Creek in Russell and Tazewell counties, and Big

Tumbling Creek forming the boundary between Russell and Smyth counties and Russell and Washington counties.

Fishing permits are available at the wildlife management area headquarters.

Douthat Lake State Park and Wilson Creek

Douthat State Park is on the Alleghany-Bath counties line, but the lake and the upper reaches of Wilson Creek are in the Bath County portion of the park. Wilson Creek forms in the George Washington National Forest to the north of the park and lake. It is the major feeder stream for the sixty-acre lake.

Fee-fishing waters include the lake and Wilson Creek north to the park border.

Rental boats are available, and there is a gravel boat-launching ramp at the upper end of the lake. Only electric motors are allowed. Fishing permits are available at the boat rental dock.

There are developed campgrounds in the state park.

The lake, stream, and park are reached by Secondary Route 629 north from Clifton Forge.

Crooked Creek Wildlife Management Area

The fee-fishing section of Crooked Creek is within the wildlife management area. It is stocked frequently during the fee-fishing season. There is also a three-mile stretch of the stream that offers fishing for native brook trout.

The wildlife management area and the stream are located in Carroll County just east of Galax.

Fishing permits are available at the concession stand near the wildlife management area headquarters. Camping in self-contained units only is allowed.

The stream is reached by Secondary Routes 620 and 720, with 720 passing through the wildlife management area. The stream is approximately four miles southeast of Galax and three miles south of U.S. Highway 58.

FISH-FOR-FUN WATERS

The Rapidan River in the Madison County section of the Shenandoah National Park and the Rapidan Wildlife Management Area is the only fish-for-fun stream in Viginia, but one of the most popular in the East. The fish-for-fun section begins at the park boundary and extends upstream the length of the river to include its tributaries. The Staunton River is the major tributary. Since all trout must be returned to the water, there is no closed season. Only artificial lures with single, barbless hooks are permitted.

There are developed campgrounds in the Shenandoah National Park.

The Rapidan River is reached by Secondary Road 662 north from Graves Mill or by Secondary Road 649 west from Criglersville, both in Madison County.

Special Trout Waters

Special trout streams and lakes are another group of waters subject to special regulations that include put-and-take, put-and-grow, and wild-trout waters. On most such streams artificial lures with single hooks only are required, and special creel and size limits are imposed.

On the following streams, or sections of them, only artificial lures with single hooks are allowed, the minimum size limit is twelve inches, and the creel limit is six.

SMITH CREEK: In Alleghany County: that section downstream from the Clifton Forge Dam to a George Washington National Forest sign above the Chesapeake and Ohio Railroad dam.

SNAKE CREEK: In Carroll County: that section upstream from its mouth to Hall Ford on Big Snake Creek and to the junction of Secondary Routes 674 and 922 on Little Snake Fork.

On the following streams the minimum size limit is nine inches (with the exception of the Conway River) and the creel limit is six.

CONWAY RIVER: In Greene and Madison counties: that section of the stream within the Rapidan Wildlife Management Area. A special size limit of eight inches applies here.

GREEN COVE CREEK: In Washington County: that section of the stream from its mouth upstream to Secondary Route 859.

LITTLE STONY CREEK: In Giles County: that section of the stream within the Jefferson National Forest.

LITTLE STONY CREEK: In Shenandoah County: that section upstream from the Woodstock Water Supply Dam.

NORTH CREEK: In Botetourt County: the stream and its tributaries upstream from the first bridge above the North Creek Campground.

ST. MARY'S RIVER: In Augusta County: the stream and its tributaries upstream from the gate at the George Washington National Forest border.

WHITETOP LAUREL: In Washington County: that section upstream from the first railroad trestle above Taylor Valley to the creek junction where Green Cove Creek enters the stream.

On the following streams the creel limit is two and the minimum size limit is sixteen inches.

BUFFALO CREEK: In Rockbridge County: that section from the confluence of Collier's Creek upstream to the confluence of North and South Buffalo creeks.

MOSSY CREEK: In Augusta County: that section upstream from the Augusta-Rockingham County line to a sign at the mouth of Joseph's Run. Only fly-fishing is permitted in this section of Mossy Creek.

SMITH RIVER: In Henry County: that section for three miles downstream from a sign below the east bank of Towne Creek.

Special regulations also apply to the waters of the Blue Ridge Parkway, Shenandoah National Park, and the upper and lower Sherando lakes. Collectively, these waters offer fishing for wild trout as well as put-and-take trout.

Live or dead fish and fish eggs are prohibited baits in the Blue Ridge Parkway waters, though other natural baits can be used in most of the streams. Artificial lures with single hooks only are required in Abbott Lake, the popular Peaks of Otter lake where fingerling brown trout are released to grow. Creel and size limits and other special regulations are posted on the shore of the lake.

The Shenandoah National Park trout season runs from the opening of the general trout season through October 15. Only artificial lures with single hooks are permitted. The minimum size limit is eight inches and the creel limit is five.

In the upper and lower Sherando Lakes in Augusta County, five-day nonresident and resident fishing licenses are valid from June 1 through Labor Day, but at other times a trout license is required.

Put-and-Grow Waters

The put-and-grow trout program is limited to waters that will carry trout from one season to the next, and particularly through the hot summer months. Fingerling trout, under the minimum size limit of seven inches, are released in these waters in the hope that they will survive, grow, and reproduce. Some Virginia waters are capable of this.

The special streams mentioned above are good examples, streams such as Beaver Creek, Buffalo Creek, Green Cove Creek, Little River, Mossy Creek, Snake Creek, Skidmore Lake, and Whitetop Laurel.

Trout survive well in tailwaters, those streams immediately below mountain lakes. The Smith River below Philpott Dam in Henry County is a good example. Brown trout enjoy good natural reproduction in these waters. The Jackson River below Gathright Dam offers a good potential, but for legal reasons it is an untapped one.

There are also the deep, two-story reservoirs where the water in the bottom half of the lake remains cold enough for trout throughout the year. Year-round fishing is available in Moomaw, Philpott, and South Holston lakes. Trout released in these deep lakes grow to trophy size, though they do not often reproduce. Abbott is another good put-and-grow lake.

NATIVE BROOK-TROUT STREAMS

Wild brook trout, or native trout, are found in cold mountain streams from the eastern slopes of the Blue Ridge Mountains west to the Kentucky and West Virginia borders. An inventory made by the Department of Game and Inland Fisheries revealed over 400 of them, offering over 2,000 miles of fishing. Some are probably so small and remote that no one has bothered to name them.

Many of the native brook-trout streams are found in the George Washington and Jefferson national forests, and some of the very best are in the Shenandoah National Park. There are also a number of excellent native-trout streams on private lands, where the permission of the landowner is needed to fish.

Some of these streams are small, so small in fact that the average angler will pass them up, not realizing that a few hundred yards upstream or down there is some excellent trout fishing.

A complete list of the native brook-trout streams in Virginia would be too long to include here—even if it was available. Attempting to name a few of the better ones would imply that they are the very best in Virginia, an erroneous assumption that could place too mcuh pressure on a few good streams. But there is no need for such a list. A Sunday afternoon drive over national-forest roads or other back roads in high country will turn up dozens of them. Just about any such stream will hold brook trout. Or buy some topographic maps of the region and study them for the thin blue lines that represent likely trout streams. Appalachian Trail Club maps are also good.

Some of the best native-trout fishing in Virginia is found in the over thirty trout streams in the Shenandoah National Park. Maps and a list of these streams are available from the park headquarters. Most are best reached by parking on the Skyline Drive and hiking down the mountain to their headwaters.

Part of the joy of fishing for the colorful little brook trout is discovering new waters.

Department of Game and Inland Fisheries Lakes _____

Few public waters in Virginia are managed specifically for fishing, but those owned and managed by the Department of Game and Inland Fisheries are. There are over twenty of them, ranging in size from 19-acre Horsepen Lake in Buckingham County to 845-acre Briery Creek Lake in Prince Edward.

Most of these public waters furnish fishing for bluegill, crappie, largemouth bass, and shellcrackers, but Bark Camp Lake in Scott County is stocked with trout, and Burke Lake in Fairfax County is noted for its muskie fishing. Lake Conner has given up some trophy largemouth bass and crappie, and Orange

County Lake is noted for its northern pike fishing. Hidden Valley Lake also offers trout fishing, and Laurel Bed Lake is part of the Big Tumbling Creek trout fee-fishing complex.

Because these lakes were built specifically for fishing and funded by fishing-license revenues plus excise taxes levied at the federal level on fishing-tackle sales, other water activities such as sailing and swimming are prohibited. Generally, outboard motors are prohibited, though electric motors are allowed. Most offer launching facilities for small boats, and camping is allowed near some of them. On a few lakes where the demand warrants it, concessionaires provide rental boats and electric motors, bait, and limited supplies of fishing tackle.

Generally, there is no charge for fishing these lakes, though the concessionaires may charge a modest boat-launching fee on some of them.

The Department lakes are scattered throughout the state from east to west and from north to south. Brief sketches of the twenty-odd lakes follow.

Airfield Lake

LOCATION: Five miles south of Wakefield on Secondary Route 628 in Sussex County.

SIZE: 105 acres.

SPECIES: Chain pickerel, crappie, largemouth bass, and sunfish.

FACILITIES: Undeveloped dirt boat-launching ramp, parking area, and lodging in 4-H center.

Albemarle Lake

LOCATION: In Albemarle County, and reached by Secondary Route 680 north from the intersection of U.S. Highway 250 and Primary Highway 240 west of Charlottesville. Follow Route 680 to 810, turn right, and then make a second right on 614 in the town of White Hall. Take 614 to 675 and turn right to the lake.

SIZE: 35 acres.

SPECIES: Catfish, crappie, largemouth bass, northern pike, sunfish, and walleye.

Department of Game and Inland Fisheries Lakes

1. Airfield Lake
2. Albemarle Lake
3. Amelia Lake
4. Bark Camp Lake
5. Briery Creek Lake
6. Brunswick County Lake
7. Burke Lake
8. Lake Burton
9. Chandlers Millpond
10. Lake Conner
11. Lake Curtis
12. Fluvanna Ruritan Lake
13. Frederick County Lake
14. Game Refuge Lake
15. Gardy's Millpond
16. Lake Gordon
17. Hidden Valley Lake
18. Horsepen Lake
19. Lake Keokee
20. Laurel Bed Lake
21. Nelson County Lake
22. Nottoway County Lake
23. Orange County Lake
24. Phelps Pond
25. Powhatan Lakes
26. Lake Robertson
27. Rural Retreat Lake
28. Lake Shenandoah
29. Thompson Lake

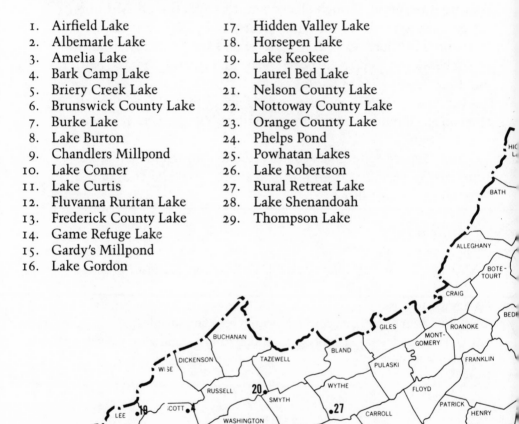

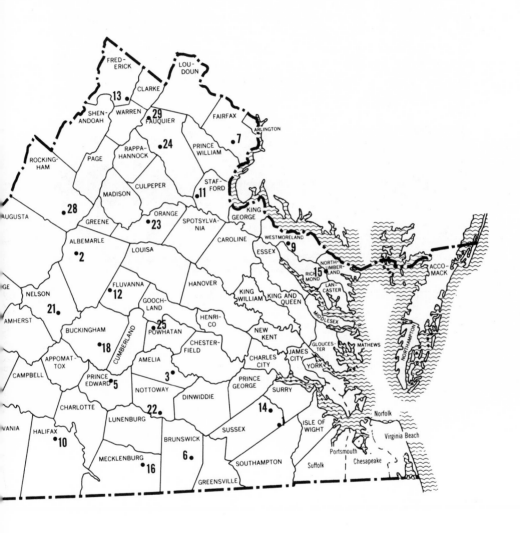

Highway sign pointing to Orange County Lake.

FACILITIES: Launching ramp for small boats.

Amelia Lake

LOCATION: In Amelia County, and reached by taking Secondary Route 604 off of U.S. Highway 360 just south of the Appomattox River and following the signs to Amelia Wildlife Management Area.

SIZE: 100 acres.

SPECIES: Catfish, crappie, largemouth bass, sunfish, and walleye.

FACILITIES: Launching ramp for small boats. Camping in self-contained units is allowed. A fishing pier will accommodate handicapped anglers.

Bark Camp Lake

LOCATION: In the Jefferson National Forest in Scott County, and seven miles north of Dungannan on Secondary Routes 653 and 706.

SIZE: 66 acres.

SPECIES: Largemouth bass, sunfish, and trout.

FACILITIES: Launching ramp for small boats, and primitive camping in the national forest.

Briery Creek Lake

LOCATION: In Prince Edward County, and reached from U.S. Highway 15 or off of 15 via Secondary Routes 701 or 604 and 705. Routes 604 and 705 provide access from the west.

SIZE: 845 acres.

SPECIES: Catfish, chain pickerel, crappie, largemouth bass, and sunfish.

FACILITIES: Several boat-launching ramps, and camping in self-contained vehicles is allowed.

Lake Brittle

LOCATION: In Fauquier County, and reached by Secondary Route 600 east of New Baltimore to Route 676.

SIZE: 77 acres.

SPECIES: Catfish, crappie, largemouth bass, sunfish, tiger muskie, and walleye.

FACILITIES: Launching ramp for small boats, and a concessionaire offering rental boats, bait, and other supplies. Fishing pier for handicapped anglers.

Brunswick County Lake

LOCATION: In Brunswick County, and reached by Secondary Route 638 off of U.S. Highway 58 east of Edgerton.

SIZE: 150 acres.

SPECIES: Catfish, crappie, largemouth bass, and sunfish.

FACILITIES: Launching ramp for small boats.

Burke Lake

LOCATION: In Fairfax County on Secondary Route 123 between Fairfax and Occoquan.

SIZE: 218 acres.

SPECIES: Catfish, crappie, largemouth bass, muskie, sunfish, and walleye.

FACILITIES: Two boat-launching ramps, and a concessionaire offering rental boats, bait, and other supplies. Campground in surrounding park.

Lake Burton

LOCATION: In Pittsylvania County, and reached by Secondary Routes 800 and 969, approximately six miles north of Callands.

SIZE: 76 acres.

SPECIES: Catfish, crappie, largemouth bass, and sunfish.

FACILITIES: Launching ramp for small boats.

Chandlers Millpond

LOCATION: On Virginia Primary Highway 3 just west of Montross in Westmoreland County.

SIZE: 75 acres.

SPECIES: Catfish, chain pickerel, crappie, largemouth bass, and sunfish.

FACILITIES: Undeveloped boat-launching ramp.

Lake Conner

LOCATION: In Halifax County, and reached by Secondary Route 624 off of Route 623, and approximately five miles from Secondary Route 603 west of Whitesville.

SIZE: 111 acres.

SPECIES: Catfish, crappie, largemouth bass, and sunfish.

FACILITIES: Launching ramp for small boats.

Lake Curtis

LOCATION: In Stafford County, and reached by U.S. Highway 17 to Secondary Route 612 and then Route 622 to the lake, or take Route 616 off of U.S. 17 to 662.

SIZE: 91 acres.

SPECIES: Catfish, crappie, largemouth bass, sunfish, tiger muskie, and walleye.

FACILITIES: Launching ramp for small boats.

Fluvanna Ruritan Lake

LOCATION: In Fluvanna County, and reached by Secondary Route 619 off of Virginia Primary Highway 53 at Cunningham.
SIZE: 50 acres.
SPECIES: Catfish, crappie, largemouth bass, sunfish, and walleye.
FACILITIES: Launching ramp for small boats.

Frederick County Lake

LOCATION: In Frederick County off of U.S. Highways 340 and 522 just north of Warren County line.
SIZE: 120 acres.
SPECIES: Crappie, largemouth bass, and sunfish.
FACILITIES: Launching ramp for small boats.

Game Refuge Lake

LOCATION: In Sussex County, and reached off of U.S. Highway 460 at Waverly by Secondary Routes 602 and 625.
SIZE: 40 acres.
SPECIES: Chain pickerel, crappie, largemouth bass, and sunfish.
FACILITIES: Launching ramp for small boats.

Gardy's Millpond

LOCATION: In Northumberland County off of U.S. Highway 360 on Secondary Route 617 west of Hyacinth.
SIZE: 75 acres.
SPECIES: Crappie, largemouth bass, and sunfish.
FACILITIES: Launching ramp for small boats, but no bank fishing permitted.

Lake Gordon

LOCATION: In Mecklenburg County, and reached west of South Hill by Secondary Routes 664 and 799 off of U.S. Highways 1 and 58.

SIZE: 157 acres.

SPECIES: Catfish, crappie, largemouth bass, and sunfish.

FACILITIES: Launching ramp for small boats.

Hidden Valley Lake

LOCATION: In Washington County on Hidden Valley Wildlife Management Area, and reached off of Secondary Route 690 approximately ten miles northwest of Abingdon.

SIZE: 61 acres.

SPECIES: Rock bass and smallmouth bass.

FACILITIES: Launching ramp for small boats, but no camping except in self-contained units.

Horsepen Lake

LOCATION: In Buckingham County on Horsepen Wildlife Management Area, and reached by taking Secondary Route 638 for three miles south of Buckingham Court House.

SIZE: 19 acres.

SPECIES: Chain pickerel, crappie, largemouth bass, northern pike, and sunfish.

FACILITIES: Launching ramp for small boats, and camping in self-contained units only.

Lake Keokee

LOCATION: In Lee County in Jefferson National Forest, and reached by Secondary Route 623.

SIZE: 98 acres.

SPECIES: Crappie, largemouth bass, and sunfish.

FACILITIES: Launching ramp for small boats, and camping in the national forest.

Laurel Bed Lake

LOCATION: In Russell County on the Clinch Mountain Wildlife Management Area, and reached by Secondary Routes 613 and 747 approximately five miles north of Saltville.

SIZE: 300 acres.

SPECIES: Trout.

FACILITIES: Launching ramp for small boats, and camping in a developed campground.

Nelson County Lake

LOCATION: In Nelson County and reached from the intersection of U.S. Highway 29 and Secondary Route 655 at Colleen, east of Route 655 to Route 812, and east on 812 east of Arrington to the lake.

SIZE: 41 acres.

SPECIES: Catfish, crappie, hybrid striped bass, largemouth bass, and sunfish.

FACILITIES: Launching ramp for small boats, and a concessionaire offering rental boats, bait, other supplies, and camping.

Nottoway County Lake

LOCATION: In Nottoway County and six miles south of Blackstone. Reached by Secondary Route 606.

SIZE: 188 acres.

SPECIES: Catfish, crappie, largemouth bass, and sunfish.

FACILITIES: Launching ramp for small boats.

Orange County Lake

LOCATION: In Orange County, and reached by Secondary Route 629 off of Virginia Primary Route 20 approximately two miles east of Orange.

SIZE: 124 acres.

SPECIES: Catfish, crappie, largemouth bass, northern pike, sunfish, and walleye.

FACILITIES: Launching ramp for small boats, and a concessionaire offers rental boats, electric motors, bait, tackle, and snacks. Fishing pier for handicapped anglers.

Phelps Pond

LOCATION: In Fauquier County on the C. F. Phelps Wildlife Management Area, and reached by Secondary Route 651 off of U.S. Highway 17.

SIZE: 3 acres.

SPECIES: Catfish, largemouth bass, and sunfish.

FACILITIES: No formal boat-launching ramp, and camping limited to self-contained vehicles.

Powhatan Lakes

LOCATION: In Powhatan County on Powhatan Wildlife Management Area and reached by Secondary Routes 684 and 625 north off of U.S. Highway 60.

SIZE: 66 acres.

SPECIES: Catfish, crappie, largemouth bass, northern pike, and sunfish.

FACILITIES: Launching ramp for small boats, and camping in self-contained vehicles only.

NOTE: Bass, Bullhead, and Sunfish ponds, all under ten acres, offer much the same kind of fishing.

Lake Robertson

LOCATION: In Rockbridge County west of Collierstown on Secondary Routes 646 and 653.

SIZE: 31 acres.

SPECIES: Catfish, crappie, largemouth bass, and sunfish.

FACILITIES: Launching ramp for small boats, and a concessionaire offers rental boats, bait, and other supplies. Camping in a developed campground.

Rural Retreat Lake

LOCATION: In Wythe County and south of Rural Retreat on Secondary Routes 677 and 671 off of Route 749.

SIZE: 90 acres.

SPECIES: Crappie and largemouth bass.

FACILITIES: There is a launching ramp for small boats, and a concessionaire offers rental boats, bait, and other supplies. Camping is a developed campground.

Lake Shenandoah

LOCATION: In Rockingham County on Virginia Primary Highway 276 near Penn Laird, and off of U.S. Highway 33 east of Harrisonburg.

SIZE: 37 acres.

SPECIES: Crappie, largemouth bass, and sunfish.

FACILITIES: Launching ramp for small boats.

Thompson Lake

LOCATION: In Fauquier County in the G. Richard Thompson Wildlife Management Area reached by Secondary Routes 638 and 688 off of Interstate Highway 66.

SIZE: 10 acres.

SPECIES: Catfish, largemouth bass, and sunfish.

FACILITIES: No boat ramp; camping in self-contained units only.

Other Lakes and Ponds _____

In addition to the major public lakes and reservoirs, Department of Game and Inland Fisheries lakes, and the trout lakes and ponds, there are dozens of other small lakes and ponds that offer good fishing. Many are privately owned, but open to the public—sometimes for a modest fee, but often by simply asking for permission. Others are on public lands such as the military reservations, state forests, state parks, or the lands of county or city governments.

Most of the lakes and ponds on public lands are managed for fishing under cooperative agreements between the Department of Game and Inland Fisheries and the state or local governments or the military authorities.

In some instances rental boats are available, and often there are good boat-launching ramps. In others, however, launching a private boat or canoe may mean simply sliding it down a grassy bank. Some of the private lakes are owned and maintained in connection with developed campgrounds, and fishing is limited to campers registered in the campgrounds.

In addition to these man-made impoundments, there are thousands of farm ponds scattered the length and breadth of the Old Dominion, fertile waters that give up some of the largest bass caught each year. The farm ponds also offer excellent fishing for bluegills, red-eared sunfish, and sometimes crappie and other sunfish. Many can be fished by simply asking for permission. The panfish populations in most of them are under-harvested, and more fishing pressure would improve the fishing. Bluegills, particularly, are highly prolific, and they tend to over-populate the small bodies of water and become stunted.

Not to be overlooked are the thousands of beaver ponds found throughout the state. Some of them are sizable, and they offer good fishing during the early years of their lives. It is a transitional kind of fishing, however, as the ponds eventually fill with silt.

The county-by-county listing of lakes and ponds that follows includes most of those open for public fishing in one way or another. Others are added yearly, however, and the list is probably not complete. Most of these waters offer fishing for largemouth bass and the various panfish.

Accomack County

DRUMMOND'S MILLPOND: 14 acres.

POND NUMBER 1: Owned by the Virginia Truck and Ornithopter Research Station, and open to public fishing from March 1 through November 30. Located 1½ miles west of Painter on Secondary Route 614. 10 acres.

A lone angler works the calm waters of Lee Hall Lake.

Albemarle County

BEAVER CREEK LAKE: Owned by the County of Albemarle, and open to public fishing. Gasoline motors prohibited. Launching ramp reached by Secondary Route 680 off of U.S. Highway 250 west of Charlottesville. 103 acres.

CHRIS GREENE LAKE: Owned by the county of Albemarle, and open to public fishing. Gasoline motors prohibited. Launching ramp reached by Secondary Route 649 and then 606 north of Charlottesville-Albemarle Airport. 62 acres.

LAKE REYNOVIA: Privately owned, but open for a fee to campers registered in campground on the lake. Rental boats available. Located 3½ miles south of Charlottesville on Secondary Route 742 off of Primary Route 20. 8½ acres.

PACE'S POND: Privately owned, but open to public fishing by permit. Located off of Secondary Route 620 approximately two miles south of Woodridge. 20 acres.

SUPERIOR STONE CORPORATION LAKE: Privately owned, but open to public fishing by a permit. Located off of Secondary Route 708 north of Hardware River bridge on U.S. Highway 29. 10 acres.

TOTIER CREEK LAKE: Owned by the County of Albemarle, and open to public fishing. No gasoline motors allowed. Launching ramp off of Secondary Route 726 near Scottsville. 66 acres.

Amelia County

BEAVER POND: Privately owned, but open to public fishing for a fee. Rental boats available, and located off of Primary Route 153, approximately 4½ miles south of its intersection with U.S. Highway 360. 62 acres.

Amherst County

BIG ISLAND RESERVOIR: Owned by Bedford Pulp and Paper Company, but open to public fishing by permit. Reached by U.S. Highway 501 northwest from Lynchburg to Big Island and then right on a light-duty road to the lake.

COLEMANS FALL RESERVOIR: Owned by Bedford Pulp and Paper Company, but open to public fishing by permit. Reached by U.S. Highway 501 southeast from Big Island, turning left on unimproved road just beyond Secondary Route 752 to the reservoir. 1,700 acres.

CUSHAW LAKE: Owned by Virginia Power Company, and open to public fishing. Reached by U.S. Highway 501 and Primary Highway 130 past Cashaw Creek. Dam in on the right. 1,800 acres.

ELON WATERWORKS RESERVOIR: Owned by county of Amherst, and open to fishing upon purchase of permit at waterworks in Madison Heights. Located off of Primary Route 130 approximately 3 miles west of its intersection with U.S. Highway 29. Gasoline motors prohibited. 45 acres.

IZAAK WALTON LAKE: Owned by Izaak Walton League, and open to public fishing. Accessible by Secondary Route 604 south, left on Route 663, and right on first light-duty road. 15 acres.

LYNCHBURG RESERVOIR: Also known as Pedlar Lake. Owned by the city of Lynchburg, and open to public fishing upon purchase of a permit at city water department. Permit includes rental boat. No gasoline motors permitted. Located in the George Washington National Forest off of forest service road 39 south of U.S. Highway 60 bridge over the Pedlar River. Provides fishing for trout as well as largemouth bass and panfish. 92 acres.

MAYS LAKE: Privately owned, but open to public fishing. Reached by light-duty road from Secondary Route 631 off of U.S. Highway 60. 12 acres.

REUSENS LAKE: Owned by Appalachian Power Company, and open to public fishing. Reached by Secondary Route 685 north past Union Chapel, then left on first unimproved road to the dam. 500 acres.

STONEHOUSE LAKE: Owned by the county of Amherst, and open to public fishing. Reached by Secondary Route 625 south, then Route 610 west, and then right on first unimproved road. 34 acres.

THRASHER'S LAKE: Owned by the county of Amherst, and open to public fishing. Accessible by Secondary Route 610 east, then Secondary Route 617 northwest, and unimproved road to the left. 34 acres.

Bedford County

BEAVERDAM CREEK LAKE: Owned by the city of Roanoke, and open to public fishing. Accessible by Secondary Route 635 north beyond Jeters Chapel, then left on unimproved road. 66 acres.

BEDFORD COUNTY LAKE: Privately owned, but open to public fishing for a fee. Rental boats only may be used. Camping available. Located on Secondary Route 639 off of Primary Highway 122 west of Colton's Mill. 36 acres.

FALLING CREEK RESERVOIR: Owned by the city of Roanoke, and open to public fishing. Reached by Primary Route 24 west, then right on Secondary Route 651 to the lake. 21 acres.

Brunswick County

PICKETT RESERVOIR: Owned by the U.S. Army, but open to public fishing upon purchase of a permit at Fort Pickett Headquarters. Located near Blackstone. 384 acres.

Buckingham County

HOLIDAY LAKE: Owned by the Virginia Division of Parks. On Appomattox-Buckingham county line. See Appomattox County for details.

Campbell County

BROOKNEAL RESERVOIR: Owned by the city of Brookneal, and open to public fishing upon obtaining a permit from the city water department. Located off of Secondary Route 601 approximately 1 mile north of Brookneal. 25 acres.

COLLEGE LAKE: Owned by Lynchburg College, and open to public fishing by obtaining a permit from the college administrative offices. Located off of U.S. Highway 460 approximately one mile west of Lynchburg. 35 acres.

DAM NUMBER 2 WATER SUPPLY: Privately owned, but open to public fishing upon securing permission from the owner. Located off of Secondary Route 834 north from Secondary Route 615. 12 acres.

Caroline County

BOWIE, DELOS, HEARN'S LONESOME GULCH, SMOOTS, TRAVIS, AND WHITE'S PONDS ON FORT A. P. HILL: Owned by the U.S. Army, and open to public fishing by purchase of a permit from Fort A. P. Hill headquarters. Located near Bowling Green. Private boats, but no motors, permitted. Size of ponds vary from 6-acre Hearn's to 100-acre Smoots.

Carroll County

BYLLSBY RESERVOIR: Owned by Appalachian Power Company, and open to public fishing. Located on Secondary Route 602, approximately 5 miles south of the county line. 335 acres.

BUCK RESERVOIR: Owned by the Appalachian Power Company, and open to public fishing. Located on Secondary Route 658 off of Primary Route 94 near Wythe County line. 262 acres.

Charles City County

HARRISON LAKE: Owned by the U.S. Fish and Wildlife Service, and open to public fishing. Gasoline motors of five horsepower or less are allowed. Located off of Primary Route 5 west of Charles City. 125 acres.

Charlotte County

KEYSVILLE LAKE: Owned by the town of Keysville, and open to public fishing. Located off of Secondary Route 653 west of Keysville. 42 acres.

Chesterfield County

BEAVER LAKES: Owned by the Virginia Division of Parks, and open to public fishing. Located in Pocahontas State Park on Secondary Route 655 off of Primary Highway 10. Rental boats May to September. 156 acres.

FALLING CREEK RESERVOIR: Owned by the city of Chesterfield, and open to public fishing. Permit needed to fish from the shore. Located at Falling Creek, between Primary Highway 10 and Secondary Route 627. Access poor. 110 acres.

LAKE DALE: Privately owned, but open to public fishing by permit. Located off of Secondary Route 632, approximately 3 miles south of Chesterfield Courthouse. 46 acres.

LAKEVIEW RESERVOIR: Owned by the city of Colonial Heights, and open to public fishing. Located near Swift Creek off of Secondary Route 625 at the bridge. Good concrete launching ramp. 50 acres.

REIVES POND: Privately owned, but open to public fishing by permit. Located off of Primary Highway 114, approximately 1 mile south of Chester. 13 acres.

SWIFT CREEK LAKE: Owned by the Virginia Division of Parks, and open to public fishing. Located in Pocahontas State Park on Secondary Route 655 off of Primary Highway 10. Rental boats from May to September. 156 acres.

SWIFT CREEK MILLPOND: Owned by the city of Colonial Heights, and open to public fishing. Located ½ mile north of Colonial Heights between the railroad and U.S. Highway 1. 11 acres.

Craig County

MCDANIEL POND: Privately owned, but open to the public by fee. Open from April through October. Rental boats available. Located off of Secondary Route 632 approximately 3½ miles west of Maggie.

Culpeper County

LAKE PELHAM: Owned by the city of Culpeper, and open to public fishing upon obtaining a permit from the city treasurer. Launching ramp, but no gasoline motors permitted. Located 3 miles west of Culpeper on Henretty Drive, off of Secondary Route 718 and U.S. Highway 29. 255 acres.

MOUNTAIN RUN LAKE: Owned by the city of Culpeper, and open to public fishing upon obtaining a permit from the city treasurer. Gasoline motors are prohibited. Located on Secondary Route 718 off of U.S. Highway 29, approximately 4 miles west of Culpeper. Launching ramp. 75 acres.

Cumberland County

ARROWHEAD, BONBROOK, OAK HILL, AND WINSTON LAKES: Owned by the Virginia Division of Forestry, and open to public fishing. Located in Cumberland State Forest north of Cumberland Court House. Boat ramps. All small, ranging from 6 to 10 acres.

BEAR CREEK LAKE: Owned by the Virginia Division of Parks, and open to public fishing. Located in Bear Creek State Park on Secondary Route 629 five miles north of Cumberland Court House. Rental boats from May to September. 55 acres.

SPORTS LAKE: Privately owned, but open to public fishing upon payment of a fee, which includes rental boat. Located on Secondary Route 609 off of Route 610 near western county line. 75 acres.

Dickenson County

LAUREL LAKE: Owned by Breaks Interstate Park, and open to fishing upon paying a fee. Located in the park off of Primary Highway 80, north of Haysi. 12 acres.

Dinwiddie County

COLEMAN'S LAKE: 63 acres.

HOBB'S MILLPOND: 25 acres.

JORDAN LAKE: 84 acres.

MCKENNY LAKE: 21 acres.

TOMMEHETON LAKE: Owned by the U.S. Army, but open to public fishing upon the purchase of a permit at the Fort Pickett headquarters. Located on the Fort Pickett Military Reservation near Blackstone. 150 acres.

TWIN LAKES: Owned by the U.S. Army, and open to public fishing upon purchasing a permit at the Fort Pickett Military Reservation near Blackstone. 16 acres.

WHEELER'S LAKE: Privately owned, but open to public fishing for a fee, which includes use of a launching ramp. Located two miles south of Five Forks on Secondary Route 645. 75 acres.

Essex County

HUNDLEYS POND: Privately owned, but open to public fishing by permit. Located off of Secondary Route 631 east of Champlain. 27 acres.

SPINDLES MILLPOND: Privately owned, but open to public fishing. Located off of Secondary Route 635, 3 miles east of Loretta. 21 acres.

Fairfax County

HUNTSMAN LAKE: A flood-control lake owned by the county of Fairfax. No boat ramp. Access by Old Keene Road and Huntsman Boulevard. 27 acres.

ROYAL LAKE: A flood-control lake and open to fishing, with Fairfax County Park Authority operating a boat-rental concession and a launching ramp. Access is off of Primary Route 123. 38 acres.

Franklin County

BOWMAN'S LAKE: Privately owned, but open to public fishing by permit. Access by Secondary Routes 684 and 615. 5 acres.

FERRUM COLLEGE LAKE: Owned by Ferrum College, and open to public fishing. Accessible from Primary Route 40 and Secondary Route 602. 6 acres.

PIGG LAKE: Owned by Virginia Power Company, and open to public fishing. Access is poor, and only bank fishing is permitted. Access off of Secondary Routes 674 and 713. 15 acres.

Frederick County

COVE LAKE: Privately owned, but open to public fishing by permit. Located off of Secondary Route 704 south of Gore. 44 acres.

Giles County

MOUNTAIN LAKE: Privately owned, but open to guests of hotel. Located on Secondary Route 613 north, off of U.S. Highway 460 at Hoges Chapel. 60 acres.

Gloucester County

CYPRESS SHORES LAKE: Privately owned, but campers registered in the campground can fish. Located west of Harcum on Primary Highway 198. 16 acres.

HAYNES POND: Privately owned, but open to public fishing by permit. Located west of U.S. Highway 17 on Secondary Route 614. 45 acres.

LEIGHT POND: Privately owned, and fishing limited to campers who are registered in the campground. Located southwest of Gloucester Court House on Secondary Route 614 just off of Route 616. 10 acres.

Greensville County

EMPORIA LAKE: Owned by the city of Emporia and open to public fishing. Located on Secondary Route 611 west of Interstate 95. 210 acres.

RAINEY'S LAKE: Privately owned, but open to the public for a fee. Located off of Secondary Route 600, 1 mile west of Barley. 20 acres.

SLAGLE'S LAKE: Privately owned, but open to public fishing on a fee basis. 200 acres.

SMITHS PONDS: Privately owned, but open for public fishing for a fee. Located off of Secondary Route 633 south of Brink. 18 acres.

Halifax County

HALIFAX RESERVOIR: Owned by the county of Halifax, and open for public fishing. Located north of Halifax on U.S. Highway 501. 400 acres.

Henry County

BRYANTS FISH LAKE: Privately owned, but open to public fishing for a fee. Located off of Primary Highway 57, approximately six miles west of Bassett. 3 acres.

FAIRY STONE LAKE: Owned by the Virginia Division of Parks, and open to public fishing. In Fairy Stone State Park, approximately 9 miles west of Bassett. Reached by Primary Route 57, then north on Secondary Route 623. Rental boats available from May to September. 45 acres.

FISHER'S POND: Owned by the county of Henry, and open to public fishing. Reached by Secondary Routes 642 and then 782 approximately 4 miles south of Martinsville off of U.S. Highway 220. 11 acres.

HALE'S FISH LAKE: Privately owned, but open to public fishing for a fee. Located 7 miles west of Bassett via Secondary Routes 687 and then 677, three miles from Primary Route 57. 5 acres.

HORSEPASTURE LAKE 1-C: Privately owned, but open to public fishing by permit. Located off of Secondary Routes 687 and 695 at Mount Olive Church. 18 acres.

HORSEPASTURE LAKE 2: Privately owned, but open to public fishing by permit. Located off of Secondary Route 696 north of Blue Ridge Airport.

LANIER LAKE: Privately owned, but public fishing by permit. Located off of Secondary Route 650. 30 acres.

LAUREL PARK LAKE: Privately owned, but open to public fishing by permit. Located off of U.S. Highway 58 approximately two miles east of Martinsville. 13 acres.

LEATHERWOOD LAKE 2A: Privately owned, but open to public fishing by permit. Located off of Secondary Route 655. 24 acres.

LEATHERWOOD LAKE 4: Privately owned, but open to public fishing by permit. Located on Secondary Route 628 off of Primary Highway 57. 13 acres.

LEATHERWOOD LAKE 5: Privately owned, but open to public fishing by permit. Located off of Secondary Route 619. 39 acres.

MARROWBONE RESERVOIR: Privately owned, but open to public fishing by permit. Located off of Secondary Route 688. 28 acres.

MARTINSVILLE RESERVOIR: Owned by the city of Martinsville, and open for public fishing. Fee required for use of private boats, and they are limited to six-horsepower maximum. Open during day only. Located off of Primary Highway 108, 2 miles north of Martinsville. 175 acres.

SMITH RIVER HYDRO DAM: Owned by the city of Martinsville, and open to public fishing. Located south of Martinsville on U.S. Highway 58. Land around the lake is privately owned. 42 acres.

Isle of Wight County

LEE'S MILLPOND: Owned by the Union Camp Company, and open to public fishing. Located approximately 3 miles east of Frankin, and reached by U.S. Highway 58 and Secondary Route 616. 45 acres.

SMITHFIELD WATERWORKS: Owned by the town of Smithfield, and open to public fishing upon the purchase of a permit from the town treasurer. Located west of Smithfield on Secondary Route 680 off of U.S. Highway 258. 32 acres.

James City County

BRACKENS POND: Owned by the National Park Service, and open to public fishing. Located on the Colonial Parkway near College Creek. 6 acres.

LAKE POWELL: Privately owned, but open to public fishing on a fee basis. Rental boats available. Located off of Primary Highway 31 between Jamestown and Williamsburg. 62 acres.

WALLER MILL LAKE: Owned by the city of Williamsburg, and open to public fishing. Rental boats, launching ramp, and pier fishing. Located in Waller Mill Park on Secondary Route 645 west of Williamsburg between Interstate 64 and U.S. Highway 60. 365 acres.

Loudoun County

GOOSE CREEK RESERVOIR: Owned by the city of Fairfax, and open to public fishing. Gasoline motors are prohibited. Located west of Ashburn on Secondary Routes 643 and 659. 140 acres.

Lunenburg County

LUNENBURG BEACH: Owned by the city of Victoria, and open to public fishing. Located approximately three miles north of Victoria off of Street T1011. 13 acres.

NOTTOWAY FALLS: Owned by the city of Victoria, and open to public fishing. Located at Primary Highway 40 bridge over the Nottoway River. 60 acres.

WHITTLES MILL: Owned by the city of South Hill, and open for public fishing. Located at Secondary Route 636 bridge over the Meherrin River. 40 acres.

Mecklenburg County

WHITTLE'S MILL POND: Owned by the city of South Hill, and open to public fishing. To reach the lake, take Primary Route 47 west out of South Hill to Secondary Route 654, then turn left on Route 636 to the lake. 60 acres.

Montgomery County

LITTLE RIVER RESERVOIR: Owned by the city of Radford, and open to public fishing. Located off of Secondary Route 605 below Claytor Lake Dam. 113 acres.

PANDAPAS POND: Owned by the U.S. Forest Service, and open for public fishing. Located on U.S. Forest Service Road 808 off of U.S. Highway 460 west of Blacksburg. 9 acres.

City of Newport News

LAKE MAURY: Owned by the Mariners Museum, and available for public fishing on a fee basis. Fishing fee includes the use of a boat. Located approximately 2 miles north of the James River bridge off of U.S. Highway 60. 165 acres.

City of Norfolk

LAKE SMITH: Owned by the city of Norfolk, and open to public fishing upon purchasing a city boat permit. Located three miles south of the Chesapeake Bay Bridge-Tunnel on U.S. Highway 13. 200 acres.

LAKE TAYLOR: Owned by the city of Norfolk, and open to public fishing upon obtaining a boat permit from the city. Located approximately three miles south of the Chesapeake Bay Bridge-Tunnel off of U.S. Highway 13. 64 acres.

Northumberland County

GARDY'S MILL POND: Privately owned, but open to public fishing from boats only. No bank fishing. Located on Secondary Route 617 west of Hyacinth, off of U.S. Highway 360. Launching ramp. 75 acres.

Nottoway County

LAKE BIRCHEN AND TWIN LAKES: Owned by the U.S. Army, and open to public fishing by permit available at Fort Pickett headquarters. Located on Fort Pickett Military Reservation off of Primary Highway 40 west of Blackstone. 96 and 16 acres.

VIRGINIA RAILWAY FALLS: Owned by the city of Victoria, and open to public fishing. Located off of Primary Route 49 at Nottoway River. 60 acres.

Page County

LAKE ARROWHEAD: Owned by the city of Luray, and open to public fishing. City permit required, however. Located on Secondary Route 669 south of Luray.

LURAY POWER DAM: Owned by the Potomac Edisor Power Company, and open to public fishing. Located 4 miles west of Luray off of Secondary Route 615 north from U.S. Highway 211. Access at Massanutten Landing. 125 acres.

NEWPORT DAM: Owned by the Potomac Edison Company, and open to public fishing. Located off of U.S. Highway 340 near Newport. Limited bank fishing. 102 acres.

SHENANDOAH POWER DAM: Owned by the city of Shenandoah, and open to public fishing. Located near Shenandoah off of U.S. Highway 340. Launching ramp. 100 acres.

Patrick County

COCKRAM MILL POND: Privately owned, but open to public fishing by permit. Located on U.S. Highway 58 east of Meadows of Dan. 14 acres.

JIM BOAZ LAKE: Privately owned, but open to public fishing by permit. Located just off of Secondary Route 652. 25 acres.

SQUALL CREEK LAKE: Privately owned, but open to public fishing by permit. Located off of Secondary Route 614. 8 acres.

TALBOTT RESERVOIR: Owned by the city of Danville, and open to public fishing. Reached by Secondary Routes 601 and 602 off of U.S. Highway 58 west of Meadows of Dan. 165 acres.

Pittsylvania County

FUZZY'S LAKE: Privately owned, but open to public fishing on a fee basis. Located off of Secondary Route 605 approximately 8 miles west of Gretna by way of Primary Rotue 40. 14 acres.

Prince Edward County

GOODWYN AND PRINCE EDWARD LAKES: Owned by the Virginia Division of Parks, and open for public fishing.

GOODWYN LAKE: Prince Edward State Park approximately two miles south of Burkeville off of U.S. Highway 360, and reached by Secondary Routes 621 and 697. Rental boats are available from May to September. 40 and 30 acres.

Prince William County

SILVER LAKE: Privately owned, but open to public fishing on a fee basis. Located approximately two miles north of Haymarket on U.S. Highway 15. 30 acres.

PLEASANT CAMP: Owned by the National Park Service, and open for public fishing. Located in the Prince William Forest Park just off of Primary Route 234 west of Dumfries. 10 acres.

LAKE JACKSON: Owned by the county of Prince William, and open for public fishing. Located off of Primary Route 234 south of Manassas. 250 acres.

Pulaski County

HOGAN LAKE: Owned by the city of Pulaski, and usually open for public fishing. Located on Secondary Route 610 approximately 2 miles west of Pulaski. 41 acres.

GATEWOOD RESERVOIR: Owned by the city of Pulaski, and open to public fishing on a fee basis. Fee includes the use of a boat. Only electric motors are allowed, and private boats are prohibited. Located approximately 7 miles west of Pulaski on Secondary Route 710.

City of Richmond

BRYAN AND BYRD PARKS LAKES: Owned by the city of Richmond, and open for public fishing. 10 and 20 acres.

Roanoke County

NIAGARA DAM: Owned by Appalachian Power Company, and open for public fishing. Located on Secondary Route 749. 85 acres.

Shenandoah County

CEDAR CREEK TROUT FARM: Privately owned, but open to the public on a fee basis. Located on Secondary Route 600 approximately 10 miles west of U.S. Highway 11.

ORNDORFF'S RAINBOW TROUT POND: Privately owned, but open to the public on a fee basis. Located approximately ten miles west of U.S. Highway 11 on Secondary Route 600.

Smyth County

HUNGRY MOTHER LAKE: Owned by the Virginia Division of Parks, and open for public fishing. Located in Hungry Mother State Park, approximately 3 miles west of Marion on Virginia Primary Route 16. Rental boats available from May to September. 108 acres.

Southampton County

RIVERS MILL POND: Privately owned, but available for public fishing on a fee basis. Located on Secondary Routes 659 and 612 off of Route 308. Rental boats. 60 acres.

Spotsylvania County

EMBRY RESERVOIR: Owned by the city of Fredericksburg, and open for public fishing. Actually an impounded section of the Rappahannock River just west of Fredericksburg. Located off of Secondary Route 639. 100 acres.

NOTTS RUN RESERVOIR: Owned by the city of Fredericksburg, and open to public fishing for a fee. Open from March to October. 160 acres.

Stafford County

ABEL RESERVOIR: Onwed by the county of Stafford for water supply, and open for public fishing. Developed boat ramp. Reached by Secondary Routes 616 and 651 off of U.S. Highway 17. 185 acres.

City of Suffolk

CREATH POND: Privately owned, but open for public fishing on a fee basis. Located northeast of Jarratt off of Secondary Route 645. 20 acres.

HARGRAVES MILL POND: Privately owned, but open to public fishing for a fee. Located one mile south of Sussex off of Secondary Route 735. 31 acres.

KILBY LAKE: Owned by the city of Portsmouth for water supply, and open for public fishing by permit from the city. Located in the city of Suffolk. Boat rentals and permits are available at the Lake Kilby filtration plant on U.S. Highway 58 in Suffolk. Concrete boat-launching ramp. 222 acres.

LONE STAR LAKES: Owned by the city of Suffolk for water supply, and open for public fishing. The lakes are a series of connected borrow pits ranging in size from an acre or so to 49 acres. Very deep, with boat-launching ramps on a few of them. Shore fishing is prohibited. Located in the city of Suffolk. 159 acres total.

M. M. MAYES LAKE: Privately owned, but open for public fishing on a fee basis. Located on Secondary Route 649 west of Peanut. 25 acres.

ROUNDTREE POND: Privately owned, but available for public fishing for a fee. Located two miles north of the Suffolk business district off of Primary Route 10. 25 acres.

SPEIGHTS RUN LAKE: Owned by the city of Portsmouth for water supply, and open for public fishing. Located in the city of Suffolk and accessible by Secondary Route 646 south of U.S. Highway 58 in Suffolk. Launching ramp, but no fishing from the shore. 197 acres.

City of Virginia Beach

LAKE JOYCE: Owned by the city of Virginia Beach, and open for public fishing. Located off of U.S. Highway 60 at Bayside. 150 acres.

LAKE LAWSON: Owned by the city of Norfolk, and open to the public for fishing on a fee basis. Outboard motors of ten horsepower or less are permitted. Located 3 miles south of the Chesapeake Bay Bridge-Tunnel on U.S. Highway 13. 98 acres.

Warren County

RIVERTON DAM: Owned by the city of Front Royal, and open to the public for fishing. Located just off of U.S. Highway 340 north of Front Royal. Access at Riverton Landing. 60 acres.

WARREN HYDRO DAM: Owned by the Potomac Edison Company, and open to the public for fishing. Located just off of U.S. Highway 340 just north of Front Royal. Access at Riverton Landing. 189 acres.

Washington County

CLEAR CREEK: Owned by the city of Bristol, and open for public fishing. Located approximately 5 miles north of Bristol by way of Secondary Routes 645 and 625. 40 acres.

EDSMOND DAM: Owned by the Appalachian Power Company, and open for public fishing. Located north of Damascus off of Primary 91 near Lodi. 60 acres.

Wise County

NORTH FORK OF POUND RESERVOIR: Owned by the U.S. Army Corps of Engineers and open for public fishing. Located west of Pound on U.S. Highway 23. 154 acres.

NORTON RESERVOIR: Owned by the city of Norton, and open for public fishing by permit. Obtain permit from city hall. Located approximately 2 miles south of Norton on High Knob Road. 8 acres.

BIG CHERRY LAKE: Owned by the city of Big Stone Gap, and open to public fishing by permit from the city. Located approximately 8 miles southeast of Big Stone Gap. 100 acres.

WISE LAKE: Owned by the city of Wise, and open to public fishing by permit. Located east of Wise on Secondary Route 646. 8 acres.

York County

HARWOOD MILL POND: Owned by the city of Newport News, and open to public fishing on a fee basis. Located off of Primary Route 173 near Burts. Open from April to November. Fee for launching private boat. 244 acres.

The Chesapeake Bay _____

Many authorities regard the Chesapeake Bay as the most valuable estuary in the world. To Virginia anglers, however, it is the state's biggest fishing hole, and the fact that this unique body of water serves many needs does not alter that. There are the inevitable conflicts, of course, conflicts between commercial and sports fishermen, between shipping interests and pleasure boaters, and even between anglers and hunters, but over the years the bay has managed to serve them all.

The Chesapeake Bay is a large body of water, with a surface area of 4,300 square miles and a 4,500-mile shoreline. Its 74,000-

square-mile drainage system includes the East's largest river, the Susquehanna. Other major feeder streams include the James, Potomac, Rappahannock, and York rivers. There are, of course, many other, smaller streams that flow into the bay, adding to its riches.

The waters of the bay range from fresh water at its northern end, where the Susquehanna enters, to salt water where it enters the Atlantic Ocean between the famous capes, Cape Charles on the Easten Shore and Cape Henry on the mainland.

Virginia, of course, shares the Chesapeake Bay with Maryland, and it is important that the angler know where the Maryland-Virginia line divides the waters between the two jurisdictions. Fishing regulations vary between the two states. The boundary begins at Smith Point, where the Potomac River enters the bay. The Potomac River belongs to Maryland. From Smith Point the line runs east and slightly north to cut through the lower part of Smith Island, an island mostly in Maryland. It runs almost due east through the island and then dips sharply south in Tangier Sound to again head abruptly east through the Cedar Straits, just south of Maryland's Cedar Island Wildlife Management Area. Then it continues into Pocomoke Sound, where it runs a crooked course to the mouth of the Potomac River. To the south of this imaginery line, the Chesapeake Bay and its sounds and tidal rivers belong to Virginia.

Just about every square mile of the big inland estuary offers the possibility of good fishing, particularly for roaming gamesters such as the slashing bluefish that enter the bay in the spring to linger well into the fall. Over the seasons anglers and charter-boat skippers have uncovered the more productive waters, where they concentrate their efforts. These include natural features such as bars, points, shallows, and sounds, and man-made ones such as buoys, bridges and tunnels, docks, and wrecked ships. The more prominent ones are listed below.

Getting an early start for a day on the Chesapeake Bay.
(Photo courtesy of Mercury Marine Corp.)

Angler's Reef

This is an artificial reef located just west of Onancock.

FISH: Gray trout, spot, and whiting.

ACCESS: Department of Game and Inland Fisheries boat-launching ramp at Onancock.

Back River

Back River is a tidal estuary fed by the Northwest Branch and the Southwest Branch, and it is located between the city of Hampton and Plumtree Island. Shallow Plumtree Bar protects it from the stormy waters of the bay.

FISH: Bluefish and striped bass.

ACCESS: The Department of Game and Inland Fisheries maintains a boat-launching ramp at the end of Dandy Point Road on the Back River in the city of Hampton. There are also several commercial launching ramps in the area.

Beach Rock

A flat beneath 5 to 20 feet of water here offers good fishing along a 90-foot deep channel in Pocomoke Sound.

FISH: Black drum, gray trout, spot, and whiting.

ACCESS: The Department of Game and Inland Fisheries maintains a boat-launching ramp at Saxis, and there are also commercial ramps on the sound.

Big Rock

Located just west of Eastville, the water here is 25 to 30 feet deep.

FISH: Gray trout.

ACCESS: Commercial launching ramps near Eastville.

Big Shell Rock

This is a small mount or rise in the bottom of the bay at the mouth of Pocomoke Sound.

FISH: Gray trout, spot, and whiting.

ACCESS: The Department of Game and Inland Fisheries maintains a boat-launching ramp at Saxis, and there are also commercial launching ramps on the sound.

Bird Rock

This is a small mount or rise in the bottom of Pocomoke Sound, and a rich fishing ground.

FISH: Black drum, channel bass, gray trout, spot, and whiting.

ACCESS: The Department of Game and Inland Fisheries maintains a boat-launching ramp at Saxis, and there are commercial launching ramps on the sound.

Bluefish Rock

Located just east of the city of Hampton, this is a hump in the bottom of the bay that rises to 12 feet from depths of 15 to 20 feet.

FISH: Bluefish and cobia.

ACCESS: The Department of Game and Inland Fisheries maintains a boat-launching ramp a mile north of Fox Hill at the end of Dandy Point Road in Hampton.

Buoy Rock

This is a small, shallow stretch of water just off of North End Point near the town of Saxis.

FISH: Speckled trout.

ACCESS: The Department of Game and Inland Fisheries maintains a boat-launching ramp in Saxis, and there are also commercial boat-launching ramps in the area.

Cabbage Patch

The Cabbage Patch, one of two fishing holes in the bay so named, is one of the most popular fishing areas in the Chesapeake Bay. It is located just offshore, southwest of Cape Charles. Most of the water is 25 to 35 feet deep.

FISH: Black drum, channel bass, and cobia.

ACCESS: The Department of Game and Inland Fisheries maintains a boat-launching ramp in Cape Charles at the end of Secondary Route 642. There are also commercial launching ramps in Cape Charles.

Cabbage Patch

This Cabbage Patch is located in the upper bay midway between Smith Point and Smith Island. It is located near an old wreck that rests in 45 to 50 feet of water.

FISH: Gray trout.

ACCESS: There are commercial ramps near Smith Point.

California

Here a ledge in Pocomoke Sound drops quickly from 10–20 feet to over 50 feet.

FISH: Gray trout, spot, and whiting.

ACCESS: The Department of Game and Inland Fisheries maintains a boat-launching ramp in Saxis, and there are commercial ramps on the sound.

Cape Charles Reef

A sudden drop-off from 15–25 feet to over 100 feet creates a good fishing area just off of Cape Charles. In adition, Old Dominion University has constructed an artificial reef in this general area.

FISH: Black drum and cobia.

ACCESS: The Department of Game and Inland Fisheries has a boat-launching ramp at the end of Secondary Route 642 in Cape Charles, and there are several commercial ramps in the area.

The Cell

An old house and its surroundings in 35 to 40 feet of water just west of Mattawoman Creek offer good fishing.

FISH: Channel bass, cobia, gray trout, spadefish, spot, striped bass, tautog, and whiting.

ACCESS: There are commercial launching rammps in the vicinity of Matta-woman Creek, or it can be reached from the western shore of the bay.

Cherrystone Channel

This is a big patch of shallow water just west of Cape Charles that is less than 5 feet deep, but pitches gradually to depths of 15–20 feet, then to 20–25 feet, and finally to 30 feet or more— but all close to shore.

FISH: Black drum, cobia, croakers, spot, and striped bass.

ACCESS: The Deprtment of Game and Inland Fisheries maintains a launch-ing ramp at the end of Secondary Route 642 in Cape Charles.

Chesapeake Bay Bridge-Tunnel

This 17-mile-long bridge and tunnel that connects the eastern and western shores of the Chesapeake Bay has become one of the most popular fishing spots in the bay. The Sea Gull Fishing Pier near the southern end of the bridge-tunnel offers pier fish-ing, but the water is generally fished by private or charter boats out of Lynnhaven Inlet or Rudee Inlet in Vrginia Beach. Anglers take some trophy fish from these waters, often fishing at night in the glow of the bridge-tunnel lights. The fishing is concen-trated around the north and south islands, the Baltimore chan-nel, the third and fourth islands, the bridge-tunnel trestle, and the high-level bridge. This is a busy area for commercial and military vessels, and anglers should keep an eye open for them.

FISH: Black drum, bluefish, channel bass, cobia, croaker, flounder, gray trout, hogfish, sea bass, spadefish, spot, striped bass, and tautog.

ACCESS: The Department of Game and Inland Fisheries maintains boat-launching ramps at Willoughby in the city of Norfolk and in Cape Charles. There are also commercial ramps in Cape Charles and in the cities of Norfolk and Virginia Beach.

City of Annapolis

This is an old wreck located in 40 to 45 feet of water just east of Reedville.

FISH: Bluefish, gray trout, and striped bass.

ACCESS: There is a Department of Game and Inland Fisheries boat-launching ramp at Shell in Northumberland County, and there are commercial ramps in the general area.

Crammy Hack

Crammy Hack is located in the mouth of Pocomoke Sound, and it is a shallow point extending out into a deep channel of over 60 feet.

FISH: Gray trout and spot.

ACCESS: The Department of Game and Inland Fisheries maintains a boat-launching ramp in Saxis, and there are commercial ramps in the area.

Cut Channel

This is a popular fishing area located east of Windmill Point. The water ranges in depth from 40 to 45 feet.

FISH: Cobia and striped bass.

ACCESS: The Department of Game and Inland Fisheries maintains a boat-launching ramp at Mill Creek in Middlesex County, and there are several commercial launching ramps in the Deltaville area.

Cut Channel Rock

This popular fishing area is located southwest of the southern tip of Tangier Island. The water average twenty-five to forty feet in depth.

FISH: Gray trout.

ACCESS: The Department of Game and Inland Fisheries maintains a boat-launching ramp at Mill Creek in Middlesex County, and there are commercial launching ramps in the Deltaville area.

Dameron Marsh Area

The popular Dameron Marsh is a broad tidal flat that runs south from the Great Wicomico River to Dividing Creek. It features many acres of shallow water of less than 5 feet in depth. These shallows extend well offshore before dropping abruptly to depths of over 20 feet.

FISH: Cobia and striped bass.

ACCESS: There is a Department of Game and Inland Fisheries boat-launching ramp at Coopers in Northumberland County, and there are several commercial ramps.

Davidson *Wreck*

This is an old wreck located just west of the southern tip of Tangier Island. The water is relatively shallow, averaging only 10 to 15 feet in depth.

FISH: Bluefish, cobia, and striped bass.

ACCESS: There is a Department of Game and Inland Fisheries boat-launching ramp at Shell in Northumberland County, and there are several commercial ramps in the Reedville area.

Ditchbank

This is a picturesque patch of 20- to 25-foot-deep water off of the Parkers Marsh Natural Area on the eastern side of the Chesapeake Bay.

FISH: Black drum, cobia, croaker, gray trout, spot, and whiting.

ACCESS: There are commercial boat-launching ramps on Onancock Creek.

Dividing Creek

The Dividing Creek area is a popular fishing hole on the western side of the bay. It is a small tidal estuary between Dameron Marsh and the city of Kilmarnock, with a 15-foot channel at its confluence with the bay. It is flanked on the north by narrow

Hughlett Point, which extends out into the bay to provide some shallow-water fishing.

FISH: Cobia, croaker, spot, and striped bass.

ACCESS: There are commercial boat-launching ramps on Indian Creek southeast of Kilmarnock.

Dogfish

Both Maryland and Virginia can claim part of this hot spot on the border in Pocomoke Sound.

FISH: Gray trout, spot, and whiting.

ACCESS: The Department of Game and Inland Fisheries maintains a boat-launching ramp at Saxis, and there are commercial ramps on the sound.

The Dorothy

This old wreck rests in 60 to 70 feet of water just east of Reedville.

FISH: Bluefish, gray trout, and striped bass.

ACCESS: There are Department of Game and Inland Fisheries boat-launching ramps at Coopers and Shell, and commercial ramps in the Reedville area.

Fox Island Buoy

Just south of the Maryland-Virginia border, this fishing area is in the mouth of Pocomoke Sound.

FISH: Channel bass.

ACCESS: There is a Department of Game and Inland Fisheries boat-launching ramp at Saxis, and there are commercial ramps on the sound.

Great Wicomico River

This popular river is a broad tidal estuary entering the bay just south of Reedville. Its channel is up to 20 feet in depth.

FISH: Cobia and striped bass.

ACCESS: The Department of Game and Inland Fisheries maintains a boat-launching ramp at Shell, and there are commercial ramps on the river.

Gwynns Island

Gwynns Island is a very popular spot on the western shore of the bay. It is a large island separated from the mainland by Queens Creek. The creek, however, is bridged, and access to the island is easy. The waters around the island are relatively shallow, and anglers like to wade and cast for striped bass. Off the bay side of the island the water drops off quickly to 20 feet or more, and an artificial reef has been established there by Old Dominion University. Milford Haven and the Hole in the Wall to the south of the island are popular fishing spots. The artificial reef is located near the Hole in the Wall.

FISH: Croaker, flounder, gray trout, spot, striped bass, and tautog.

ACCESS: The Department of Game and Inland Fisheries maintains a boat-launching ramp on the island, and there are also commercial launching ramps.

Hack's Rock

This is a shallow, broad point that extends west of Onancock, where the water drops off from approximately 10 feet to 40 feet or more.

FISH: Channel bass, cobia, croaker, and gray trout.

ACCESS: The Department of Game and Inland Fisheries maintains a boat-launching ramp at Onancock, and there are commercial ramps on Onancock Creek.

Hampton Bridge-Tunnel

Connecting the city of Hampton with Willoughby Spit, this bridge-tunnel carries Interstate 64 to Norfolk and Virginia Beach, and it has become a popular fishing area near the mouth of the James River. Inside of the bridge-tunnel is Hampton Roads, the Hampton Bar, and Hampton Flats, all good shallow-water fishing. Outside of the bridge-tunnel is Willoughby Bank. Fishing at night under the lights of the bridge-tunnel is popular.

FISH: Croaker, flounder, gray trout, spot, and striped bass.

ACCESS: The Department of Game and Inland Fisheries maintains a boat-launching ramp at Willoughby off of View Street in the city of Norfolk. There are also a number of commercial ramps in the area.

Hill Rock

This is a popular fishing spot in Pocomoke Sound just west of the Saxis Wildlife Management Area. The water here averages 7 to 12 feet in depth.

FISH: Channel bass and gray trout.

ACCESS: The Department of Game and Inland Fisheries maintains a boat-launching ramp at Saxis, and there are commercial launching ramps nearby.

Hurdle Drain

Hurdle Drain is one of many good fishing spots in Pocomoke Sound. Located in the mouth of the sound, the water drops off from 2–3 feet to 10–15 feet.

FISH: Gray trout, spot, and whiting.

ACCESS: The Department of Game and Inland Fisheries maintains a boat-launching ramp at Saxis, and there are commercial launching ramps on the sound.

Inner Middle Ground

Generally considered a part of the rich fishing water around the Chesapeake Bay Bridge-Tunnel complex, some of this patch of water is less than 5 feet deep. It is located north of the bridge-tunnel in the high-level bridge area and just west of Fisherman Island Wildlife Refuge at the northern end of the bridge-tunnel.

FISH: Black drum, channel bass, and cobia.

ACCESS: The Department of Game and Inland Fisheries maintains a boat-launching ramp at Cape Charles. There are also commercial launching ramps at Cape Charles.

Kiptopeke Breakwater

Here there is some deep water just off of the Kiptopeke Beach that drops quickly to 35–40 feet.

FISH: Bluefish, cobia, croaker, flounder, hogfish, spot, striped bass, and tautog.

ACCESS: The Department of Game and Inland Fisheries maintains a boat-launching ramp in Cape Charles, and there are also commecial ramps nearby.

Latimer Shoal

This is a popular Eastern Shore fishing area jut west of Cape Charles. The water over the shoal is 15 feet or less, but channels on either side of the shoal drop off to 30 feet or more. Anglers are warned that rough water can develop quickly on the shoals.

FISH: Black drum and cobia.

ACCESS: The Department of Game and Inland Fisheries maintains a boat-launching ramp at the end of Secondary Route 642 in Cape Charles. There are also commercial ramps in the Cape Charles area.

Little Rock

This is a long, narrow stretch of water just west of Eastville that drops suddenly from approximately 2 feet to depths of 15–20 feet.

FISH: Channel bass and gray trout.

ACCESS: The nearest Department of Game and Inland Fisheries boat-launching ramp is at Cape Charles, but there are commercial ramps closer.

Little Shell Rock

This is a shallow fishing ground southwest of Freeschool Marsh in Pocomoke Sound. The water ranges in depth from 2 to 10 feet.

FISH: Gray trout, speckled trout, spot, and whiting.

ACCESS: The Department of Game and Inland Fisheries maintains a boat-launching ramp in Saxis, and there are commercial ramps on Pocomoke Sound.

Lynnhaven Inlet and Shoals

This popular fishing area is located between the Chesapeake Bay Bridge-Tunnel and Seashore State Park, and behind the inlet are Broad and Lynnhaven bays, good fishing waters in their own right. The shoals are just offshore from the inlet.

FISH: Croaker, flounder, hogfish, puppy drum, speckled trout, and spot.

ACCESS: The Division of State Parks maintains a boat-launching ramp on Broad Bay that provides access to the inlet and shoals, and there are also commercial launching ramps that provide quick access.

Mattawoman Creek

This is a shallow Eatern Shore fishing spot where Hunger and Mattawoman creeks join to flow into the bay.

FISH: Speckled trout.

ACCESS: There is a Department of Game and Inland Fisheries boat-launching ramp at Morley's Wharf, and there are commercial ramps on Nassawadox Creek to the north.

Mobjack Bay

Inshore from a line drawn between New Point Comfort and the Guinea Marshes is Mobjack Bay, with water ranging up to 25 feet in depth. The North and Severn rivers are its major tributaries.

FISH: Croaker, flounder, gray trout, spot, striped bass.

ACCESS: The Department of Game and Inland Fisheries maintains boat-launching ramps at Warehouse in Gloucester County and at Town Point in Mathews County. There are also good commercial ramps on the bay.

Mudhole

This is a shallow area at the mouth of the Eastern Shore's Pungoteague Creek. The flats are only 2–3 feet deep, but the creek channel may be as much as 10–20 feet deep.

FISH: Cobia, croaker, gray trout, kingfish, spot, striped bass, and white perch.

ACCESS: There are commercial boat-launching ramps on Pungoteague Creek.

Nassawadox Creek

The shallow water at the mouth of Nassawadox Creek on the Eastern Shore offers good trout fishing, but the offshore water drops to 20 or 30 feet, offering fishing for cobia and other species. There are good eelgrass areas close to shore.

FISH: Cobia, croaker, flounder, speckled trout, spot, striped bass, and tautog.

ACCESS: There are good commercial boat-launching ramps on Nassawadox Creek.

Nigger Lump

Also known as Black Buoy, this is a fishing hot spot in the mouth of Pocomoke Sound. The water here is 10–15 feet deep.

FISH: Gray trout, spot, and whiting.

ACCESS: The Department of Game and InlandFisheries maintains a boat-launching ramp at Saxis and also one at Chesonnessex.

Occohannock Rock

This is a popular fishing area just west of Silver Beach on the Eastern Shore. Water of 30–35 foot depths drops quickly to 45–50 foot depths.

FISH: Gray trout.

ACCESS: The Department of Game and Inland Fisheries maintains a boat-launching ramp at Morley's Wharf, and there are commercial launching ramps on Occohannock Creek.

Old Plantation Flats and Lights

Just west of Cape Charles the bay bottom rises from depths of 20–25 feet to only 10–12 feet and then drops quickly to 50–75 foot depths. The result is a rich fishing area.

FISH: Cobia, croaker, and spadefish.

ACCESS: The Department of Game and Inland Fisheries maintains a boat-launching ramp at Cape Charles, and there are commercial ramps in the area.

Onancock-Pungoteague Flats

The Onancock Creek flows into the bay here from the Eastern Shore and forms a broad area of shallow flats.

FISH: Channel bass and cobia.

ACCESS: The Department of Game and Inland Fisheries maintains a boat-launching ramp in the town of Onancock, and there are commercial ramps on Onancock Creek.

Peaceful Beach

The water just offshore from Peaceful Beach in Northampton County is shallow and offers good fishing for channel bass in 3 to 6 feet of water.

FISH: Channel bass.

ACCESS: There are commercial boat-launching ramps on Nassawadox Creek, and the Commission of Game and Inland Fisheries maintains a ramp at Morley's Wharf.

Piankatank River

The Piankatank is a picturesque, but small, tidal estuary that enters the bay between Stingray Point on the north and Gwynn's Island on the south. It is a reasonably shallow estuary, less than 20 feet deep in most parts.

FISH: Bluefish, croaker, gray trout, flounder, spot, and striped bass.

ACCESS: The Department of Game and Inland Fisheries maintains a boat-launching ramp on Gwynn's Island, and there are convenient commercial ramps on the river.

Plumtree Island

Forming the northern shore of Back River where it enters the bay, Plumtree Island and Plumtree Bar in the mouth of Back

River offer limited fishing, because the island serves as a bombing range for military planes.

FISH: Bluefish and striped bass.

ACCESS: The Department of Game and Inland Fisheries maintains boat-launching ramps at Messick in the town of Poquoson and at Fox Hill in Hampton. There are also commercial ramps on Back River that offer access to the bar and the waters around the island—but the area is often closed to fishing because of bombing practice.

Poquoson River

Protected from the bay by the broad and shallow Poquoson Flats, and Poquoson River is mostly a broad bay lying between Goodwin Islands to the north and Plumtree Island to the south. Most of the water in the river is less than 20 feet deep, and it offers reasonably protected fishing.

FISH: Bluefish, croaker, flounder, gray trout, spot, and striped bass.

ACCESS: The Department of Game and Inland Fisheries maintains boat-launching ramps at Mesick in the town of Poquoson and at Tide Mill northeast of Tabb. There are also good commercial ramps on the river.

Potters Rock

This is a shallow fishing area on the Maryland-Virginia border in Pocomoke Sound. It is noted for its gray-trout fishing.

FISH: Gray trout.

ACCESS: The Department of Game and Inland Fisheries maintains a boat-launching ramp at Saxis, and there are commercial ramps on the sound.

Rappahannock River

One of the bay's major feeder streams, the lower reaches of the river and its confluence with the bay offer excellent fishing. Upstream from its entrance to the bay the channel is deep, up to 70 feet, but the river becomes more shallow as it broadens to enter the bay.

FISH: Croaker, flounder, gray trout, spot, striped bass, tautog, and white perch.

ACCESS: There are a number of commercial boat-launching ramps on the river, and the Department of Game and Inland Fisheries maintains a ramp at Mill Creek, just north of Hartfield.

Robin Hood

This is a drop-off of from 20 to over 60 feet in Pocomoke Sound.

FISH: Black drum, gray trout, spot, and whiting.

ACCESS: The Department of Game and Inland Fisheries maintains boat-launching ramps at Saxis and Chesconnessex, and there are commercial ramps on the sound.

Smith Point and Smith Point Light

Where the southern banks of the Potomac River merge with the western shore of the bay, there is a broad point that runs well out into the bay. Water from 5 to 10 feet deep extends well out from shore.

FISH: Bluefish, cobia, gray trout, and striped bass.

ACCESS: The Department of Game and Inland Fisheries maintains a boat-launching ramp at Shell, southeast of Reedville, and there are commercial ramps in the area.

South Channel

This is a patch of shallow water close to the eastern shore of the bay and located just north of Mattawoman Creek.

FISH: Flounder and speckled trout.

ACCESS: There are commercial launching ramps on Nassawadox Creek.

Spoil Area Ground

This is a popular fishing area in the lower bay midway between Plumtree Island on the mainland and Kiptopeke Beach on the Eastern Shore. Water depths range from 25 to 35 feet.

FISH: Black drum, channel bass, and cobia.

ACCESS: The Department of Game and Inland Fisheries maintains boat-launching ramps at Cape Charles on the Eastern Shore and in Hampton on the mainland. There are also a number of commercial ramps that provide access to this fishing area.

S.S. Brazilia

An old wreck in deep, 90-to-100-foot water located just southeast of the Smith Point Light.

FISHING: Bluefish, gray trout, and striped bass.

ACCESS: The Department of Game and Inland Fisheries maintains boat-launching ramps at Coopers and Shell in the Smith Point area, and there are commercial launching ramps.

Stingray Point

The tip of the peninsula formed by the Rappahannock River on the north and the Piankatank River on the south is known as Stingray Point. Shallow waters surround the point and extend well into the bay, offering good fishing.

FISH: Bluefish, croaker, flounder, gray trout, spot, striped bass, and tautog.

ACCESS: The Department of Game and Inland Fisheries maintains boat-launching ramps on Gwynn's Island and at Mill Creek on the Rappahannock River. There are also a number of commercial ramps in the area.

Stone Rock

This is a reasonably shallow area in Pocomoke Sound that drops from depths of 15–20 feet to 80–90 feet in a deep channel.

FISH: Black drum, cobia, croaker, gray trout, spot, and whiting.

ACCESS: The Department of Game and Inland Fisheries maintains a boat-launching ramp on Chesconessex Creek reached by Secondary Route 655 northwest of Onancock.

Tangier Lumps

This is a popular fishing hole in 25 to 35 feet of water and located midway between Tangier Island and the mainland.

FISH: Bluefish and striped bass.

ACCESS: The Department of Game and Inland Fisheries maintains boat-launching ramps at Coopers and Shell in the Smith Point area, and there are also commercial ramps in the area.

The Targets

This is a popular Chesapeake Bay fishing hole located just west of Tangier Island and approximately a third of the distance toward the mainland.

FISH: Bluefish, cobia, and striped bass.

ACCESS: The Department of Game and Inland Fisheries maintains boat-launching ramps at Coopers and Shell in the Smith Point region, and there are also commercial ramps in the vicinity.

The Old Texas

A popular fishing area located southwest of the southern tip of Tangier Island, the Old Texas offers good fishing at depths of 30 to 45 feet.

FISH: Gray trout, spot, and white perch.

ACCESS: There are commercial boat-launching ramps in the Kilmarnock area.

Thimble Shoal–Ocean View Oyster Grounds

This is a shallow, shoals, area in the lower bay and just east of Old Point Comfort. Depths range up to 15 or 20 feet.

FISH: Croaker, flounder, gray trout, and spot.

ACCESS: The Department of Game and Inland Fisheries maintains boat-launching ramps in Hampton and at Willoughby in Norfolk.

Watts Island

This is a small island in the mouth of Pocomoke Sound. It is surrounded by shallow water that offers good fishing.

FISH: Black drum, striped bass, and whiting.

ACCESS: The Department of Game and Inland Fisheries maintains boat-launching ramps at Saxis and Chesconnessex, and there are commercial ramps on the sound.

Windmill Point

Windmill Point guards the northern entrance to the Rappahannock River from the bay. A narrow point extending deeper into the bay from this point is known as the Rappahannock Spit. The water over the point is less than 10 feet deep.

FISH: Bluefish, cobia, croaker, flounder, gray trout, striped bass, and tautog.

ACCESS: The Department of Game and Inland Fisheries maintains a boat-launching ramp at Mill Creek on the Rappahannock River, and there are commercial ramps in the area.

Winter Harbor

Generally included here are the shallow waters and marshes between Gwynn's Island and New Point Comfort.

FISH: Striped bass.

ACCESS: The Department of Game and Inland Fisheries maintains boat-launching ramps on Gwynn's Island and at Town Point in Mathews County. There are also commercial ramps that provide quick access to this water.

York River

A broad tidal river and a major tributary of the bay, the York enters the bay between the Guinea Marshes and the Goodwin Islands. Though the river channel is over 50 feet deep just before the river enters the bay, the York spit just beyond the mouth is less than 5 feet deep in places. Just northeast of the Goodwin Islands is Roast Meat Flats, only 5 to 10 feet deep.

FISH: Bluefish, croaker, flounder, gray trout, spot, and striped bass.

ACCESS: The Department of Game and Inland Fisheries maintains boat-launching ramps at Gloucester Point, Messick, Tanyard, Tide Mill, and West Point, and there are a number of commercial ramps on the river.

The Offshore Waters   ———————————————

Fishing the big ocean waters of the Atlantic off Virginia's coast is one of the youngest kinds of angling in Virginia, although the fish have been there for generations. The first white marlin taken from Virginia waters was caught off Chincoteague in 1937, and it was not until the boom years following World War II that modern fishing boats equipped with electronic fishing gear and navigational aids helped anglers open up this rich offshore fishery.

Contributing to the rich fishing grounds are the blue waters of the Atlantic Ocean, the gently sloping continental shelf, the Labrador Current, and the famous Gulf Stream.

The golden sand that draws summer visitors to Virginia's beaches by the thousands every summer actually extends far off-shore. The continental shelf, a rich ocean plateau that stretches far out into the ocean, has a predominantly sandy bottom. This water-covered plateau slopes gently initially as it extends toward the mysterious depths of the Atlantic Ocean, reaching a depth of approximately 120 feet during the first 40 miles. For the next 20 miles, however, it pitches more rapidly to depths of 250 to 300 feet, and then it drops abruptly—and out of sight as far as fishermen are concerned. It is the first 40 to 60 miles of the continental shelf that are of interest to oceangoing anglers, an underwater plateau marked by small hills called shoals, by craters, and by the rusting hulks of several centuries of wrecked ships.

The continental shelf is a rich fishing area, made even richer by the Labrador Current and the Gulf Stream, big ocean rivers that bring food-laden currents to the area. The Labrador Current moves slowly south from the Arctic, while the Gulf Stream sweeps in from the tropics. Their fertile waters mix over this ocean plateau off the Virginia coast. The result is a rich offshore fishing ground, but one that Virginia anglers did not discover until well into the twentieth century.

Virginia anglers generally concentrate their offshore efforts on an area between Chincoteague to the north and Virginia Beach to the south.

Good though the fishing is off Virginia's coast, these ocean waters are not to be taken lightly. This is the stormy Atlantic Ocean, to be tackled only by experienced sailors and navigators in seaworthy boats outfitted with modern navigational aids and radios tuned to the latest weather reports. Even the most experienced don't hesitate to crank up their two-way marine radios and call on the Coast Guard when trouble arises.

The offshore fishing season is a long one, beginning in March with the arrival of big schools of Atlantic or Boston mackerel. The bluefish arrive in April and May. There are tautog over the wrecks at that time. Bluefin tuna and king mackerel show up in June, and by late June or early July there are blue and white marlin, dolphin, wahoo, and yellowfin tuna to replace the bluefins.

Famous people sample Virginia's offshore waters. Former President and Mrs. Jimmy Carter after a successful offshore trip. (Photo courtesy of Virginia Beach Convention Bureau)

Fishing is strong well into October, when the battling bluefish and white marlin finally desert cooling Virginia waters for the more comfortable ones to the south.

Offshore fishing in Virginia usually means trolling for such exciting fish as bluefin tuna, bluefish, blue marlin, dolphin, false albacore, king mackerel, wahoo, white marlin, and yellowfin tuna. There is also a growing interest in the rich offshore shark fishery, one that produces some of the largest fish caught in Virginia waters. This is big-game fishing. While white marlin averaging 30 to 50 pounds outnumber the larger blues five to ten, the occasional blues that are caught run to several hundred pounds. Tuna average 20 to 40 pounds, and even dolphin run 5 to 20 pounds.

Offshore anglers also often resort to bottom fishing from anchored or drifting boats. The catch is primarily black sea bass, porgy, and tautog.

Offshore fishing boats head for the blue waters out of such popular ports as Cape Charles, Chincoteague, Hampton, Norfolk, Oyster, Quinby, Wachapreague, and Lynnhaven and Rudee inlets in Virginia Beach. Surveys made by the Virginia Institute of Marine Science show that Rudee Inlet and Wachapreague are by far the busiest ports used by offshore anglers, however.

For the average angler, enjoying a day of offshore fishing means boarding a charter or head boat out of one of these ports. Charter boats carry four to six fishermen, but a head boat may carry twenty to sixty. A head-boat trip is within the limits of any angler's fishing budget. The usual crew of sports-fishing boats includes the skipper and a mate to serve the anglers. Most boats are equipped with bait and tackle so the angler needs no special tackle to enjoy this unique fishing.

There is a growing conservation ethic among serious offshore anglers. The greater percentage of white marlin now caught in Virgnia's offshore waters are released, and most fishing tournaments are catch-and-release tournaments. Also, there are often self-imposed catch limits on tuna and other popular fish.

During the past half century adventuresome anglers have unraveled bit by bit some of the mysteries of the continental shelf off the Virginia coast. Good fishing spots have been uncovered and pinpointed on navigational and other maps. There may still be others waiting to be discovered. Here are thumbnail sketches of the better-known ones. All are easily accessible from Rudee Inlet, Wachapreague, and other Virginia ports.

Blackfish Bank

A little more than 5 miles east of the Chincoteague Inlet a narrow, underwater ridge rises from depths of 45 to over 70 feet to shallows in the 15- to 20-foot range. The ridge runs in a northeastern direction.

FISH: Bluefish, bonito, cobia, false albacore, and gray trout.

Boomerang

This is a tuna and billfish hot spot approximately 35 miles east of Virginia Beach.

FISH: Bluefish, bonito, false albacore, marlin, and tuna.

Captain Rick

The *Captain Rick* is an old wreck on the ocean floor, located approximately 25 miles east of Virginia Beach.

FISH: Bluefish, bonito, false albacore, marlin, and tuna.

Cigar

Approximately 50 miles east of the North Carolina–Virginia border a long, narrow ridge rises in the ocean floor. Known as the Cigar, it is one of the more popular offshore fishing spots. The depths on the top of the ridge range from 100 to 120 feet.

FISH: Bonito, dolphin, false albacore, mackerel, tuna, wahoo, and white marlin.

Coral Beds

This is a small patch of productive water located approximately 15 miles east of Garathy Inlet. The ocean floor rises here from a depth of approximately 70 feet to depths of 50–55 feet.

FISH: Codfish, porgy, sea bass, and tautog.

David H. Atwater *Wreck*

Resting on the ocean floor approximately 10 miles east of Assateague Island is the rusty hulk of the *David H. Atwater*. It is in approximately 40 feet of water.

FISH: Codfish, porgy, sea bass, and porgy.

The Fingers

Located approximately 50 miles east of the mouth of the Chesapeake Bay is The Fingers, a finger-shaped formation on the ocean floor and at depths of from 100 to 130 feet.

FISH: Bonito, dolphin, false albacore, king mackerel, tuna, wahoo, and white marlin.

First Lump

The First Lump is the northernmost of several formations on the ocean floor just northwest of the Washington Canyon, located approximately 50 miles east of Quinby Inlet.

FISH: Blue marlin, bonito, dolphin, false albacore, king mackerel, tuna, wahoo, and white marlin.

The Fish Hook

The Fish Hook is a hook-shaped formation on the ocean floor located approximately 20 miles east of the Virginia Beach resort area. The water here ranges from 50 to 75 feet in depth.

FISH: Amberjack, bluefish, bonito, dolphin, false albacore, king mackerel, and tuna.

4A Buoy Lumps

Approximately 10 miles east of False Cape State Park there is a group of little hills that rise 10 to 20 feet above the ocean floor. The depths here range from 45 to 70 feet.

FISH: Bluefish, bonito, dolphin, and false albacore.

Francis E. Powell *Wreck*

Back in 1948 the *Francis E. Powell* sank approximately 30 miles east of the Virginia Beach resort center, and it now serves as a haven for various species of fish.

FISH: Bluefish, bonito, dolphin, false albacore, mackerel, tautog, tuna, wahoo, and white marlin.

Green Run Buoy

This marks a rise in the ocean floor approximately 10 miles offshore, near the Maryland border. The ocean bottom rises from approximately 50 feet to depths of 30 feet or less.

FISH: Albacore, bluefish, bonito, dolphin, and mackerel.

Gulf Hustler

Approximately 30 miles east of Virginia Beach the wreck of the *Gulf Hustler* provides a fishing hot spot.

FISH: Bluefish, tuna, and white marlin.

Hambone

Also known as twenty-six Mile Hill, this is a small ocean-bottom hill located approximately 30 miles east of Cobb Island off the Eastern Shore. Its peak is 50 to 60 feet deep, and the water around it drops quickly to depths of 90 to 100 feet or more. It draws a rich variety of fish.

FISH: Bluefish, bonito, dolphin, false albacore, king mackerel, tuna, wahoo, and white marlin.

Honey Hole

The Honey Hole is located approximately 50 miles east of False Cape State Park near the edge of the continental shelf.

FISH: Blue marlin, bonito, dolphin, false albacore, king mackerel, tuna, and white marlin.

Horseshoe

This is a horseshoe-shaped formation on the ocean floor, located approximately 25 miles east of Virginia Beach.

FISH: Bluefish, bonito, dolphin, and false albacore.

Hot Dogs

Located approximately 30 miles east of False Cape State Park, this is a slight rise in the ocean bottom from depths of 70–80 feet to 40–50.

FISH: Bluefish, tuna, and white marlin.

Jackspot

This fishing area is located near the Maryland line and about 20 miles east of the Assateague National Seashore. It is a rise in the ocean floor marked by wrecked ships and a whistle buoy. The depth above the rise is approximately 50 feet, but most of the surrounding water is 75 to 100 feet deep.

FISH: Bluefish, bonito, dolphin, false albacore, tuna, wahoo, and white marlin.

The Lump

This is a slight rise in the ocean floor approximately 20 miles east of the Assateague Island National Seashore. It attracts a good variety of fish.

FISH: Bluefish, bonito, dolphin, false albacore, tuna, wahoo, and white marlin.

The Lumps

The Lumps consist of a series of rises in the ocean bottom approximately 30 miles east of False Cape State Park. The water here ranges in depth from 70 to 120 feet.

FISH: Bluefish, bonito, dolphin, false albacore, king mackerel, and white marlin.

Mona Island

This is the rusting hulk of a wrecked ship located approximately 45 miles east of the mouth of the Chesapeake Bay and not far from the Parramore artificial reef.

FISH: Bonito, dolphin, false albacore, king mackerel, tuna, wahoo, and white marlin.

Monroe Slough

This is a long, narrow valley in the ocean floor running generally between The Lump and the Jackspot. It is located approximately 20 miles east of the Assateague Island National Seashore.

FISH: Bluefish.

Monroe *Wreck*

The *Monroe* wreck is a rusting ship, wrecked and in approximately 60 feet of water about 20 miles east of Parramore Island. A variety of fish are found here.

FISH: Codfish, ling cod, porgy, sea bass, and tautog.

No Name

An unnamed, but productive, area between Quinby Inlet and twenty-one Mile Hill approximately 25 miles offshore, this area is worth attention.

FISH: Bluefish, bonito, dolphin, false albacore, king mackerel, tuna, and white marlin.

Norfolk Canyon

This is a deep ocean canyon and one of the most popular fishing holes off the Virginia coast. The canyon runs generally in an east-west direction, with the bottom of the canyon estimated at depths of from 1,000 to 4,000 feet. The ocean floor along its rim is in the 200 to 300 foot range. It is located approximately 60 miles east of the mouth of the Chesapeake Bay.

FISH: Blue marlin, bonito, dolphin, false albacore, king mackerel, tuna, and white marlin.

One Hundred Fathom Curve

A popular blue and white marlin-fishing area at the very edge of the continental shelf, this area also offers fishing for dolphin, tuna, and wahoo. The water drops off here from depths of 150–300 feet to over 600 feet and then quckly to over 5,000 feet. It is located approximately 60 miles east of the North Carolina–Virginia line and fished by anglers from both states.

FISH: Blue marlin, dolphin, tuna, wahoo, and white marlin.

Owl and Kingston Celonite

This is a wrecked and sunken ship located just 10 miles offshore from Rudee Inlet.

FISH: Bluefish, codfish, king mackerel, ling cod, porgy, sea bass, and tautog.

Parramore Artificial Reef

The Parramore artificial reef, marked by a buoy, has been embellished by the Virginia Marine Resources Commission with two sunken liberty ships, the *Mona Island* and the *Walter Hines Page*. It is located approximately 40 miles east of the mouth of the Chesapeake Bay.

FISH: Bluefish, bonito, dolphin, false albacore, and white marlin.

Poor Man's Canyon

This is an ocean canyon located approximately 50 miles east of the Maryland-Virginia border.

FISH: Blue marlin, bonito, dolphin, false albacore, king mackerel, tuna, wahoo, and white marlin.

The Reef

A 55 to 70 foot deep fishing area located approximately 15 miles off the Virginia Beach resort strip, the Reef is noted for a rich variety of fish.

FISH: Bluefish, dolphin, flounder, ling cod, and sea bass.

Rockpile

The Rockpile is a billfish and tuna fishing area just northwest of the Washington Canyon and approximately 50 miles east of Quinby Inlet.

FISH: Blue marlin, bonito, dolphin, false albacore, king mackerel, tuna, wahoo, and white marlin.

R6 Whistle Buoy

This buoy, located approximately 12 miles east of Assateague Island, is attractive to cobia.

FISH: Bluefish and cobia.

Santore

This is the rusty hulk of the ship *Santore,* which sank in 1948 approximately 20 miles east of Cape Henry.

FISH: Amberjack, flounder, sea bass, and tautog.

Second Lump

This fish-attracting formation on the bottom of the ocean is located approximately 30 miles east of the Maryland-Virginia border. It is noted for its billfish and tuna.

FISH: Bluefish, bonito, dolphin, false albacore, tuna, wahoo, and white marlin.

Smith Island Shoal—Buoy 14 Area

This patch of shallow water, with depths of less than 30 feet in places, is located approximately 15 miles east of the southern tip of the Eastern Shore.

FISH: Bluefish.

Southeast Lumps

The Southeast Lumps consist of a bottom formation located approximately 40 miles east of the mouth of the Chesapeake Bay, and it is noted for its billfish and tuna.

FISH: Bonito, dolphin, false albacore, king mackerel, tuna, and white marlin.

Spring Chicken

Located approximately 30 miles east of Virginia Beach, the wreck of the *Spring Chicken* rests on the ocean floor.

FISH: Codfish, king mackerel, porgy, sea bass, and tautog.

Stove Pipe Buoy

Just south of Chincoteague Shoals, this area is located approximately 10 miles east of Assawoman Inlet in water of 25 to 40 feet.
FISH: Bluefish, bonito, flounder, and tuna.

Submarine Slough

This is a 10- to 20-foot-deep slough in the ocean floor, approximately 15 miles east of the Chincoteague Inlet. It runs in a northeasterly direction.
FISH: Bluefish.

Submarine Wreck

A wrecked submarine rests in water of approximately 60 feet about 15 miles east of Assawoman Inlet.
FISH: Bonito, sea bass, and tuna.

Sugar Lumps

This is a small hump in the ocean bottom approximately 5 miles offshore near the Maryland border.
FISH: Bluefish, bonito, dolphin, false albacore, and mackerel.

Tarav Reef and The Tower

Here there is a reef in 50 to 70 feet of water and marked by a Coast Guard Light Station and an artificial reef buoyed by the Marine Resources Commission. It is located approximately 15 miles east of Cape Henry.
FISH: Amberjack, bluefish, bonito, dolphin, false albacore, king mackerel, sea bass, and tuna.

Three Mile Hill

Located approximately 15 miles east of Parramore Island, this is a sudden rise in the ocean floor from depths of 75–80 feet to only 35–40 feet.

FISH: Bluefish, bonito, dolphin, and false albacore.

Tiger *Wreck*

The rusting hulk of a wrecked ship is located here in approximately 40 feet of water and about 8 miles east of the Virginia Beach resort strip.

FISH: Amberjack, flounder, sea bass, and tautog.

Tiger Wreck Lumps

This is a group of tiny hills on the ocean floor just south of the *Tiger* wreck and located approximately 9 miles east of Virginia Beach. The water varies from depths of 45 to 65 feet.

FISH: Bluefish, bonito, dolphin, and false albacore.

Triangle Artificial Reef and Wrecks

This is a hot fishing area located approximately 40 miles east of the mouth of the Chesapeake Bay, featuring the wreck of the *Lillian Luckenback* and four liberty ships sunk by the Virginia Marine Resources Commission.

FISH: Bluefish, codfish, king mackerel, ling cod, porgy, sea bass, and tautog.

Twenty Fathom Finger

Located approximately 40 miles east of Quinby Inlet, this is one of the far-offshore fishing grounds. The Finger is a mitten-shaped formation on the ocean floor in 75 to 150 feet of water.

FISH: Bonito, dolphin, false albacore, king mackerel, tuna, wahoo, and white marlin.

Twenty-One Mile Hill

This underwater hill is a long, reasonably narrow rise in the ocean floor from depths of over 100 feet to depths of 60 to 90 feet. It is located approximately 25 miles east of Quinby Inlet. The vaiety of fish is rich.

FISH: Bluefish, bonito, dolphin, false albacore, king mackerel, tuna, and white marlin.

Washington Canyon

This is one of the more popular far-offshore fishing grounds, located approximately 60 miles east of Quinby Inlet. The ocean bottom here pitches from depths of 150–200 feet to 300 feet or more.

FISH: Blue and white marlin, bonito, dolphin, false albacore, king mackerel, tuna, and wahoo.

Winter Quarter Shoals

This is a long-popular offshore fishing area located approximately 8 miles east of Assateague Island. The water here is less than 5 feet deep in places, but it averages 10 to 25. Several old wrecks rest on the bottom. It is a good area for trolling as well as bottom fishing.

FISH: Bluefish, cobia, codfish, porgy, sea bass, and tautog.

NOTE: The depths and distances give here are estimates only, and the directions are general. None of this information should be used for navigation purposes. While the listing of fishing areas is reasonably complete, it does not include all of unnamed wrecks and other underwater obstructions that attract fish. These and others are being discovered and charted every fishing season.

The Inshore Waters

Technically, all of Virginia's salt waters could be divided into offshore and inshore waters. Offshore would include the Atlantic Ocean from three miles off the coast to the edge of the continental shelf and possibly beyond, while inshore would encompass the great variety of inland waters including the Chesapeake Bay, the surf, the tidal rivers, and the rich fishing waters along the ocean side of the Eastern Shore. The Chesapeake Bay, the surf, and the tidal rivers are discussed elsewhere, however, and this chapter will be devoted primarily to the broad tidal creeks along the ocean side of the Eastern Shore, the inlets, the rich maze of islands, the sounds, and the strips of golden sand washed clean by the ocean surf.

Inshore fishing changes dramatically south of Cape Charles, but it should not be overlooked. The broad mouth of the Chesapeake Bay is often hard to distinguish from the rolling ocean, but its Chesapeake Bay Bridge-Tunnel and wrecks and other obstructions off of Cape Henry offer a unique kind of inshore fishing. On the mainland there are the broad waters back of Lynnhaven Inlet, Rudee Inlet, and other inshore possibilities, but they taper off rapidly from Cape Henry to the North Carolina line.

Here are thumbnail sketches of some of the major inshore fishing spots.

Assawoman Island

The Intracoastal Waterway separates this Eastern Shore island from the mainland. It is surrounded by Assawoman Inlet to the north, Kegotank Bay to the south, and Northam Narrows to the west. All offer good fishing.

LOCATION: Accomack County.

ACCESS: Commercial boat ramp on Assawoman Creek.

FISH: Black drum, gray trout, and hickory shad.

The Black Can Area

This is a popular inshore trolling area just east of Cape Henry. Boats work from a half mile to a mile or two offshore.

LOCATION: City of Virginia Beach.

ACCESS: The Virginia Division of Parks maintains a public boat-launching ramp on Broad Bay, and there are commercial ramps on Lynnhaven Inlet.

FISH: Bluefish and striped bass.

Cape Henry Wreck

The wreck of the *Chilore* rests on the bottom of the Chesapeake Bay approximately a mile north of Fort Story. Anglers know this

Anglers work the inshore waters along the ocean side of the Eastern Shore from Chincoteague Island.

area as the Cape Henry Wreck, and it is a popular inshore fishing area. The water averages 35 to 70 feet in depth.

LOCATION: City of Virginia Beach.

ACCESS: The Virginia Division of Parks maintains a boat-launching ramp on Broad Bay, and there is a commercial ramp on Lynnhaven Inlet.

Cedar Island

Cedar Island just north of the Wachapreague Inlet is primarily a surf-fishing area, but dozens of creeks and inlets offer limited inshore fishing.

LOCATION: Accomack County.

ACCESS: The Department of Game and Inland Fisheries maintains a boat-launching ramp on Folly Creek, and there is a commercial ramp at Wachapreague.

FISH: Black drum, channel bass, flounder, gray trout, sand mullet, spot, and whiting.

Chincoteague Bay

Chincoteague Bay, which Virginia shares with Maryland, is one of the most popular fishing areas on the Eastern Shore. The city of Chincoteague and Chincoteague Island are in the center of the Virginia portion of the bay and connected to the mainland by a causeway. Assateague Island protects the bay from the ocean. The water in the bay is generally shallow, with maximum depths of approximately 15 feet, but much of it is less than 5 feet deep.

LOCATION: Accomack County.

ACCESS: There are a number of commercial boat-launching ramps on the bay.

FISH: Black drum, bluefish, channel bass, croaker, gray trout, sand mullet, striped bass, and white perch.

Chincoteague Inlet

Chincoteague Inlet is the entrance to Chincoteague Bay from the ocean. It lies between the southern tip of Assateague Island and Wallops Island and is one of the most popular fishing spots on the Eastern Shore. The water in the channel reaches a maximum of 15 to 20 feet in depth, and much of it is shallower.

LOCATION: Accomack County.

ACCESS: The Department of Game and Inland Fisheries maintains a boat-launching ramp on Wishart Point at the end of Secondary Route 695, and there are commerical launching ramps on Chincoteague Bay.

Chincoteague Shoals

This is a patch of shallow water near Chincoteague Inlet and Assateague Island. Its outer edge is approximately 3 miles off-shore. The water averages 10 to 20 feet in depth.

LOCATION: Accomack County.

ACCESS: The Commission of Game and Inland Fisheries maintains a boat-launching ramp on Wishart Point at the end of Secondary Route 695, and there are commercial ramps on Chincoteague Bay.

FISH: Bluefish, channel bass, false albacore, gray trout, and whiting.

Hog Island and Great Machipongo Inlet

Hog Island is a large barrier island lying between Quinby Inlet on the north and Great Machipongo Inlet on the south. The Great Machipongo Channel and other inlets offer fishing for various bottom fish, and the Great Machipongo gives up some tarpon, one of the few places in Virginia where this exciting fish can be caught.

LOCATION: Accomack County.

ACCESS: The upper island waters and North Channel Inlet can be reached by boat from the Department of Game and Inland Fisheries launching ramp at Quinby, but the lower part of the island is more accessible from Oyster, where the Department also maintains a launching ramp. There are also commercial ramps in the general area.

FISH: Black drum, channel bass, croaker, flounder, gray trout, spot, and whiting.

Lynnhaven Inlet

This popular inshore fishing spot has already been discussed above in the chapter on the Chesapeake Bay, but it is also important to the inshore angler who may never venture far up in the bay. Rather than repeat the discussion here, I refer the reader to chapter 6, where this popular fishing area is discussed in full.

Metomkin Island

Metomkin Inlet to the south of this barrier island leads to Metomkin Bay and some excellent inshore fishing. There is also good fishing in the inlet itself, particularly during the spring shad run.

LOCATION: Accomack County.

ACCESS: The Department of Game and Inland Fisheries maintains a boat-launching ramp on Folly Creek just south of Accomac. There is also a commercial ramp on Parkers Creek.

FISH: Flounder, gray trout, and shad.

New Inlet

New Inlet provides access to South Bay from the ocean. The inlet is between Ship Shoal Island to the south and Wreck Island to the north. South Bay is part of the Mockhorn Island Wildlife Management Area. Mockhorn, Ramshore, and Sand Shoal channels lead inshore from South Bay.

LOCATION: Northampton County.

ACCESS: The Department of Game and Inland Fisheries maintains a boat-launching ramp in Oyster.

FISH: Black drum, channel bass, croaker, flounder, gray trout, tarpon, and whiting.

Parramore Banks

Approximately three miles east of the Wachapreague Inlet a series of ridges rise from depths of 45–50 feet to only 25–30 feet. Deep water to the west of the banks is only two miles offshore.

LOCATION: Accomack County.

ACCESS: There is a commercial boat-launching ramp at Wachapreague.

FISH: Bluefish and gray trout.

Parramore Island

Parramore is a large barrier island almost due east from Quinby and located between Wachapreague Inlet to the north and Quinby Inlet to the south. Both inlets offer good fishing, and so do the channels and creeks behind the island.

LOCATION: Accomack County.

ACCESS: Wachapreague Inlet and the creeks and channels to the north are best reached from Wachapreague, where there is a commercial boat-launching ramp, but Quinby Inlet and those creeks and channels to the south are accessible from a Department of Game and Inland Fisheries boat-launching ramp at Quinby.

FISH: Black drum, channel bass, croaker, flounder, gray trout, sand mullet, shad, spot, and whiting.

Red Can Buoys

Red Can Buoys, located just south of Cape Charles and east of the Chesapeake Bay Bridge-Tunnel, mark the entrance to the Chesapeake Bay. The water here ranges in depth from 15 to 20 feet.

LOCATION: Accomack County.

ACCESS: The Department of Game and Inland Fisheries maintains a boat-launching ramp at Cape Charles, but there are also commercial ramps in the area.

FISH: Black drum and striped bass.

Sand Shoal Inlet and Southeast Channel

The Sand Shoal Inlet and Southeast Channel provide the entrance to Sand Shoal Channel from the ocean. This inshore water is located between Cobb Island on the north and Wreck Island to the south. Sand Shoal Channel is a broad tidal river that connects with Eckichy, Mittigy, Mockhorn, and Ramshorn channels.

LOCATION: Accomack County.

ACCESS: The channels and inlet can be reached from the Department of Game and Inland Fisheries boat-launching ramp at Oyster.

FISH: Black drum, croaker, flounder, gray trout, hogfish, and tarpon.

Smith Inlet Shoal Area

The Smith Inlet Shoal Area is located just south of Cape Charles between Fisherman Island Wildlife Refuge and the Red Can Buoys. It is a popular and accessible fishing area.

LOCATION: Northampton County.

ACCESS: The Department of Game and Inland Fisheries maintains a boat-launching ramp at Cape Charles.

FISH: Black drum, bluefish, channel bass, gray trout, and striped bass.

Smith Island and Magothy Bay

Smith Island, Magothy Bay, and Fishermans Island are located in the Cape Charles area at the very southern tip of the Eastern

Shore. Fishermans Island is now the Fishermans Island National Wildlife Refuge, and it guards the Magothy Channel entrance to Magothy Bay. This entire region is a rich inshore fishing area.

LOCATION: Northampton County.

ACCESS: The Department of Game and Inland Fisheries maintains a boat-launching ramp at Cape Charles.

FISH: Black drum, channel bass, croaker, flounder, gray trout, hogfish, spot, striped bass, and tarpon.

Turner Lump and Turner Lump Buoy

This is a shallow area only 10 feet deep in places and located approximately 2 miles offshore between Chincoteague Inlet and Chincoteague Shoals.

LOCATION: Accomack County.

ACCESS: There are commercial boat-launching ramps on Chincoteague Bay.

FISH: Channel bass, gray trout, and whiting.

Westmoreland *Wreck*

The rusting hulk of the *Westmoreland* rests a little less than 3 miles east of the Fort Story lighthouse in approximately 30 feet of water. It is a popular inshore fishing area.

LOCATION: City of Virginia Beach.

ACCESS: There are commercial and public boat-launching ramps at Lynnhaven and Rudee inlets in the city of Virginia Beach.

FISH: Bluefish, spot, and striped bass.

NOTE: There are a number of wrecks and other fish-drawing obstructions off of Cape Henry that are unnamed. Additionally, the Chesapeake Bay Bridge-Tunnel, covered in chapter 6 on the Chesapeake Bay, is considered an inshore fishing area and a good one. Many anglers out of Rudee Inlet head into the bay for this popular fishing grounds—or inshore as opposed to going offshore.

The Surf _____

Just about every foot of Virginia's coast from the Maryland border to the North Carolina line is a possibility for surf-fishing, though federal, state, or local regulations may stand in the way. So are the eastern and western shores of the Chesapeake Bay. Over the years some nice striped bass have been taken by surf fishermen working the relatively mild surf of the bay.

The very best surf-fishing, however, is concentrated along the broad beaches of Assateague Island and along several of the barrier islands off the ocean side of the Eastern Shore. South of Cape Henry there is some surf-fishing along the resort beaches, at

There are many miles of surf-fishing along the Virginia coast.

Sandbridge, and to a lesser degree south to the North Carolina line. Access, however, south of the Virgina Beach resort strip is limited. Regardless of the other possibilities, the more serious surf fishermen concentrate on the Assateague Island beaches and the barrier islands.

Generally, the beach buggy, long the vehicle to successful surf-fishing, is prohibited along the Virginia beaches, and this has been a handicap to this fascinating approach to saltwater fishing. In fact, the only beach open to beach buggies or 4 × 4 vehicles is a designated stretch on Assateague Island in the Chincoteague National Wildlife Refuge. To reach the best fishing along other beaches, the angler must either walk or go by boat.

Following is a thumbnail sketch of the more popular surf-fishing spots along Virginia's Atlantic Coast.

Assawoman Island

Assawoman Island is owned by The Nature Conservancy, and managed by the Virginia Coast Reserve, Brownsville, Nassasadox, Virginia 23413. Permission to fish from its shores can be obtained from that organization.

LOCATION: Accomack County.

ACCESS: The island is accessible from Assawoman Creek, where there is a commercial launching ramp.

FISH: Black drum, gray trout, shad, and whiting.

Assateague Island

Part of Assateague Island is managed by the National Park Service as a national seashore, and the remainder is the Chincoteague National Wildlife Refuge, managed by the U.S. Fish and Wildlife Service. The beach is reached from the city of Chincoteague.

LOCATION: Accomack County.

ACCESS: The island is accessible by a causeway from Chincoteague Island.

FISH: Black drum, channel bass, flounder, gray trout, shad, and whiting.

Back Bay National Wildlife Refuge

The Back Bay National Wildlife Refuge controls the beaches between Sandbridge and False Cape State Park. The supervising office is Back Bay National Wildlife Refuge, Pembroke no. 2 Building, Suite 218, 287 Pembroke Office Park, Virginia Beach, Virginia 23462. A paved road behind the sand dunes follows the beach for approximately four miles. Vehicles are not allowed on the beaches.

LOCATION: City of Virginia Beach.

ACCESS: By walking from road behind the sand dunes.

FISH: Albacore, black drum, bluefish, channel bass, croaker, flounder, gray trout, hogfish, speckled trout, spot, striped bass, and whiting.

Cedar Island

Cedar Island, one of the more popular of the barrier islands among anglers, is owned by The Nature Conservancy with the Virginia Coast Reserve, Brownsville, Nassawadox, Virginia 23143, supervising the area. It is generally available for surf-fishing.

LOCATION: Accomack County.

ACCESS: There is a Department of Game and Inland Fisheries boat-launching ramp on Follys Creek and commercial ramps at Wacha-preague.

FISH: Black drum, gray trout, and whiting.

Cobb Island

One of the major barrier islands, Cobb Island is owned by The Nature Conservancy and open to surf-fishing. The angler should contact the Virginia Coast Reserve, Brownsville, Nassasadox, Virginia 23413, regarding details.

LOCATION: Northampton County.

ACCESS: The island can be reached by boat from the Department of Game and Inland Fisheries launching ramp at Oyster.

FISH: Black drum, channel bass, and gray trout.

False Cape State Park

The approximately seven miles of beach between the Back Bay National Wildlife Refuge and the North Carolina line is managed by the False Cape State Park under the jurisdiction of the Virginia Division of Parks. There is no vehicle access to this long stretch of ocean beach, but it is available for surf-fishing.

LOCATION: City of Virginia Beach.

ACCESS: The only access is by boat or by foot from trails within the state park.

FISH: Albacore, black drum, bluefish, channel bass, croaker, flounder, gray trout, hogfish, speckled trout, spot, striped bass, and whiting.

Hog Island

Owned by The Nature Conservancy, Hog Island is one of the more popular spots for catching channel bass in the surf. Information on fishing from the island are available from the Virginia Coast Reserve, Brownsville, Nassawadox, Virginia 23413.

LOCATION: Northampton County.

ACCESS: The island is accessible by boat from the Department of Game and Inland Fisheries boat-launching ramps at Quinby or from a commercial ramp on Parting Creek.

FISH: Black drum, channel bass, croaker, flounder, gray trout, spot, and whiting.

Metomkin Island

Metomkin is one of the barrier islands owned by The Nature Conservancy and open to the public for fishing. Information is available from the Virginia Coast Reserve, Nassawadox, Brownsville, Virginia 23143.

LOCATION: Accomack County.

ACCESS: The island can be reached from commercial boat-launching ramps on Gargathy and Parkers creeks.

FISH: Channel bass, flounder, gray trout, and whiting.

Myrtle Island

Located near the southern reaches of the Eastern Shore, Myrtle is a small barrier island owned by The Nature Conservancy, and permission to fish it is available from the Virginia Coast Reserve, Brownsville, Nassawadox, Virginia 23413.

LOCATION: Northampton County.

ACCESS: The island is accessible by boat from the Department of Game and Inland Fisheries boat-launching ramp at Oyster.

FISH: Black drum, channel bass, croaker, flounder, gray trout, and whiting.

Smith Island

Smith is the southernmost of the barrier islands owned by The Nature Conservancy, and it is open to the public for surf-fishing.

Interested anglers should contact the Virginia Coast Reserve, Brownsville, Nassasadox, Virginia 23413, for information on the fishing.

LOCATION: Northampton County.

ACCESS: The island is accessible by boat from the Department of Game and Inland Fisheries launching ramp at Oyster.

FISH: Black drum, channel bass, gray trout, and whiting.

Virginia Beach Resort Beaches

Surf-fishing along the many miles of broad, sandy beaches that make up the Virginia Beach resort area is a hit-and-miss proposition and certainly not the most productive fishing area. The beaches are crowded with swimmers during the vacation season, but fishing is permitted all year. Access is easy by walking to the beach, but vehicles are not allowed on the sand. The military areas, Fort Story in the Cape Henry area and Camp Pendleton south of Rudee Inlet, are generally off-limits to fishermen.

LOCATION: City of Virginia Beach.

ACCESS: Generally the beaches can be reached by foot only from the boardwalk or resort-strip streets.

FISH: Albacore, black drum, bluefish, channel bass, croaker, flounder, gray trout, hogfish, speckled trout, spot, striped bass, and whiting.

Wallops Island

Located just south of Assateague Island, Wallops Island is owned by the federal government and controlled by the National Aeronautics and Space Administration. It is generally not open to the public for fishing, but this could change.

LOCATION: Accomack County.

ACCESS: It is accessible from commercial boat-launching ramps on Chincoteague Bay and from the Department of Game and Inland Fisheries ramp at Wishart Point near the end of Secondary Route 695.

FISH: Black drum, channel bass, flounder, gray trout, shad, and flounder.

Wreck Island

Wreck is also a barrier island, but it is owned by the Virginia Division of Parks, and it is open to public fishing. It is located between New Inlet on the north and Ship Shoal Inlet on the south.

LOCATION: Northampton County.

ACCESS: The island can be reached by boat from the Department of Game and Inland Fisheries launching ramp at Oyster.

FISH: Black drum, channel bass, and gray trout.

NOTE: Parramore, Revel, and Ship Shoal are also barrier islands owned by The Nature Conservancy, but they are not now open for fishing. Fisherman Island, located at the tip of the Eastern Shore, is owned by the U.S. Fish and Wildlife Service, but it is not open for surf-fishing.

The Black Bass

Three members of the black bass family, the largemouth, small-mouth, and spotted bass, fin Virginia's varied waters. The large-mouth is the largest and most widely distributed, but the smallmouth is more popular among some anglers. The smaller spotted bass is often confused with the largemouth and is less well known than the other two. All three, however, are fine game fish, and as a family the black bass is one of the most popular in the state.

The largemouth bass is native to much of Virginia, but both the smallmouth and the spotted bass were originally found only

The largemouth black bass is one of Virginia's most popular game fish.

in the streams of Southwest Virginia. Both are native to the Ohio River drainage system. Modern fishery management, however, has changed the distribution pattern considerably. While the spotted bass is still pretty much limited to Southwest Virginia, the smallmouth occurs in fast streams and cold lakes from the fall line west.

DESCRIPTION: The largemouth bass typically has a green back and upper sides that fade gradually to a near-white belly. An irregular horizontal line runs from the rear of the gill cover to the tail. The corner of its mouth is normally to the rear of its eyes, and unlike the other black bass, the forward spiny rays of its dorsal fin and the soft rear ones are almost completely separated.

The color of the smallmouth is more bronze than dark green, and spectacular horizontal bars mark its flanks. The corner of its mouth extends no further back than the eye, and a shallow notch separates the forward spines and the rear soft rays of its dorsal fin.

The coloration of the spotted bass is much like that of the largemouth, though its sides tend to be more olive or bronze. Diamond-shaped spots dot its sides, and a series of such markings form the horizontal line that runs from its gill covers to its tail. The corner of its mouth may extend rearward to the eye, but never beyond it. The spines and soft rays of its dorsal fin are not separated but joined by a shallow notch. Unlike the other black bass, it has fine teeth on its tongue.

While 10- and 12-pound largemouth bass are not uncommon in Virginia, a 3-pound fish is probably closer to the average. Smallmouth anglers take 5- and 6-pound fish every season, but a 1 pounder is a good average for the bronzeback, as it is fondly called. A 2-pound spotted bass is a good one, and the average fish is probably a pound or less. The spotted bass is also called Kentucky bass in Virginia.

HABITAT: The largemouth bass is a fish of the slow and still waters. Though sometimes found in fast-flowing streams, it will seek the quieter pools in such streams. It likes cover in the way of aquatic grass and weeds, brush, logs, and even docks. During the heat of the summer it may sink to depths of 30 feet or more to avoid the sun and find comfortable water temperatures. The smallmouth bass, on the other hand, prefers fast water and cold lakes. It prefers rock- and boulder-strewn water and rock cliffs, but it often feeds in water filled with aquatic grass. Vegetation close to boulders and rock cliffs is always worth the angler's attention. The larger fish spend much of the time in the deeper pools, but move into the shallows to feed. The spotted bass likes water and habitat much like that of the smallmouth, but is more tolerant of warmer water.

SEASONS: There are no closed seasons on the black bass in Virginia. Fish can be caught at every season, but spring and fall are good seasons. The summer months can also be good, particularly for stream fishing.

GOOD WATER: The Piedmont and Coastal Plains waters offer the best largemouth-bass fishing. Good tidal streams include the James and Rappahannock rivers and their tributaries. Farm ponds produce some of the largest bass every season, and the big lakes such as Anna, Buggs Island, Gaston, Flannagan, and South Holston usually produce. Back Bay in Virginia Beach is famous for its shallow-water bass fishing. The James, New, Rappahannock, and Shenandoah rivers are among the best smallmouth-bass streams in the country. Their tributaries are also often good. Claytor is one of the best smallmouth lakes, but Philpott, and Smith Mountain lakes are also good. Just about any stream or lake in Southwest Virginia is likely to produce some spotted bass. There is also a population of spotted bass in the Appomattox River in eastern Virginia.

FISHING METHODS: Casting popping bugs with a fly rod or surface poppers or chuggers with casting tackle is one of the most popular methods for largemouth bass, but such fishing is limited to shallow water and generally the shorelines. At other times successful anglers fish deep with crankbaits, plastic worms, or spinnerbaits. Baitcasting tackle is the usual choice for fishing underwater lures, though some anglers like spinning tackle. When fishing underwater, anglers work drop-offs, points, and other fish-holding structures. Smallmouth-bass anglers fish smaller lures, and fly fishermen like streamers. Small surface lures with noisy spinners are good and so are minnow-shaped lures that can be made to imitate a crippled minnow. Smallmouth anglers work the midstream boulders, rock cliffs, and other cover that attract their favorite fish. Smallmouth fishing methods will also take spotted bass.

CARE, CLEANING, AND COOKING: Ideally, bass should be kept alive as long as possible. This may mean placing them in a live well as soon as they are caught or stringing them through both lips on a chain stringer and lowering them into the water. If the surface water is warm, it may be necessary to use a cord extension and get them deeper. Live wells are not available in all boats, however—a canoe, for example. And on a float trip down a river, fish placed on a stringer can be hung up on rocks or other obstructions and lost. When this is the case, an ice chest is the best solution. Keep plenty of ice in the chest, and ice the fish down as soon as they are caught.

Even when a live well or a stringer is used to keep the bass alive while fishing, they should be iced down in a chest for the trip home.

Cleaning should be done as quickly as possible. Bass can be either scaled and gutted or cut into fillets. The tools needed are limited and inexpensive. For scaling, a clamp to hold the fish by the tail, a simple scaler to remove the scales, and a knife for gutting will do the job. Place the fish on a flat surface, and clamp it by the tail; simply work the scaler against the scales (from the tail toward the head), and the scales are quickly removed. Now slit the fish through the belly from gills to the tail and remove the viscera. Finally, use the tip of the knife blade and remove the blood along each side of the spine.

Filleting a fish is less time-consuming. All that is needed is a sharp fillet knife. Work from the head toward the tail. With the knife, make a cut just behind the gills all the way to the spine, then twist the knife and cut along the spine to approximately an inch from the tail. This will remove one side of the bass. Now flip the loose side over, go to the tail, and work forward between the meat and the skin. This removes the skin, and one of the fillets is ready for the pan. Turn the fish over and repeat the process. Leaving an inch of flesh and skin near the tail on the initial cut makes it easier to hold the fish for the second effort.

There are many ways to cook bass for the table, but as is often the case, the simplest method may produce the tastiest dish. *Bass fillets* are delicious and quick and easy to prepare. Begin by dipping the fillets in melted butter. Then place them on an oiled grill, put it in the oven, and set the oven on broil. Broil until they turn a golden brown. This will take 3 to 7 minutes, depending upon the thickness of the fillets. It may be necessary to turn the larger fillets. When the fillets have reached the desired degree of color, remove them and sprinkle them with seafood dressing. Serve with cut lemon.

The Other Sunfish _____

The sunfish family is a large one. It includes the black bass, which were discussed in chapter 10, and the crappie, which will be discussed in chapter 12. Here the emphasis will be upon the *other* sunfish, primarily the bluegill, the redbreast sunfish, and the rock bass. There are others, however, the little banded sunfish of the tidal regions of Virginia, the flier of Lake Drummond and other Coastal Plain waters, the green sunfish, the pumpkinseed, the red-eared sunfish, and the warmouth.

The bluegill is found in still waters, lakes and ponds, statewide. It could well be our most popular sunfish. The rock bass

Bluegills are fun to catch and tasty to eat.

is most abundant from the eastern slopes of the Blue Ridge Mountains west, and the redbreast, like the bluegill, is found just about statewide. Both the rock bass and the redbreast are primarily stream fish, and often share the fast, clear streams with the smallmouth bass.

The red-eared sunfish, better known as shellcracker, is not a native of Virginia waters, but introduced fish do well. Many farm ponds are stocked with this colorful sunfish.

DESCRIPTION: All of the sunfish are more or less saucer-shaped, or built along the lines of the human hand. "About the size of your hand," is the phrase often used to describe the sunfish. Coloration and markings vary. The banded sunfish, the bluegill, and to a lesser extent the warmouth and green sunfish have vertical bars that run from the dorsal fin to a usually well-colored belly. The shellcracker has a bright orange or red earflap, and the earflap of the redbreast is dark and very pronounced. The redbreast is a particularly colorful fish with a bright orange belly. Both the rock bass and warmouth have large mouths and red eyes much like the smallmouth bass. Few fish have a smaller mouth than the bluegill, a feature that calls for small lures and hooks. Often distinguishing between the various sunfish boils down to counting the rays and spines in the dorsal fins. Markings and coloration may vary between waters, but the rays and spines are infallible. Field guides available from the Department of Game and Inland Fisheries are helpful.

While rock bass occasionally tip the scales at 2 pounds or more and bluegills and red-eared sunfish might approach 4 or 5 pounds, a 1-pound sunfish in any of the species is a good fish. The average is probably considerably under a half pound.

HABITAT: Most of the sunfish prefer quiet, still water such as that found in sluggish creeks, ponds, and lakes. Banded sunfish, bluegills, fliers, green sunfish, pumpkinseed, red-eared sunfish, and warmouth all prefer that kind of water. Each has its own preference within that broad habitat, however. The bluegill, pumpkinseed, and warmouth like weeds and other aquatic vegetation. The little green sunfish prefers small creeks and streams, and the warmouth likes water over a muddy bottom. The redbreast sunfish and the rock bass, on the other hand, prefer reasonably fast, clear streams. Most of the sunfish, bluegills particularly, live in schools, so once they are located, a great many fish can be caught from the same spot. Redbreast and rock bass, however, are not as noted for schooling habits.

SEASONS: There are no closed seasons on any of these sunfish in Virginia, and many are taken all year. May and early June are popular weeks for bluegill anglers because the fish are spawning then, and casting small popping bugs on light fly-fishing tackle can be a delight. Sunfish usually hit well throughout the warm summer months, when fishing for other species can be poor. The redbreast sunfish and the rock bass of the fast streams hit well throughout the summer, and they often salvage smallmouth-bass trips that would otherwise produce nothing because the bronzebacks refuse to strike.

GOOD WATER: The Suffolk Lakes, particularly Lake Prince, offer some of the best bluegill fishing in Virginia, but there are farm ponds throughout the state that might be even more productive. There probably isn't a county in the state that does not have some private or public water to thrill the bluegill angler. For good redbreast sunfish, the James River and its tributaries would be hard to beat, but all of the major river systems from the fall line west offer excellent fishing for this colorful little sunfish. Included are the Clinch, Holston, New, Rappahannock, Roanoke, and Shenandoah river systems. Good rock-bass streams are in the western part of Virginia. Include here the Clinch, Holston, New, and Roanoke (where there is a subspecies called the Roanoke bass) rivers. The Cowpasture and the Jackson, which form the headwaters of the James, are also good. Highly acidic Lake Drummond is probably the best flier water in the state, and the sluggish streams and millponds of eastern Virginia all offer fishing for warmouth.

FISHING METHODS: One of the beauties of sunfish angling is that sophisticated methods are not needed to catch them. A cane pole and bobber and a can of garden worms can be just as productive as the most expensive fly-fishing tackle. The fish are usually so abundant and so accessible that the most casual angler can catch all he wants. On the other hand, the fly-fishing purist can also fill a stringer on dainty dry flies. In between there are the minnow dunkers, spinning tackle anglers, and all the rest. Crickets are a top bait for most of the sunfish, particularly for bluegills. Except during the spring spawning season, when the sunfish are on their beds, the bigger fish will usually be found deeper in the water, often near or on the bottom.

CARE, CLEANING, AND COOKING: The sunfish fall into the panfish class, meaning they are easy to catch and tasty on the table. The proper care soon after they are caught will help assure good eating fish. This means keeping them alive in a live well or strung through both lips and lowered into cool water on a stringer. If neither is possible, place them immediately on ice. They should be transported home on ice in any event and cleaned as quickly as possible. They can be scaled and gutted by making a slit along the belly and removing the viscera. When the fish is clamped to a flat board, the scales can be removed by working a scaler toward the head from the tail. Even small fish can be filleted, and this eliminates the bones. To fillet a sunfish, use a sharp knife and make a cut just behind the gill cover all the way to the backbone, and then along the backbone almost to the tail. With the fillet still attached to the fish by a small strip of skin and flesh, flip it over and work forward between the flesh and skin to remove the skin. Repeat this process on the other side of the fish. Because sunfish are reasonably lean they can be *fried*. It matters not whether they are filleted or cooked whole. Cook the fish in a heavy skillet with ¼ inch of vegetable oil. Dry the fish thoroughly, and roll in seasoned corn meal, fine bread crumbs, flour, or pancake mix. Heat the oil until a drop of water sizzles on it, and place the fish in the oil. Fry the fish over moderate heat for 3 to 5 minutes, depending upon the thickness, then turn and cook another 2 to 5 minutes. When the flesh can be separated easily from the backbone, the fish is ready to serve.

The Crappie

The crappie rounds out the sunfish family. We discussed the black bass in chapter 10 and the other sunfish in chapter 11.

There are two crappie in Virginia waters, the black and the white. Most anglers make little effort to distinguish between the two, and often both occur in the same body of water. The black crappie, however, is most abundant in the coastal plains, while the white is found most abundantly from the Piedmont region west. Only the black is a native of Virginia, but today both are found throughout the state. The crappie is a popular fish, very prolific, and widely stocked in Virginia waters. It is primarily a lake fish, but is also found often in quiet streams.

The crappie is a good school fish. Catch one and there are probably others in the same place.

DESCRIPTION: The basic coloring of both the black and white crappies is black and white, but the tones vary depending upon the water in which they live. The white may become light gray or olive, and the black markings range between green and black. The green to black markings on the black crappie are mottled and tend to run well down on its belly, while those of the white form irregular bars that run vertically along its flanks. Both fish are saucer-shaped, like the bluegill, but the back outline of the white forms a more S-shaped curve than that of the black. The black may have 6 to 10 spines in the dorsal fin, whereas the white will have from 5 to 7. While both crappie may exceed 5 pounds in weight, the average fish will weigh less than a pound. A 1-pound crappie is a good one in Virginia waters.

HABITAT: Both crappie prefer clear, quiet water such as that found in lakes, ponds, and the quieter stretches of streams. Water containing vegetation is preferred, and the fish are attracted to submerged brush and other cover. Bridge abutments and similar objects attract many fish. The white is more tolerant of turbidity than the black. Crappie tend to travel in schools, and once they are located, the angler can often anchor and catch all he wants.

SEASONS: There are no closed seasons on crappie in Virginia, but spring and fall are primary fishing seasons. March, April, and May can be particularly good.

GOOD WATER: Lake Drummond in the Great Dismal Swamp National Wildlife Area is noted for its large black crappie, but the fish is also found in the Suffolk Lakes and the slow streams of the coastal plains. The white crappie is more widespread, and it occurs in both public and private lakes and ponds throughout most of the state. Buggs Island Lake is noted for its jumbo crappie, but the fish are also abundant in Lake Anna, and in Gaston, Smith Mountain, Leesville, and Philpott lakes, and many others. The tidal stretch of the James River is good. There is probably not a county in Virginia without some good crappie-fishing water.

FISHING METHODS: Long cane poles, tiny bobbers, and lively 1-inch minnows account for thousands of crappie every spring in Virginia. The small minnow is probably the most popular bait. Catching crappie is as simple as locating a school of fish, lowering anchor carefully, and dunking the minnows at the depth the fish are located. Locating the fish is the first problem. They are attracted to submerged brush, trees, and other debris in reasonably deep water—water a minimum of 5 to 6 feet in depth. The crappie is not a shallow-water fish. The fish are usually located by fishing such cover until one is caught. While live minnows are probably the most used bait, crappie can be caught on a variety of artificial lures. Fly fishermen use small streamers and other wet flies, and spinning anglers fish doll flies, tiny spinners, and other small lures. Artificial lures should be worked *very* slowly. Some anglers permit their boats to drift as they trail live minnows or cast flies or lures until they locate the fish. Crappie will hit surface lures and dry flies, but usually underwater lures or wet flies and streamers are the most productive.

CARE, CLEANING, AND COOKING: The crappie is the first choice of many who like fish in their diet. Its flesh is firm and sweet and contains a minimum of bones. The few there are can be removed by filleting the fish. Like most fish, the crappie should be kept fresh as long as possible, and the sooner it is placed on the table the better it will taste. If possible, keep the crappie alive in a boat live well or by stringing through both lips and lowering the stringer into cool water. If this is not possible, place the fish on ice as soon as it is caught. Crappie can be scaled and gutted and cooked whole or filleted. To scale, clamp the fish on a flat surface, and remove the scales by working a knife or scaler against the scales and toward the head. This done, open the fish by slitting the belly from the throat to the tail and removing the viscera. Use the tip of a knife blade to scrape the blood from alongside its backbone. To fillet, place the fish on a flat surface; using a fillet knife or a sharp knife, make a cut just back of the gills all the way to the backbone, and then work the knife along the backbone almost to the tail. Now flip the fish over, and remove the skin by working the knife forward between the skin and the fillet. This produces one fillet. Flip the fish over and repeat the process on the other side. For *crispy fried crappie* gather 2 teaspoons of garlic salt, 1½ teaspoons of onion powder, 2 pounds of crappie fillets, 48 finely crushed buttery crackers, ½ cup of beer, 1 beaten egg, and vegetable oil. Combine the garlic salt and the onion powder, and sprinkle the fillets with ½ teaspoon of the mixture. Mix the remainder of the mixture with cracker crumbs on a sheet of aluminum foil. Combine the beer and egg in a shallow dish, and place the fillets in the beer and egg mixture. Coat both sides of the fillets with seasoned cracker crumbs, and place in a fry pan with ⅛ to ¼ inches of vegetable oil. Heat over medium heat until a bread cube dropped into the oil sizzles. Fry a few fillets at a time, 3 to 5 minutes on each side. Cook to a golden brown and until the fish flakes in the center. Drain the fillets on paper towels, and keep them warm in a 175° F oven until ready to serve.

The Freshwater Trout _____

There are three trout in Virginia's cold-water lakes and streams: the brook, the brown, and the rainbow. All three are popular fish that provide trout anglers with many hours of angling pleasure.

The brook trout is the only native fish. It is found at the higher elevations from the eastern slopes of the Blue Ridge Mountains west to the Kentucky and West Virginia borders. The little brookie enjoys good natural reproduction in Virignia waters. The brown trout, a native of Europe, has been successfully introduced to American waters, but its numbers are maintained in Virginia primarily with hatchery-reared fish. There is

Native brook trout caught in a Shenandoah National Park stream.

some natural reproduction in a few waters. The rainbow is a native of the western United States, but has also been successfully introduced in eastern waters. While there is some natural reproduction of rainbows in Virginia, the fishing is basically put-and-take fishing and is supported by hatchery-reared trout.

Like the brook trout, browns and rainbows are found from the eastern slopes of the Blue Ridge Mountains west. Both will tolerate water slightly warmer than that demanded by the native brookie.

DESCRIPTION: The three trout found in Virginia are alike in many ways. All have soft dorsal fins free of spines, and their body build is much the same. All are colorfully marked fish, but each has its own distinctive markings. The brook trout is a colorful fish with vermicular or wormlike brown markings on its back and upper sides. The true native has a bright orange belly, and its flanks are dotted with red, gray, or yellow spots surrounded by a blue circle. The leading edges of the lower dorsal fins are creamy white and very striking. Its tail is square, a feature that helps distinguish it from the brown and rainbow trout. Its scales are minute. The brown trout is sometimes confused with the brookie in stocked waters because of the red spots on its sides. These spots, however, are surrounded by light rings instead of blue ones. The general tone of its color is brown. It has a large adipose fin and fairly large scales, larger than those of the brook and rainbow. The brightly colored pink, purple, or red band that runs horizontally along the flanks of the rainbow trout gives it its name. The vivid colors in this band vary considerably between fish, however. The rainbow's basic color is silvery on its flanks to greenish blue on its back; its back, caudal and dorsal fins, and sides are pock-marked with tiny black spots. Generally, the brook is the smallest of the trout and the brown is the largest, but all three can attain good size. In Virginia a 1-pound brook, 3-pound rainbow, and 5-pound brown are good fish, even though larger fish are caught from time to time. Native brook trout probably average 6 to 7 inches, and hatchery-reared browns and rainbows average less than a pound—or 10 to 12 inches in length.

HABITAT: All three trout are cold-water fish and reasonably demanding of water quality. None of them will accept much siltation or general pollu-tion, though the brown is more tolerant in this respect than the other two. Brown trout sometimes thrive alongside smallmouth bass. They will accept warmer water than will the brook and rainbow. All the trout are primarily stream fish in Virginia, and they do best in the cold waters at the higher elevations. Rainbow trout sometimes fare well in the lower levels of the deep, two-story reservoirs such as Philpott and South Hol-ston lakes. In streams the flashy rainbow is a fish of the rapids and fast water, whereas the brook and brown prefer the quiet pools. All trout seek the shallows for food, however, and can be caught there at feeding time—usually early and late in the day.

SEASONS: The trout is the only fish in Virginia's fresh waters on which there is a closed season. On most trout waters the season opens at noon on the third Saturday in March to run through February 1. Generally, there are no closed seasons on the large lakes where trout are stocked. Trout fish-ing is generally best in April and May in Virginia, when the stocking program is heaviest, but the fall fishing can also be good on the better streams. Anglers who know Virginia's trout waters also catch fish through the hot summer months.

GOOD WATERS: There are over 200 trout streams and lakes in Virginia that are stocked with trout, and at the peak of the spring season the fishing is equally good in just about all of them. By late June, however, the fishing is beginning to fade in the marginal waters, and then the real trout waters come to the fore. At such times streams such as the Bullpasture and Smith rivers and Whitetop Laurel can be depended upon to produce. The Jackson River is also good. The Smith River below Philpott Dam is a tailwaters stream kept cool by the icy waters released from the bottom of the deep lake. Fee-fishing waters such as Big Tumbling Creek and Laurel Bed Lake, Douthat Lake and Wilson Creek, and Crooked Creek are always good choices for summer fishing. Also try some of the special regulation waters such as Conway River and St. Mary's River and Buffalo, Mossy, and Snake creeks. There are also the native-brook-trout streams in the Shenandoah National Park. They offer good summer fishing except during very dry seasons.

FISHING METHODS: Trout-fishing methods vary from casual fishermen who dunk garden worms on the opening day of the season to dry-fly fishermen who seek seclusion on the quiet pools of some remote mountain stream. In between are the more sophisticated bait fishermen who fish for big brown trout and the spinning enthusiasts who use ultralight tackle and catch good fish on tiny lures. Fortunately, in Virginia there is room for all. Regardless of the lures or tackle they use, trout fishermen should keep in mind the fact that trout like a moving lure or bait, particularly stream fish that look to the current for their food. Allow the lure or bait to move naturally with the current; try to avoid any drag that slows it unnaturally; and maintain a tight line, so that a quick strike can be detected. It is easy to get an argument over the merits of fishing down or upstream, but it is well to bear in mind that trout usually rest faced into the current, and the bait or lure should approach from that direction. This can be accomplished by fishing upstream and maintaining a tight line as the bait or lure drifts back, by making diagonal casts across the current and again maintaining a tight line, and sometimes by casting downstream and allowing the line to peel off the reel. The latter method is difficult, however, and not usually recommended except for special situations. Lake- and pond-trout fishermen troll or fish deep with bait or lures.

CARE, CLEANING, AND COOKING: Rarely is it possible to keep trout alive in a live well. Lake or pond anglers may be able to do so, but stream fishermen cannot. The fish can be strung through both lips and lowered in cool water. Stream anglers can even trail the stringer from their belt. Generally, however, trout are kept cool in other ways—cool but not alive. The age-old wicker creel is still one of the best ways to keep trout while on the stream. The air circulates through it and trout placed in wet ferns or other vegetation in the creel will keep well. Sprinkle the fish and ferns with cool water occasionally. As soon as possible, however, get those trout in a chest and iced down. Trout can be filleted like other fish, but there is something about a whole trout simmering in a hot pan that makes the lips water. Trout are good, particularly those little native brookies caught high in the Allegheny or Blue Ridge mountains, and they are best cooked whole. To clean a trout for cooking, scale it by clamping it by the tail and working the knife or scaler forward against the scales. Even the brookie has small scales that should be removed. Leave the head on, but remove the gills; slit the belly from the head to the tail, and remove the viscera. Finally, take the point of a knife and scrap away the blood along the backbone. Wash the trout, and it is ready for the pan. For *grilled trout with a butter baste,* dress and clean two ½ to ¾ pound trout, and assemble vegetable oil, salt and pepper, garlic powder, ¼ cup of melted butter, ½ teaspoon of grated lemon peel, 1 tablespoon of lemon juice, ¼ teaspoon of salt, and ⅛ teaspoon each of pepper, garlic powder, and paprika. Line the fire bowl of the grill with heavy-duty aluminum foil, and generously oil the grid of the barbecue grill. Sprinkle the cavity of the fish with seasonings, and bind each fish with two aluminum foil loops. Slash skin crosswise in three places on each side. Make the butter baste by combining all of the ingredients. Grill the fish over medium-hot direct heat, and brush with the baste during cooking. Turn the fish halfway through the cooking time. Grill 8 to 10 minutes, or until the fish flakes easily with a fork. Finally, garnish with lemon slices.

The Pikes ———————————————————

The pickerels (the chain, the grass, and the redfin) are the only members of the pike family native to Virginia waters, and even the grass pickerel is questionable. It is native to the Ohio River, and a few possibly live in Southwest Virginia. Neither the northern pike nor the muskellunge are native to the state, but introduced fish provide some exciting angling.

The little redfin pickerel is limited to streams in the extreme eastern part of Virginia, but the chain pickerel is more widespread. It is found throughout the eastern part of Virginia and as far west as the eastern slopes of the Allegheny Mountains. They are reasonably abundant in both the Cowpasture and Jackson

The chain pickerel is Virginia's native pike.

rivers. Both pike and muskellunge have been stocked in suitable waters throughout the state.

DESCRIPTION: The various members of the pike family are easily confused as they all have the same general body build. All are long-bodied fish with long, flat, duckbilled jaws and anal and dorsal fins set far back on their bodies. The experienced pike angler has no trouble distinguishing between the fish. He is guided by distinctive markings, but markings might confuse the novice. To eliminate doubt, examine the gill covers and cheeks. On the pickerels both are fully scaled. On the northern pike only the upper half of the gill covers are scaled, but the cheeks are fully scaled. The muskellunge has scales only on the upper half of both the cheeks and gill covers. Body markings also vary, though all have green to olive backs and sides, and lighter shades of green and white on their lower sides and bellies. The chain pickerel has chainlike markings over much of its body, hence its name. The little redfin has dark bars that run diagonally down its flanks, and the green body of the grass pickerel is coverd with wavy dark lines. Light beanlike markings against a dark background make the pike easy to spot. The muskellunge is a fish that can be confused with the redfin or grass pickerel, though the size alone usually eliminates any doubt. The little pickerels (grass and redfin), as they are often called, seldom exceed 10 inches in length. The muskellunge generally has a green to grayish-brown back and on its upper sides this is covered with dark spots and markings. All of the pikes have soft fins void of spines, but big mouths lined with sharp teeth. Both pike and muskellunge grow big, and even in Virginia waters muskellunge of over 20 pounds are fairly common. The average, however, is probably 10 pounds or less. Pike run smaller. Many fish in the 10- to 15-pound range turn up every season, but the average fish is probably closer to half that weight. The chain pickerel is probably the most popular of the pikes, though fish in excess of 5 or 6 pounds are somewhat scarce. A 3-pound chain is a good fish. Tiger muskies, a pike-muskellunge hybrid, are also being stocked in Virginia waters.

HABITAT: All of the pikes like quiet water, lakes and ponds or the slow stretches and backwaters of streams. They also prefer vegetation and reasonably shallow water. Northern pike sometimes hang out around rocks and boulders, and both the northern pike and the muskellunge prefer cool water. Both are most abundant in Canada and the northern states. In the absence of vegetation, look for the fish around logs and other debris.

SEASONS: While there are no closed seasons on the pikes in Virginia, fishing is often best during the cooler or even cold months. They can be caught all year, however.

GOOD WATER: Just about any slow-flowing stream or reasonably shallow lake or pond from the western Piedmont to the coast is likely to hold some chain pickerel. They are often found in streams that are so small no one bothers to fish them. Few streams really stand out, but Speights Run is good. So are many of the creeks draining into the lower James River and the Rappahannock River. Good lakes include Burnt Mills, Chickahominy, Cohoon, Diascund, Lee Hall, Prince, and Whitehurst. The James and New rivers lead the state in the production of musekllunge, but the Clinch and Cowpasture rivers are also good. Good lakes include Burke, Claytor, Smith Mountain, and South Holston. Good northern-pike streams are a bit limited, but the James, Occoquan, and Pamunkey rivers give up a few. The best pike lakes include Hungry Mother, Lee Hall, Occoquan, and Orange County. Smith Mountain Lake is one of the better tiger-muskellunge waters.

FISHING METHODS: All of the pikes are vicious predators. They are also slinky fish that like to hide in weeds or other cover to ambush some unsuspecting victim—usually a small fish. They will also gobble up frogs, small birds, or just about anything else that ventures too near their lair. From that point of ambush the pikes can dart forward with amazing speed and grab the victim. Pike anglers take advantage of these habits by concentrating on weed beds when they are available. Bait-casting tackle is probably the most popular tackle for pike fishing, but spinning tackle is also popular, and some anglers like the challenge of fly tackle. Casting and spinning anglers like spoons and lures that resemble crippled minnows, but the fly fishermen usually go with streamers. All will take pike. So will surface lures. The explosive strike of a big pike hitting a topwater lure can be unnerving. Generally, pike like a fairly fast-moving lure. Even bait fishermen get into the act with live minnows, 5- to 6-inch ones for pickerel, but much larger ones for northern pike and muskellunge. Most pike are probably caught in reasonably shallow water, water not too deep for aquatic weeds. Pickerel and northern pike can be reasonably easy to catch, but most anglers put in many hours of fishing between muskellunge. It is a trophy fish worth working for. All of the pike have needle-sharp teeth, and for muskellunge and northern pike particularly, wire leaders are recommended. A pickerel may occasionally slash a monofilament leader, but the small leaders seem to slip between the teeth. Few pickerel fishermen use wire leaders.

CARE, CLEANING, AND COOKING: As is true of most fish, the pikes should be kept fresh, and this is best accomplished by keeping them alive for as long as possible. They are hardy fish and can be kept alive with a minimum of effort on the part of the angler. This usually means stringing them through both lips and lowering them into cool water. Most pike are too large for the average live well. Once removed from the stringer, they should be placed on ice and kept there until they can be cleaned. All of the pikes are bony fish and best cleaned by filleting. To do so, use a fillet knife or other sharp knife, and make a cut just behind the gills all the way to the backbone. Then turn the knife, and cut along the backbone to a point an inch from the tail. Now flip the fillet over, and work back between the skin and the flesh to remove the skin. Repeat the process on the other side of the fish. *Pike patties* are a popular dish in northern fishing camps. The ingredients are 2 cups of water, ½ teaspoon of salt, 1 medium red potato, 1 pound of pike fillets, 1 egg, 1 cup of milk, ½ cup of cracker crumbs, 2 tablespoons of finely chopped onion, 1 teaspoon of Worcestershire sauce, ½ teaspoon of salt, ¼ teaspoon of pepper, 1 cup of dry bread crumbs, 2 tablespoons of vegetable oil, and 1 tablespoon of butter or margarine. Heat water and ½ teaspoon of salt to boiling point in a 1-quart saucepan, and add the potato. Continue to boil, but reduce the heat, cover the pan, and allow to simmer until the potato is tender—normally about 20 minutes. Drain and cool. Cut the pike fillets into 3-

inch pieces and place with the egg in a food processor. Process slowly, and add milk for 1 to 2 minutes—or until smooth. Mix pike, cracker crumbs, onion, Worcestershire sauce, ½ teaspoon of salt, and the pepper in a medium bowl. Peel and shred the potato, and stir it into the fish mixture before refrigerating for 30 minutes. Sprinkle bread crumbs on a plate or waxed paper, and form the pike mixture into 8½-inch thick patties. Coat with bread crumbs, pressing lightly, and place on a baking sheet or tray. Heat the oil and butter or margarine over medium-high heat in a 9-inch skillet. Place four patties in the skillet, fry for 2 minutes, and turn. Fry for about 2 more minutes, or until they are golden brown. Drain on paper towels and keep warm in 175° F oven. Handle the rest of the pike mixture in the same manner.

The Perch

The word *perch* is probably used incorrectly more often than any other word in the angler's vocabulary. Many of the sunfish, including the crappie, are often incorrectly lumped as perch. And the white perch is not a perch at all, but actually a member of the true bass family that includes the striped and white bass, which will be discussed in chapter 16.

Here, we will cover the true perch, the sauger, the yellow perch, and the walleye. All three are native to Virginia waters, but the ranges of the yellow perch and the walleye have been expanded widely by stocking in new waters.

Big yellow perch from Lake Drummond.

Both are now found just about statewide.

The yellow perch is a native of the eastern tidal streams and the New River drainage system, but it is abundant in many eastern lakes and ponds. The walleye is also a native of the New River drainage system, but it has been stocked widely throughout the state. The sauger is limited to the Clinch and Powell rivers, and other streams of deep Southwest Virginia, where it is regarded as a native fish. Its range has not been expanded by stocking.

DESCRIPTION: All members of the perch family are stubby in build, but not to the extent that the bluegill is. The major distinguishing feature is a completely divided dorsal fin on the back, with the forward, spiny portion being completely separate from the soft, rear one. The anal fin has only one or two spines. The walleye has strong canine teeth. The little yellow perch is the most colorfully marked, with black or dark vertical stripes against a yellow back and sides. The colors are particularly bright during the spawning season, when most perch are caught. The walleye is usually brown on its back and sides, but its belly is a lighter creamy white or white. The color of the sauger is much like that of the walleye, but dark markings, or saddles, on its back set it apart from the other perch. Yellow perch run small in Virginia. Most are only 7 or 8 inches long and weigh considerably less than a half pound. A 12-inch or a 1-pound perch is a good one. The walleye is the largest of the three, and in Virginia fish weighing over 10 pounds are landed every season. Walleyes of 2 to 3 pounds, however, are probably closer to the average. The sauger is a smaller fish, with the average probably being less than a pound. All of the perch are delicious eating fish, and the walleye is one of the tastiest in America.

HABITAT: The perch are primarily bottom fish, and they like reasonably deep water—and big waters. The walleye seems to prefer large lakes, though it is found in a number of Virginia's larger rivers. It likes clean, clear water and shorelines of boulders or gravel. It is usually caught in reasonably deep water. The sauger, on the other hand, will accept silty rivers, but it too likes large lakes. In Virginia, however, it is primarily a stream fish. The yellow perch prefers the calm water of lakes and quiet streams where there is a minimum of current.

SEASONS: There are no closed seasons on the perch in Virginia, but fishing for all of them is usually best during the cooler months of fall and spring and even in winter. A few fish are caught, however, just about every month of the year. February and March are the prime yellow-perch months, but the fishing also picks up when the waters cool in the fall. Like walleyes, a few perch are caught throughout the year. The sauger is primarily a late fall and winter fish.

GOOD WATER: The Mattaponi and Pamunkey rivers could well be the best yellow-perch waters in Virginia, but they are just a beginning of the possibilities. Other rivers and streams include the Chickahominy River, Dragon Run, and the James, New, Nottoway, and Occoquan rivers. The lakes also are many, including Anna, Burnt Mills, Chickahominy, Claytor, Drummond, Prince, and Western Branch. Smith Mountain Lake could well be the best walleye water in the state, but other good lakes include Buggs Island, Carvins Cove, Claytor, Philpott, Smith, and Whitehurst. Some of the rivers are also productive, including the Appomattox, James, and New rivers. Sauger fishing is limited in Virginia—mostly to the Clinch and Powell rivers.

FISHING METHODS: Fishing for the perch, whether it be sauger, yellow perch, or walleye, usually means fishing fairly deep and usually on the bottom. Sauger can be caught by jigging small spoons and lures in deep water as the fish move up Virginia streams from the big Tennessee lakes. It is a form of fishing that is not widely practiced in the state. Yellow perch can be taken by a variety of methods, but there is no better method than fishing with small 1-inch live minnows. February and March, when the fish hit best, can be cold in the Old Dominion, and a comfortable way to fish is to locate a school of the fish, anchor, and fish the live minnows with a small bobber to telegraph the action. Between bites the angler can concentrate on keeping warm. Yellow perch can also be caught on small spinning lures such as spoons, jigs, and others fished near the bottom. Fly fishermen may have trouble getting their small streamers and wet flies down where the perch are feeding, but a sinking-tip line will help. The scrappy perch can wage a good battle on light fly tackle. Walleye are caught in a great variety of ways, but trolling a spinner ahead of a night crawler is popular—and effective. The real key to catching walleyes is being able to locate them. They are usually in deep water during daylight hours, as the sun hurts their eyes. Many anglers prefer to fish for them at night, as they are usually more active after the sun leaves the water. Jigging in the deep holes with doll flies, small spoons, and other lures that sink rapidly is often productive. When trolling or casting, vary the action and speed of the retrieve until the fish begin to hit—and then stick with that particular action until they quit. The walleye is not noted as a fighter, but it is fun to catch, a real challenge in Virginia waters, and tasty on the table.

CARE, CLEANING, AND COOKING: Because they are most often caught during cool or cold weather, or at night, the perch are not difficult to keep fresh. Placing them in a live well is fine, but if one is not available, simply string them through both lips and lower them into cool water. Another solution is to place them in a well-cooled ice chest with plenty of ice. They should remain on ice until the angler is ready to clean them. Sauger and walleyes are invariably filleted. To do so make a cut just back of the gill covers all the way to the backbone. Then twist the fillet knife or other sharp knife and work along the backbone to the tail, leaving about an inch of skin and meat to hold the fillet while the skin is removed. To remove the skin, flip the fillet over, and work the knife back toward the head and between the skin and the flesh. This produces one fillet. Flip the fish over and repeat the process for the other fillet. If the fish is particularly large, the fillets will have to be cut into sections. Yellow perch can also be filleted, but because they are small, many anglers prefer to cook them whole. The fish is difficult to scale, however, and the scaling should be done while the scales are still wet. Simply lay the fish on a flat surface, clamp the tail to hold it, and work a knife or scaler forward against the scales until all are removed. To finish the job, slit the belly, remove the viscera, and use the point of the knife to remove the blood from along the backbone. *Walleye fillets* are unsurpassable in the eyes of many anglers. The ingredients include 2 to 3 pounds of walleye fillets, 1 teaspoon of salt, 1 teaspoon of tarragon leaves, 1 teaspoon of lemon-pepper seasoning, and 1 teaspoon of onion powder. Line fire bowl of a covered grill with heavy duty aluminum foil. Place individual servings of fillets on greased sheets of foil large enough to wrap the fillets. Sprinkle each with 1 teaspoon of seasoning mix, and cook on open grill over medium-hot direct heat for 6 to 8 minutes. Turn the fillets twice while cooking.

The Striped and White Bass and the White Perch _____

Like *sunfish*, the word *bass* also gets confusing when applied to Virginia fish. The largemouth bass, for example, is actually not a bass at all, but is instead a member of the sunfish family. The same is true of the smallmouth and the spotted bass. No amount of urging is going to get avid bass anglers to call their favorite fish a sunfish, so let's leave it as it is. The true bass, however, are the striped bass, the white bass, and, yes, the white perch. The striped bass and white perch are native Virginia fish, and the white bass has been widely introduced. Both the striper and the perch are primarily fish of the salt and brackish waters. The landlocked striper, however, has become one of Virginia's most

Striped bass are found in both fresh and salt water in Virginia.

popular game fish. Hatchery-reared fish do well in the major reservoirs such as Lake Anna and Smith Mountain Lake, and the Buggs Island stripers enjoy good natural reproduction on spawning runs up the Dan and Staunton rivers. Perch too can thrive in inland waters—far from the brackish water of the tidal streams. The white bass, a native of the Mississippi River region, has been successfully introduced to Buggs Island, Claytor, and South Holston lakes, and other Virginia waters. It too enjoys good natural reproduction.

DESCRIPTION: All of the true bass found in Virginia have a metallic gold to silver background, depending upon the water in which they live. The back and upper sides may be dark green or almost black, but the color fades to almost white on the belly. Landlocked fish tend to be darker than those that live in brackish or salt water. The white bass and white perch have stubby bodies when compared to the slimmer, more streamlined body of the striped bass. All have longitudinal stripes on the sides, but those of the striper are the most pronounced. They are distinct and unbroken. So are those on the white bass. The lines on the white perch are less distinctive, but it does have a pronounced lateral line approximately halfway down its flanks. The white perch is the only bass with the dorsal fins joined. The striped bass has only three or four spines in its dorsal fin, the white perch eight or nine, and the white bass ten to twelve. Striped bass, whether they are landlocked or live in brackish water, are big fish. Fish in the 30- to 40-pound class are landed every season in Virginia, and 10- to 15-pound fish are fairly common. The average, however, probably runs 5 to 10 pounds. Virginia waters produce a few 4 to 5-pound white bass and a great many in the 2 to 3-pound range, but the average is probably a half pound. It is not uncommon to find a 1- to 2-pound white perch, but the average perch, particularly of those caught on spawning migrations, is less than half a pound.

HABITAT: All the the bass are big- or open-water fish. Those caught during the spring spawning run, however, are often taken from fairly small rivers—white perch in the Rappahannock River near Fredericksburg, for example, white bass in the New River just upstream from Claytor Lake, and stripers in the Staunton River near Brookneal. When they drift back into the lakes, the big tidal rivers, or the Chesapeake Bay, however, they often travel in schools and stay in the open water. Striped bass and white perch are frequently found around rocky points. Even though they like big, open water, they tend to hug the shoreline.

SEASONS: There is a closed season on tidal-water striped bass from December 1 through May 31, but otherwise there are no closed seasons on the bass in Virginia. The fish generally prefer cold water, particularly the striped bass, and the best fishing comes in the fall and spring. Winter fishing for striped bass can be good at times. The April and May spawning runs are the peak fishing periods for white bass and white perch.

GOOD WATERS: Smith Moutain Lake is by far the most productive striped-bass lake in Virginia, but Anna, Buggs Island, Claytor, Gaston, Leesville, Prince, and Whitehurst are also good. The April and May spawning runs up the Dan and Staunton rivers are also productive. Claytor leads the white-bass lakes, but Buggs Island, Gaston, Leesville, Smith Mountain, and South Holston are also good. The New and South Holston rivers are also productive. Just about any sizable tidal stream is likely to produce some good white-perch fishing, but Back Bay is one of the best white perch waters in Virginia. Good inland waters include Lake Anna and Western Branch Lake. The good tidal streams are almost too numerous to list, but include Blackwater River, Dragon Run, and the Elizabeth, James, North Landing, Northwest, and Rappahannock rivers.

FISHING METHODS: Floating slowly down the Dan or Staunton rivers during the spring run of striped bass out of Buggs Island Lake is one of the highs of the angling year in Virginia. This usually occurs in late April and May. Anglers cast jigs, spoons, and underwater lures that imitate small bait fish. The fishing can be slow during daylight hours, but when the action does come, it usually produces a big trophy striper. Many top anglers prefer fishing at night—after the sun leaves the water. The action often picks up then. Lake anglers locate the fish with fish finders or graphs, or watch for surface activity. They then cast to the fish with jigs, spoons, and other proven striper lures. Large live minnows will also prove productive at times. Some anglers prefer trolling, fishing the same lures that are effective on casting tackle. There are two proven methods for catching white bass. One is to cast to the migrating fish in the spring using light to medium spinning tackle and fishing with small spoons and underwater lures. This fishing is often good where a major stream enters a good white-bass lake. The other method is to watch for "the jumps," surface disturbances that comes when the bass are chasing bait fish. The pursued minnows jump frantically trying to escape the hungry bass. When "jumps" are located, the angler moves in and casts tiny spoons or other lures to the feeding school of fish. Action is almost assured. Thousands of white perch are caught every spring in rivers such as the James and the Rappahannock as the fish move upstream to spawn. The usual bait is a section of bloodworm fished on a tiny hook and allowed to drift with the current. Light spinning lures cast diagonally into the current and allowed to drift with it will also produce some fast fishing and good creels of perch. Bait or lures fished along rocky shorelines can also be effective.

CARE, CLEANING, AND COOKING: Since the best bass fishing comes in the spring or in cold weather, keeping the fish fresh is rarely a problem. When the fishing is done from a boat, the white bass, perch, and smaller stripers can be kept in a live well or strung through the lips and lowered into the water. Bank fishermen can string the fish and lower them over the bank into the stream—and fasten the stringer securely. Ice chests with plenty of ice will also keep the bass in good condition. They should be cleaned as soon as possible once they are removed from the ice. All of the bass can be cleaned by scaling and gutting or by filleting. To clean and scale the fish, place it on a flat surface, clamp it by the tail, and use a knife or scaler to remove the scales. Work against the scales—from the tail toward the head. After the fish is scaled, slit it along the belly and remove the viscera, and finally use the tip of the knife to remove the blood from along the backbone. To fillet a bass, make a cut just back of the gill cover all the way to the backbone; turn the fillet knife and work along the backbone to the tail, but leave a small piece of skin to facilitate finishing the job. Flip the fillet over and work the knife forward between the skin and the meat. This produces a single fillet. Turn the fish over, and repeat the process on the other side. For *Low-Cal Striped Bass with Vegetables* the necessary ingredients include 1 tablespoon of flour, 2 striped bass fillets ½ pound each, ¼ cup of melted diet margarine, ¼ teaspoon of paprika, 2 tablespoons of water, 1 medium zucchini cut into 2 × ⅛ inch strips, ¾ cups of grated carrot, ¾ cups of thinly sliced celery, ¼ cup of finely chopped green onion, ½ teaspoon of salt, ½ teaspoon of basil leaves, and ⅛ teaspoon of pepper. Preheat the oven to 350° F, shake the flour in 10 × 16 inch cooking bag, and place in a 12 × 8 × 2 inch baking dish. Place the fillets skinned-side down in the bag. Combine margarine and paprika, and pour over the fish. In a saucepan, combine water, vegetables, salt, basil, and pepper, and cover and let simmer for 5 to 8 minutes. Spoon the drained vegetables over the fish. Close the bag with a nylon tie, and make 6 half-slits in the top. Cook for 20 to 25 minutes or until the fish flakes easily with a fork.

The Catfish

Mention catfish and you can get all kinds of reactions. Some anglers hate the whiskered fish that grub along the bottom, often in badly polluted water. Others, however, place catfish right up there at the top with bass, trout, and other popular species. In fact, a U.S. Fish and Wildlife survey made several years ago showed that the catfish ranked high with anglers of America. The same is generally true of Virginia.

Taken from reasonably clean waters, cared for and cleaned promptly, and prepared properly for the table, the catfish can be tasty. In fact catfish farming is a growing industry in America.

The catfish family is a large one, over two dozen different kinds of cats, but many are too small to be of importance. In Virginia there are four major cats, three native and one introduced. These are the blue catfish, the channel catfish, the flathead catfish, and the white catfish. Most angling interest is directed toward the first three.

The blue catfish, a native of the Mississippi River drainage system, has been introduced to suitable Virginia waters, and it shows a good deal of promise. These cats grow big, and they are found in a variety of waters just about statewide. The channel, probably the most popular catfish in Virginia, is also found statewide, and it has been stocked widely by the Department of Game and Inland Fisheries. The flathead catfish, a native of the larger streams of Southwest Virginia, is generally limited to the western part of the state. The white, a catfish that seldom reaches appreciable sizes, is found primarily in the eastern part of Virginia.

DESCRIPTION: The cats are scaleless and all have barbels (whiskers or feelers) around their mouths, which are highly sensitive and used for locating food by taste and touch. Most of the cats live in turbid waters, and they feed mostly at night. The touch and taste or smell senses are more important than vision.

Contrary to common belief, the catfish does not sting with its barbels, but sharp spines in the dorsal and pectoral fins can inflict a painful injury. In some of the catfish these spines may hold poison. Experienced anglers avoid these spines by gripping the fish firmly just behind them. The sleek channel cat is the most popular among anglers. Its tail is deeply forked, and its slate-gray or silvery body is covered with black spots. Some 25- to 30-pound channel cats are caught every season in Virginia, and fish in excess of 10 pounds are fairly common. The average fish, however, is probably in the 1- to 2-pound range. The blue catfish also has a forked tail; its color is slate gray to bluish, but it has no spots on its side. Blue cats grow large, though fish in excess of 30 pounds are rare in Virginia. Fish in excess of 15 pounds are fairly common, but the average is probably somewhere between 5 and 10 pounds. The flathead catfish is a yellow or light-brown fish with a slender body and a flat head. Its tail is not forked. Fish approaching or exceeding 50 pounds are caught in Virginia waters, and 15 to 20 pounders are fairly common. The average weight is probably less than 10 pounds. The white is a small catfish that

There is good catfish fishing in Virginia.

likely averages less than a pound. It has a deeply forked tail and a gray to greenish-blue body.

HABITAT: While the channel cat prefers clear streams with a good current, it is also found in large lakes and it is stocked in many Commission of Game and Inland Fisheries lakes. The other cats prefer slower water, and the flathead prefers sluggish water. The blue likes lakes and streams with mud bottoms, and the white will accept brackish water. Most of the cats seek some kind of cover during the daylight hours and roam mostly at night.

SEASONS: There are no closed seasons on the catfish in Virginia, and a few fish are caught just about all year. The summer months are good fishing months, however, particularly for night fishing.

GOOD WATER: Although a native of the Ohio River drainage system, which includes the streams of Southwest Virginia, the channel cat is now found statewide. All of the good waters are too numerous to list, but include Lake Anna, and Brittle, Burke, Chickahominy, Claytor, Flannagan, Diascund, Occoquan, Smith, and Whitehurst lakes. Good rivers include the Clinch, James, North Landing, Northwest, and Shenandoah. The white catfish is limited generally to the coastal streams and lakes, and the flathead fishing is best in western rivers such as the New and the Powell and lakes such as Claytor. In fact the New River and Claytor Lake are the top flathead rivers in Virginia. The fish is native to the New River. The Rappahannock River is probably the best blue-catfish stream in the state, but other good streams include the chickahominy, Clinch, James, and Occoquan. Among the better lakes are Chickahominy and Western Branch.

FISHING METHODS: While smallmouth-bass anglers take channel catfish on artificial lures every season, catfish are generally caught on natural baits or special catfish baits such as chicken livers or the prepared catfish "stink" baits. Both attract the fish because of their strong odor. Generally, catfishing means bottom fishing with such baits. The method is no more complicated than baiting up on strong tackle and lowering the baited hook to the bottom of some known catfish hole. Patience is a necessity, as there is often a lot of waiting between bites. At times, however, the action can be fast. The best catfishing usually occurs once darkness has descended upon the water.

CARE, CLEANING, AND COOKING: Catfish are tough fish and not difficult to keep alive for a long time—even out of water. Fish tossed into a wet burlap sack will keep for hours. The big cats are too large for the average live well, but even they can be hooked on sturdy fish stringers and lowered into the water. There they will keep well for many hours. Unlike most fish, the cat may still be alive when the angler reaches home, and it may be necessary to kill the fish before cleaning it. A good rap on the head or a sharp knife will do the job quickly and humanely. There are no scales to remove, but the tough skin should be removed. This can be done with pliers. Use a knife to peel off a section of the skin, grasp it with the pliers and pull. The usual approach is to slit the skin completely around the body just to the rear of the gill covers, and remove the skin with pliers. Nailing the head to an upright of some kind will make this easier. Once the skin is removed, the fish can be filleted or gutted and cooked whole. To fillet, make a cut just back of the gills all the way to the backbone and then twist the knife and cut along the bone to the tail and remove the fillet. Repeat the process on the other side. For small catfish the fillets can be cooked whole, but it will be necessary to steak the larger ones. Small cats can be cooked whole, and to prepare them for cooking slit the belly and remove the viscera and the blood along the backbone. The catfish has a minimum of bones, and the meat is very tasty. For *Corn Crispy Catfish Fillets* the needed ingredients are ¼ cup of mayonnaise, 2 tablespoons of grated Parmesan cheese, 2 tablespoons of water, 1 teaspoon of instant minced onion, 2½ cups of coarsely crushed corn chips, and 1 pound of catfish fillets. Preheat the oven to 450° F, and line a 13 × 9 × 2 inch baking pan with heavy duty aluminum foil. Grease the foil. In a shallow dish or pie pan, combine cheese, mayonnaise, onion, and water. Spread the crushed corn chips onto a sheet of aluminum foil, and heat the foil-lined pan in the oven for 5 minutes. While the pan is heating, dip the fillets in the mayonnaise mixture until both sides are lightly coated. Then coat the fillets with the crushed corn chips. Place the fillets an inch apart in the hot pan, and bake for 15 minutes, or until the fish flakes easily with a fork.

The Herring and the Shad ─────────

Several popular Virginia fish are migratory or anadromous, meaning they spend much of the year in salt water but migrate up the tidal streams in the spring to enter fresh water, where they spawn. These spawning runs have become particularly popular in recent years, and since most of the fish are caught in fresh water as opposed to salt, they are included in the freshwater section of this book. The long-popular striped bass is no longer in this group, as it is now protected during the spawning season, and most angling effort is directed toward the landlocked bass, which are discussed in chapter 16. The emphasis here will be on the shads and herring.

There are two shads, the American or white shad and the smaller hickory. The hickory usually appears first in the spring, with good runs hitting the more popular fishing spots in late March or early April. The American shad runs come later, often in late April or May. The closely related herring usually arrives at favorite fishing holes between the middle and the end of April.

All of these fish are native to Virginia waters and can be found in most streams draining into the Chesapeake Bay or into the ocean.

DESCRIPTION: The herrings and shads are generally deep-bodied fish with forked tails and a single short dorsal fin in the middle of the back. The dorsal is soft and free of spines. The fish are generally silver in color with a dark green to blue or gray back and no distinct lateral line. Large scales cover the fish, and they are easily removed. The herring has a saw-edged belly; the shad has a notch in the upper jaw, and the tip of the lower jaw fits into the notch. The American shad, the largest of the three, may grow to 15 pounds, but fish of this size are rare. The average is 2 to 3 pounds. The hickory is a smaller shad that rarely exceeds 3 pounds, and the average fish is probably closer to 1 to 1½ pounds. The herring is a much smaller fish that may grow to a pound, but probably averages half of that.

HABITAT: While herring may be found in small streams that drain into the Chesapeake Bay or into the larger tidal streams, the shads usually prefer the larger tidal rivers on inlets along the Eastern Shore, where they enter from the ocean. Migrating fish are drawn to fast water, often the boulder- and rock-strewn water that marks the fall line. They can be caught, however, in quieter water. The shad is generally a big-water fish.

SEASONS: There are no closed seasons on herring and shads in Virginia, but the busy fishing season occurs in late March or early April, with the peak of the season coming in April. There is some fishing well into May, however, particularly for American shad.

GOOD WATER: Good shad and herring fishing is likely to be found in streams just about anywhere from the fall line to the Chesapeake Bay or ocean, but the Appomattox River below Petersburg, the James River at Richmond, the Potomac River just west of Washington, D.C., and the Rappahannock River at Fredericksburg are the traditional hickory-shad fishing spots in Virginia. The inlets along the ocean side of the Eastern

Herring and shad ascend Virginia's tidal rivers in the spring.

Shore are also good. These same rivers also offer fishing for American shad, and the Nottoway River has good runs of this bigger shad as well. Herring are pretty widely scattered, but one of the most popular spots in the state is Walker's Dam on the Chickahominy River.

FISHING METHODS: Neither shad nor herring are hard to catch once the fish are running. Catching herring on hook and line is no more complicated than jigging a small gold hook (unbaited) into a school of fish. Snagging is illegal, however, and any fish hooked accidentally should be returned to the water. Probably more herring are caught in dip nets, however, and netting is generally legal—though prohibited in some waters. County permits are usually required. Shad can be taken on light spinning tackle and on fly tackle, but spinning tackle is the usual choice. Favorite lures are shad darts and small shad spoons, and both are usually available in eastern tackle shops during the spring season. Shad fishing requires no special techniques other than casting the darts or spoons into the current and working them back at a moderate pace. Sometimes it may be necessary to experiment with depths to determine where the fish are suspended. Shad often leap spectacularly, and catching them is a real joy. Many anglers release the fish immediately.

CARE, CLEANING, AND COOKING: While both herring and shad are often caught for their roe, shad, particularly, are an excellent food fish. So are the smaller herring, though they are usually salted down and preserved. Both shad and herring require care when caught if they are to provide the tastiest food, but since they are usually caught in cool weather, this is rarely a problem. Most are placed on stringers and lowered into the stream—or they can be placed on ice. Herring are usually cleaned by scaling and removing the viscera. The scales are easily removed on both shad and herring by working a scaler or knife against the scales. The belly is slit, the viscera removed, and the blood removed from along the backbone with a knife blade. To fillet, make a cut just behind the gill covers all the way to the backbone, then cut along the backbone to the tail, leaving a piece of skin to hold the fish when the fillet is flipped over and the skin removed by working the knife forward between the skin and flesh. The fish is then turned over and the process repeated on the other side. Shad can also be cleaned for cooking whole as described for herring. The roe (eggs) of both the herring and the shad are considered a delicacy and should be removed whether the fish is filleted or cleaned whole. For *Broiled Shad Roe* the ingredients are one shad roe sac, salt, pepper, and strips of bacon. Sprinkle the shad roe sac with salt and pepper, and wrap in bacon strips. Place on a shallow rack in a heavy frying pan or broiling rack. Broil for about 20 minutes. The major problem with both herring and shad is the presence of many small bones, but they can be softened by cooking. One such recipe is for *Herbed Shad*. The ingredients are a 3- to 4-pound dressed shad, salt, lemon and pepper seasoning, 1 cup of dry wine, 3 to 4 cups of water, 2 stalks of celery, 1 medium onion chopped coarsely, and 2 bay leaves. Wash and thoroughly dry the shad, and place in a roasting pan with rack. Sprinkle the shad inside and out with salt and lemon-pepper seasoning. Add wine and water to a level just below the rack. Add the broken celery, chopped onion, and the bay leaves. Cover *tightly* and steam in 300° F oven for five hours. Baste frequently. Cooked in this manner, the bones will either disappear or become soft enough to eat.

The Nongame Fish

Webster defines a game fish as "a fish made a legal catch by law."
He also defines the adjective *game* as "having a resolute unyielding spirit." Following this line of reasoning it would seem that a
nongame fish is not protected by law and that it does not have a
resolute unyielding spirit. But that doesn't work. Some nongame
fish are stubborn, if not colorful, fighters, and all enjoy some
protection.

In any event, in Virginia's fresh waters game fish include the
trout, all of the sunfish including the black bass, walleye, white
bass, chain pickerel, muskellunge, northern pike, and striped

The sucker is one of the more popular of the nongame fish.

bass. Here, we have also treated the yellow perch, sauger, white perch, catfish, herring, and shad as game fish of the fresh waters. All others we can group as nongame fish.

The angler still needs a license to fish for the nongame fish, and he must abide by the general fishing regulations that apply to the taking of game fish. There are, however, no closed seasons on nongame fish, nor generally any size or creel limits.

The more popular nongame fish in Virginia include the carp, sucker, chub, fallfish, bowfin, gar, and eel. Most of these fish occur pretty much statewide. Most are native to Virginia waters, but the carp was introduced from Europe.

DESCRIPTION: Except for the eel, all of these fish have scales, and those of the bowfin and gar are extremely tough. None have spiny rays, but both the bowfin and the gar have sharp teeth. The gar has a long, slender body and long jaws. The bowfin is a primitive fish with a fairly short, round body and a long dorsal fin. The eel's scaleless body is long and snakelike. Both the carp and sucker have small, toothless mouths built for sucking food from the bottom, and the chubs and fallfish have larger, but also toothless mouths. The introduced carp is the largest of the nongame fish, with some outsized specimens going over 40 pounds. The suckers are smaller, but some may grow to 10 pounds. Big gar and bowfin may go to 15 or 20 pounds. A 3- to 4-pound eel is a big one, though the fish do grow bigger. An 18-inch fallfish is a big one, and the average is probably 10 inches or less. Good-sized chubs average 10 to 12 inches in length.

HABITAT: Most of the nongame fish prefer quiet water, with the fallfish probably the most likely to seek fast water. These silvery-colored fish are often caught in fast bass or trout streams. Though they prefer quiet water, suckers are also found far up many small streams, though they also live in larger rivers and lakes. The carp and chubs are also stream fish, though carp live in lakes too, usually over muddy bottoms. They seek vegetation when it is available. Both the bowfin and the gar are most abundant in the quiet waters of the coastal plain, but gar are often found far up inland streams.

SEASONS: There are no closed seasons on the nongame fish, but spring is a popular time to catch suckers as they move slowly up many inland streams on spawning runs.

GOOD WATER: While the bowfin and the gar are most abundant in the eastern part of the state, the other nongame fish occur just about everywhere.

FISHING METHODS: Carp, sucker, and eel are primarily bottom-feeding fish and best caught by fishing baits on the bottom. It can be a slow kind of fishing, for the usual approach is to toss a baited hook into seemingly good water and allow it to rest on the bottom until the fish finds it. Garden worms are the favorite of sucker fishermen, and they are also good for eel. Carp, however, are most often caught on dough or corn kernels. Chubs can also be caught in this manner. They too will hit worms, but they are just as likely to take a bait drifting with the current as they are a still one. Fallfish, bowfin, and gar are more readily taken on artificial lures. Light spinning lures are ideal for fallfish, but heavier lures and tackle are recommended for bowfin and gar. Wire leaders are not a bad idea when going after bowfin and gar.

CARE, CLEANING, AND COOKING: Of all of the nongame fish, the sucker is probably the most popular on the table. When it is taken from icy waters in late winter and spring, the flesh is firm and sweet, but also bony. The fallfish is also a good eating fish, but very bony. The chubs are less bony, and many anglers prefer them for table use. Neither the bowfin nor the gar are considered for table use. The roe of the gar is supposedly poisonous. The flesh of the carp is somewhat coarse, and while the fish is popular on European tables, it is not popular in America. The same is true of the eel. It is popular in Europe, but not particularly so in America. The flesh is somewhat oily. The nongame fish can be filleted, scaled or skinned (eel), or ground for fish cakes. Many of the recipes already recommended for game fish can be used for the nongame fish.

The Bluefish ⸺

The battling bluefish may not truly be the most popular fish in Virginia's briny waters, but a good case could be made for its having that status. Hundreds of anglers from the hinterlands visit the Chesapeake Bay or the ocean every season just to do battle with these scrappers of the salt waters, and seldom are they disappointed.

One of the joys of fishing for bluefish is the variety of waters in which it can be found. Generally, it is an open-water fish, and the big waters of the Chesapeake Bay produce untold numbers every season. It can also be taken from offshore waters, and from fishing piers and the surf. Fishing methods also vary greatly. Add the fact that, if properly cared for and prepared, it is tasty on the table, and no wonder the fish is so popular.

DESCRIPTION: The color of the bluefish is appropriate for its name. Its upper body is a striking blue or bluish-green, shading to blue-gray, and eventually silver toward its belly. The fish is noted for its sharp teeth, and they should be avoided when handling it. It is long-bodied and has very small scales. The smaller bluefish, often called tailor blues, caught in the Chesapeake Bay will average 2 to 5 pounds, but those taken from the offshore waters are much larger, with the average probably being 10 pounds or more. Fish in excess of 15 pounds are fairly common.

HABITAT: The bluefish is generally an open-water fish and a school fish, though it often enters the surf in search of bait fish and other food. Small blues may also wander far up tidal rivers, even into brackish water.

SEASONS: There are no closed seasons on bluefish in Virginia waters, and the fishing season is a long one. The first fish arrive off the Virginia coast in April, often to chase schools of mackerel north, and there are fish around well into November, when the final blues appear off Virginia Beach on their migration south.

GOOD WATER: The entrance to the Potomac River is one of the most popular fishing holes in the Chesapeake Bay, but this is Maryland water, and a Maryland license is required. The fish are found throughout the bay, however, along the bay side of the Eastern Shore, and near the mouths of the tidal rivers on the western shore. Good offshore fishing is sometimes found less than five miles off of Virginia Beach. One popular area is the Southeast Lumps.

FISHING METHODS: Bluefish can often be spotted when they surface and slash into schools of bait fish, slashing the water to a froth and drawing flocks of circling gulls. Any lure cast into the disturbance is almost sure to bring a savage strike. This is a delightful way to fish, but blues are caught by just about every method conceivable. Chesapeake Bay charterboat skippers grind up oily fish to create chumming lines to attract the fish. Then their anglers fish cut bait, crabs, and other bait or lures. Offshore anglers troll eel skins, spoons, and feathered lures. One of the nice things about bluefish is that they can be caught by just about any method the angler prefers. Keep in mind those sharp teeth, however, and use wire leaders.

CARE, CLEANING, AND COOKING: Bluefish should be placed on ice in a fish box or other container as soon as possible after being caught. Ideally, the ice should be crushed and some sea water added. Fortunately, most charter boats are equipped to give first-class care to the fish. Bluefish

The battling bluefish is one of the most popular saltwater fish in Virginia. (Photo courtesy of Virginia Beach Convention Bureau)

should be filleted. To do so, make a cut just behind the gills to the backbone and then along the backbone to the tail. To remove the skin, run the fillet knife between it and the flesh. Turn the fish over, and repeat the process. Bluefish are usually tastier if the blood line on the outer side of the flesh is removed. This can be done with the tip of the knife blade. For *Charcoal Grilled Bluefish* the ingredients are 2 pounds of fillets, about three dozen charcoal briquets, and ¾ to 1 cup of basting sauce. In addition to a charcoal grill and the briquets, a basting brush and a hinged wire hand grill are needed. As soon as the briquets become white hot, spread them evenly over the bottom of the grill. Wash and dry the fillets, and cut them into serving-size portions before placing them on the well-greased grill. Baste the fish with sauce, and grill them skin side down about 4 inches from the coals. Cook for 5 minutes, baste, and turn; cook for another 5 minutes, baste, and turn. Then cook until done, approximately 15 minutes or until the flesh flakes easily when tested with a fork.

The Croaker and the Spot ───────────────

Spot and croaker are the panfish of the salt water. They are the bluegills of the Chesapeake Bay, the tidal rivers, and the inshore waters. They are fun and easy to catch, but best of all, they are delicious on the platter. The spot is the more abundant of the two, but this has not always been so, and the roles could easily reverse. Both fish are taken by bottom fishing—from fishing piers, from bridges, from the beaches, and from private or head boats. Head boats are roomy fishing vessels that carry large numbers of anglers at so much per angler (or head). They offer an inexpensive way to enjoy saltwater fishing, and success is all but guaranteed. Spot and croaker are popular vacation fish because they are easy to catch, are reasonably abundant, and are in Virginia waters during the peak of the vacation season.

DESCRIPTION: Both the croaker and the spot are short, reasonably deep-bodied fish, gray and silver colored, with dark bars that run vertically and slightly forward down the flanks. Both also have underslung mouths. The spot, however, has a dark spot on its shoulder just to the rear of its gill covers and above and forward of its pectoral fins. The croaker does not have this spot. The two fish are easily confused, and to complicate matters they are often found in the same general area. The spot is the smaller of the two fish, averaging about a half pound, whereas the average croaker is probably closer to a pound.

HABITAT: Both the croaker and the spot are bottom fish. They seem to prefer depths of 10 to 25 feet, and they like bays and protected waters, but may occur just about anywhere in the Chesapeake Bay, the lower tidal rivers, and the inshore waters.

SEASONS: July and August are the peak months for both fish, but the croaker appears in Virginia earlier, often in early May. It is usually late June before spot show up. Both fish hang around into October.

GOOD WATER: Spot and croaker are all over the Chesapeake Bay, in the lower stretches of the tidal rivers, and croaker are found in the inshore ocean waters. Trying to name all of the possible places to fish for them would be just about impossible, but look for them in water 20 feet deep or less.

FISHING METHODS: Fishing for croaker and spot is bottom fishing at its best. It can be as simple as baiting up a hook with bloodworm or a piece of crab and lowering it to the bottom from any fishing pier along the Chesapeake Bay. Boat anglers often let their craft drift with the wind or tide and drag their baited hooks along the bottom until they catch a fish. Then the anchor is lowered carefully, and often moving never becomes necessary. Big catches of spot, particularly, are the rule rather than the exception. Light spinning tackle is just about ideal for this kind of fishing, and bottom-fishing rigs featuring two or more hooks are available at fishing piers, marinas, and tackle shops throughout the tidewater area. So is bait.

CARE, CLEANING, AND COOKING: Because of their relatively small size, spot and croaker are usually scaled and gutted, though they can be filleted. The fish are best scaled while wet. This is a simple task. Place the fish on a flat surface, grasp it by the tail (with a clamp if one is available),

Croaker and spot are the panfish of Virginia's salt water.

and work against the scales with a knife or a scaler—from the tail toward the head. Turn the fish over and scale the other side. Many anglers chop off the head, but the gills can be removed and the head left on for the sake of appearance, if desired. In either event, slit the belly; remove the viscera; and using the tip of the knife blade, remove the blood from along the backbone. Some remove the fins, others prefer to leave them intact. It doesn't matter. For *Barbecued Croaker* the ingredients are 2 pounds of croaker fillets, ½ cup of cooking oil, 1 tablespoon of salt, a dash of pepper, 1 minced clove of garlic, 1 cup of shredded cheddar cheese, 1 cup of fine bread, cracker, or cereal crumbs, and 1 cup of barbecue sauce. Combine the oil, salt, pepper, and garlic. Mix the cheese and crumbs, dip each piece of fish into the oil, and roll in the cheese-crumb mixture. Arrange the fish in a well-greased baking pan, and bake in hot oven, 450° F, 7 to 10 minutes. Heat the barbecue sauce, and spoon half the sauce over the fish. Keep the remaining sauce hot. Cook the fish an additional 5 minutes or until it flakes easily with a fork. Serve with the remaining sauce.

The Saltwater Trout —————————————

The saltwater trout—gray and speckled—are closely related fish that rank high among the saltwater anglers of Virginia. Both are actually weakfish, so named because hooks and lures tear so easily from their tender mouths. Trout is actually a misnomer, but they do resemble the freshwater trout of the mountain streams, hence the name by which they are best known. Both are fun to fish for, excellent table fish, and reasonably abundant in Virginia waters. Gray trout are popular among bottom fishermen, and they are caught from piers, in the surf sometimes, and from a

The gray trout is a favorite of Chesapeake Bay anglers.

variety of fishing craft ranging from charter and head boats to small skiffs. The gray in particular is a popular vacation fish and is often caught at night along the Chesapeake Bay Bridge-Tunnel. The gray trout is the northern species and the speckled the southern, but their ranges overlap in Virginia.

DESCRIPTION: The gray trout is a gray to silver fish, dark above and light on its belly. Dark spots or blotches cover its back and flanks. There is usually some orange in its lower fins. Its dorsal fins are separate, but together they contain 26 to 29 rays. The edge of its tail is slightly concave. The fish in Virginia waters average 2 to 5 pounds, but gray trout of 8 to 10 pounds are not uncommon. The speckled trout is much like the gray, with sides of subdued gray and silver and a dark back. It is a beautifully colored fish with dark spots along its upper sides, dorsal fins, and tail. The inside of the mouth of older fish may be yellow. Its average size is in line with that of the gray trout.

HABITAT: Gray trout are fond of channels, inlets, the surf, and rip tides, whereas the speckled trout favors sand shallows and mud flats and it will run into brackish water, though not to any degree in Virginia.

SEASON: Gray trout may enter Virginia waters as early as April, but it is usually late May or June before they are in the Chesapeake Bay in any abundance. The summer populations are strong, and the fish stay around well into October. Speckled trout usually appear near the entrances to Eastern Shore creeks in late May or early June, and from there they spread out. August, September, and October are peak months, and a few fish are caught well into November.

GOOD WATER: The Chesapeake Bay Bridge-Tunnel is one of the most popular spots in Virginia for gray trout, but it can be difficult to fish. Caution is recommended. Gray are actually caught just about all over the Chesapeake Bay and in the tidal rivers as well. They are also caught along the ocean side of the Eastern Shore—in the inlets and offshore. Speckled trout are probably most abundant in the shallow bays and inlets of the Eastern Shore, but they offer good fishing in Broad Bay and in Lynnhaven and Rudee Inlets. Other good areas include Craddock, Deep, Hungars, Nandura, Nassawadox, Occahannock, and Plantation creeks, and the Onancock, Pungoteague, and Saxis waters.

FISHING METHODS: Gray trout are caught primarily by bottom fishing, both from piers and boats. Drift fishing is popular along the ocean inlets to the Eastern Shore, but the fish are also taken in large numbers by fishing squid or peeler crabs on the bottom throughout the Chesapeake Bay and in the major tidal rivers. Anglers along the Chesapeake Bay Bridge-Tunnel take some good trout jigging artificial lures, often under the lights at night. Trolling along the bridge-tunnel is also popular, but tricky. Using bait-casting or spinning tackle to cast plugs or bucktails to speckled trout schooled or scattered in inshore waters or casting the same kinds of lures into the surf are the favorite ways to fish for this colorful trout. Many are also caught fishing the bottom from boats or piers, just as gray trout are fished for. One of the secrets to fishing for speckled trout is locating the drop-offs where the fish congregate.

CARE, CLEANING, AND COOKING: A very delicious fish, the trout tends to become soft quickly once it is removed from the water. Ideally, the fish should be placed quickly in a fish box or ice chest with plenty of crushed ice. In cool weather surf fishermen sometimes bury their catch in wet sand, but ice is the better choice. Trout can be prepared whole by scaling and gutting, or they can be filleted. To prepare whole, scale the fish by placing on a level surface and grasping it by the tail with a clamp or other tool. Remove the scales by working a scaler or knife forward against the scales. To gut, remove the head and slit the belly to remove the viscera, and then use the point of the knife blade to remove the blood along the backbone. To fillet, make a cut just behind the gills to the backbone and then work the knife along the backbone to the tail. Leaving a short section to the flesh and skin attached, flip the fillet over, and work the knife forward between the flesh and skin to remove the skin. Turn the fish over, and repeat the process. For *Baked Sea Trout* the ingredients are a 3-pound trout cleaned whole, 6 medium-size white potatoes, 4 onions, 1 tablespoon of butter, 3 slices of bacon, seasoned salt, and oregano. Salt and pepper the trout well, and place it in a pan. Place sliced onions and peeled potatoes around the trout, and sprinkle it with seasoned salt and oregano. Place the strips of bacon on the fish, and add ½ cup of water and butter. Do not, however, cover the trout with water. Bake with the cover on the pan until the potatoes are tender, then remove the cover and cook until brown.

The Flatfish _____

When flatfish are mentioned in Virginia, the reference is primarily to the summer flounder, though a scattering of winter flounder may appear in the state's briny waters. The flounder is a popular vacation fish, relatively easy to catch and delicious on the table. Many fish for this flatfish just for the delicious table fare it provides. Adding to its popularity is the fact that the fish is caught frequently from fishing piers, one of the least expensive ways to fish the salt water. It is also a popular head-boat quarry, and the head boats also offer an inexpensive approach to saltwater fishing. Add the facts that the fish arrives in Virginia

Pier fishermen take a lot of flounder.

waters in April to stay well into October, is reasonably abundant, and puts up a good fight, and you have all of the ingredients for a popular saltwater fish.

DESCRIPTION: The summer founder appears to rest on its side, but the fish leads a one-sided life, with its downside white because it rarely sees the sun or light. The upper side is a reddish brown, which serves as camouflage, and the color will vary slightly, depending upon where the fish lives. The flounder has a small mouth and eyes on the top and to the left of its head. It is a left-eyed flounder as opposed to some of the other flounders, which are right-eyed. Fins all but surround the fish's flat body, and the edge of its tail is uneven and slightly concave. There are numerous white spots on its body and fins, and the body is covered with tiny scales. The mouth is lined with tiny teeth. Some outsized fish may top the 10-pound mark, but the average summer flounder will weigh from 1 to 5 pounds.

HABITAT: Summer flounder are found in the inlets along the ocean side of the Eastern Shore, the Hampton Roads area of the Chesapeake Bay, and generally in shallow water throughout the lower Chesapeake Bay. Preferred habitat seems to be reasonably shallow water with a sandy bottom and good protection from the ocean or rough seas. Cuts in the bottom are favorite hangouts. Offshore wrecks in reasonably shallow water can also be productive.

SEASONS: While flounder arrive in Virginia waters in April and remain into October, May through August are the peak months for fishing generally.

Spring fishing can be fantastic, however, out of Chincoteague, Oyster, and Wachapreague on the Eastern Shore.

GOOD WATER: Some of the best flounder fishing of the long season comes in April or early May in the inlets and small bays close to Chincoteague and Wachapreague. Later all of the Eastern Shore inlets can be good. The Chesapeake Bay Bridge-Tunnel has become a popular spot for big flounder, and all of the Chesapeake Bay fishing piers offer good flounder fishing at various times during the summer. The Cape Charles–Kiptopeke area is generally good. In the Chesapeake Bay the best fishing is found on the lower reaches of the big body of salt water.

FISHING METHODS: Generally, flounder fishing means bottom fishing, and this applies to pier fishing, surf fishing, party-boat fishing and any other method by which the flatfish are caught. Drift fishing in a small boat is very popular, particularly in the Eastern Shore inlets. This means moving slowly with the tide using live minnows for bait, though strips of squid, peeler crabs, and other popular baits can be used. While drift fishing is probably the choice of the more experienced anglers, the fish can be taken by anchoring and fishing on the bottom. Though not used extensively, flounder can also be caught on small artificial lures worked slowly near the bottom.

CARE, CLEANING, AND COOKING: The flounder is a reasonably durable fish, and in cool weather the fish can be kept alive by placing them on a stringer and keeping them in the water—particularly during the cool months of spring and autumn. Ideally, however, the catch should be placed on ice in a fish box or an ice chest. Flounders are invariable filleted, and since the fish is all back and belly with no sides, the technique is slightly different from that used for other fish. A cut is made along the backbone from the top of the back down, followed by a horizontal cut from the gill covers to the tail. This is repeated on the other side of the backbone. Flounder fishing is a gregarious activity and done where there are always other fishermen. The best plan is to get some quick advice from an experienced angler before proceeding with the cleaning. The manager of a fishing pier, for example, or the mate on a head boat, can give a quick lesson on filleting a flounder. Seek this advice. The fish can also be cleaned whole by scaling and removing the viscera. Here again, the procedure is slightly different. Seek some local advice. For *Pan Fried Flounder* the ingredients are three pounds of flounder filets, one cup of white stone-ground cornmeal, shortening, three tablespoons of melted butter or substitute, the juice of two lemons, seasoned salt, and salt and pepper to taste. Place the cornmeal in a bag, and shake the fillets, a few at a time, in the bag. Heat the shortening in a large skillet until it is hot, but not smoking; depth in pan should be a quarter inch. Place fillets in skillet in a single layer, and leave until the edges look crisp and brown. Turn carefully to avoid breaking the fillets. When the fillets are crisp and brown on both sides, place them on a paper towel to drain. Drain quickly, and place them on a warm platter; brush melted butter over each fillet, season, and sprinkle with lemon salt.

The Cobia _____

A brown or creamy-colored fish with a flat head like a catfish, the cobia is the big game fish of the Chesapeake Bay. Cobia are not limited to the bay in Virginia, but it is there that they receive the most attention. Reasonably abundant one year and scarce the next, the cobia is an unpredictable and elusive fish that, when located, can offer some exciting fishing and a home freezer half full of tasty fish. Anglers are advised against going after these big bruisers of the bay waters with tackle too light for the task at hand. Fish of 50 to 100 pounds are always a possibility. The risk is losing light tackle that could be better used on

*The cobia is the big game fish of the Chesapeake Bay.
(Bob Hutchison photo)*

smaller, but still exciting, battlers. Tackle too light could mean the loss of a trophy fish. Match the tackle to the fish.

DESCRIPTION: The cobia has a spindle-shaped streamlined body that is typically brown, but cream-colored in some fish. Its head is flat; its tail is deeply forked; and usually a long longitudinal stripe runs the length of its body. The body has no scales. It can be a vicious fish that strikes hard and fights even harder. Cobia taken in Virginia waters are probably in the 25- to 30-pound range on the average, but 50- to 75-pound fish are fairly common, and the fish grow to over 100 pounds.

HABITAT: Cobia swim alone or in twos and threes, and sometimes among schools of other fish such as rays. It is an open-water fish, but often found near pilings. They like the shade of buoys, floating objects, rock piles, and other cover.

SEASONS: The cobia is a summer fish in Virginia waters, usually arriving in June to remain well into the summer. The Chesapeake Bay is about the northern extreme of its range. It may move out of the bay in late summer to offer offshore fishing in August and September.

GOOD WATERS: The traditional cobia fishing grounds are not always reliable because of the unpredictable nature of the fish. Over the years, however, good fishing has occurred in the Deltaville–Windmill Point area of the Chesapeake Bay, the Bluefish Rock waters, and the shoal waters off of Onancock Creek. Productive ocean waters have included Blackfish Bank and Winter Quarter Shoals. These waters may or may not produce cobia fishing in the future.

FISHING METHODS: Trolling big spoons or lures, giving particular attention to buoys or other objects in open water that provide cover and shade, is one or the more popular methods of fishing for cobia. The motion of the boat provides enough action, and the fish usually hook themselves when they strike. Fishing live eels or other bait is also popular. First, however, a chum line is created with ground menhaden or other oily fish. When a cobia takes an eel, it will grab it and make a fast run that will make the reel screech. When this happens, the angler restrains himself, lets the fish have the bait for awhile, and then sets the hook with a mighty heave. It is usually best to let the fish make the first run, halt, and then take off again before striking back.

CARE, CLEANING, AND COOKING: The cobia is a durable fish, and it will remain alive for awhile in a fish box. The box is the best place to keep the fish in the best condition for eating purposes. Add plenty of ice and run some sea water over it. The average family ice chest is too small for the average cobia, so other means must be used to keep the prize cool and fresh. Once back at the dock, the fish should be gutted as soon as possible and filleted or steaked. Even if filleted, a large fish will have to be cut into smaller portions. To fillet the fish, make a cut to the backbone just to the rear of the gill cover, twist the knife, and cut along the backbone to the tail, leaving a piece of skin attached to hold it; then flip the filet over, and cut forward between the skin and flesh to remove the skin. Repeat the process on the other side. To steak the fish, make a slit along the belly, and remove the viscera and blood along the backbone. Then using a sharp knife and meat saw, cut the fish into one-inch steaks. For *Cobia Steaks with Piquant Meringue,* the ingredients are 2 pounds of cobia steaks, 1 can of tomato paste, ⅓ cup of water, 2 tablespoons of lime juice, 2 tablespoons of Worcestershire sauce, 1 tablespoon of sugar, 1 tablespoon of cooking oil, 1 teaspoon of salt, and ⅛ teaspoon of garlic powder. Sprinkle the fish steaks with salt and pepper, and brush with the melted butter. Place the fish on a well-greased broiler pan, and broil until the steaks are slightly brown, or for about 5 minutes. Turn the steaks, and repeat the process. Beat the egg white until it is stiff, and fold in the remaining ingredients. Place the mixture on the top of the steaks, and brown in the broiler for about a minute.

The Drums _____

There are a pair of drums that create rumbles along the Virginia coast in the spring and fall. They are noticeably absent in the summer, but by then saltwater anglers have too many other exciting fish to demand their attention. The two drums are related, possibly distantly, but they have enough in common to be treated together here. The name *drum* comes from the noise the drums can make with their air bladders. Schools of croaking drum can sometimes be heard from above the surface of the water. Particularly popular among surf fishermen is the red drum, or channel bass. Black drum can also be caught in the surf, and mixed catches are possible. The two fish prefer much the same kind of water, but black drum are taken mostly from fishing boats. Both fish enjoy a good deal of popularity among anglers who have learned to fish for them.

DESCRIPTION: The black drum is a stubby, deep-bodied fish with high dorsal spines and a long dorsal fin. Barbels that drop from its lower jaw give it a unique appearance. In color it ranges from dark gray to coppery. Vertical bands may appear along its body. Its throat teeth are large and blunt. The fish will average 2 to 10 pounds, though 40- to 50-pound fish are fairly common. Top weights will exceed 100 pounds. The red drum is a more streamlined fish. It is not as deep-bodied as the black drum. Typically, its color is brass or coppery, though it may run toward grayish silver. A conspicuous black spot at the base of the tail helps identify it. It has a long head and lacks scales on its dorsal fin. Red drum may go to 80 pounds or more, but the typical fish will run 10 to 20 pounds. Small red drums are called puppy drums.

HABITAT: Both the black and the red drum like inlets, sandbars, channels between the bars, and the surf. The black drum may occur around pilings. Both fish often occur in schools. They also move into inshore waters and into deep holes to feed. Both are bottom feeders.

SEASONS: Black drum appear in Virginia waters in late April and leave in June. The black-drum fishing season is a short one, and May is the big month. Red drum, or channel bass, make their seasonal appearance in May and provide fishing inshore or in the surf into June, when they scatter out into the Chesapeake Bay. Sporadic catches are made through the summer, but the fishing drops off sharply in June. The middle of September and early October finds the fish in the ocean surf again as they migrate south for the winter.

GOOD WATER: For black drum the traditional spring fishing grounds are the north end of the Chesapeake Bay Bridge-Tunnel, Fishermans Island, Smith Island, Buoy C-10, the Cabbage Patch, the Kiptopeke–Cape Charles area, and inlets and bars on both sides of the Eastern Shore. The barrier islands surf, inlets, and bars are the place to fish for red drum in the spring, but the Virginia Beach fishing piers and surf can give up some action in the fall.

FISHING METHODS: Bottom fishing with crabs and clams is the usual way to fish for black drum. Fishing is usually done from an anchored boat, but some fish are also taken from the surf and from fishing piers. Surf and pier fishermen also fish the bottom with clams and crabs. Surf-fishing off the barrier islands is the most popular way to fish for red drum. Pieces of fish or crabs are the most popular bait, but they can also

The channel bass is a favorite of Eastern Shore surf fisherman. (Joel Arrington photo)

be caught casting or trolling spoons and jigs. In addition to trolling the inshore waters, some anglers sight-cast to fish they spot feeding in the shallow waters. Fall anglers fish off the ends of the Virginia Beach fishing piers.

CARE, CLEANING, AND COOKING: Since both black and red drum are caught in the cool weather of spring or fall, they are easy to keep in good condition until they can be cleaned for the freezer or the table. Ideally, they should be placed on ice in a fish box or ice chest. Surf fishermen often bury their catches in the sand and periodically pour sea water over them. Drum can be cleaned whole by scaling, removing the viscera, and steaked if they are large, or they can be filleted. To fillet, place the fish on a level surface and make a cut to the backbone just behind the gill cover. Turn the knife sideways and cut along the backbone to the tail, leaving a small strip of skin for the next step. Flip the fillet over and remove the skin by running the knife forward between the flesh and the skin. When cleaned whole, the fish should be scaled by rubbing the scaler or a knife blade forward against the scales, removing the head, and then slitting the belly to remove the viscera. The point of the knife should be used to remove the blood along the backbone. For *Corn Crispy Black Drum Fillets* the ingredients are ¼ cup of mayonnaise, 2 tablespoons of grated Parmesan cheese, 2 tablespoons of water, 1 teaspoon of instant minced onion, 2½ cups of coarsely crushed corn chips, and 1 pound of drum fillets with the skin removed. Preheat the over to 450° F, and line a 13 × 9 × 2 inch baking pan with heavy duty aluminum foil. Grease the foil. Combine the mayonnaise, cheese, water, and onion in a shallow dish or pie pan. Spread the crushed corn chips on a sheet of aluminum foil, and heat the foil-lined pan in the oven for 5 minutes. While the pan is heating, dip the fillets in the mayonnaise mixture to coat both sides lightly, and coat with the crushed corn chips. Place the fillets 1 inch apart in the hot pan, and bake for 15 minutes, or until the fish flakes easily with a fork.

The Sharks and the Rays _____

Of the 250 sharks found around the world, 22 make appearances inshore of the Gulf Stream between Cape Cod and Cape Hatteras. The most likely rays include the bluntnose, cownose, and roughtail stingrays. While most of the sharks and rays present some risk to man, the use of common sense can usually ward off injury. There are occasional shark attacks on anglers, divers, and swimmers, and the rays have venomous spines in their tails. The best defense against injury is recognizing the risks these marine animals present. Virginia sharks include the Atlantic angel, bull, dusky, hammerhead, mako, sandbar, spiny dogfish, and tiger. An

angler might encounter any of these fish, but the most important to the fisherman are the cownose ray and the mako and
tiger sharks. All are sizable quarries for the angler, and can be
included in the big-game fish of Virginia. Fishing for them is
exciting and demanding of tackle, and prepared properly for the
table they are all excellent.

DESCRIPTION: The mako is a vicious shark with tremendous power and
with large, sharp teeth that make landing it dangerous. Its scaleless body
is streamlined and blue on top, shading to silver below. When hooked,
it can clear the surface in spectacular leaps. Its average length is 5 feet,
but big ones will go well over 10 feet, and its weight may top 1,000
pounds. The tiger shark is also streamlined, with the upper lobe of the
tail being much larger than the lower one. It has deeply notched teeth.
Its body is blue to gray above and fades to creamy white below. Vertical
bars mark its body from head to tail. Usually less than 12 feet in length,
big ones may reach 18 feet or more. A 12-foot tiger will weigh from 700
to 1,000 pounds. The cownose ray is a diamond-shaped animal, very
flat, with eyes on top of its head, brown on top, and lighter underneath.
Its long tail can inject a painful wound if not handled with care. The
average weight of the cownose ray is 30 pounds.

HABITAT: The mako is an open-water shark, usually 15 to 20 miles offshore
in water 75 to 80 feet deep. While the tiger is also an open-water fish it
will venture close to shore, and fish are sometimes taken within a quarter
mile from the beach. Both sharks like bottom structures such as old
wrecks. While cownose rays spend much of the year in the ocean waters,
they move into the Chesapeake Bay and the tidal rivers in late spring.

SEASONS: Sharks enter Virginia's offshore waters in late May and remain
into October, while cownose rays move into the Chesapeake Bay in May
and leave in September.

GOOD WATER: While the mako shark is an offshore fish found in water of
75- to 80-foot depths, the tiger favors much shallower water during the
summer months that it spends off of Virginia's coast. Both are open-
water fish that favor bottom structures such as old wrecked ships. The
sharks are fished for in Virginia's offshore waters. The Chesapeake Bay
and the lower reaches of the larger tidal rivers offer good fishing for
cownose rays.

FISHING METHODS: Shark fishermen either drift or anchor over good bottom structure and fish three lines, one on the bottom, one near the surface, and one in between the surface and the bottom. Fresh fish such as
albacore, bluefish, mullet, spot, skate, and whiting are used for bait.
Sight casting to schools of feeding rays is the usual way to fish for cow-

Sharks grow big in Virginia's salt water. (Bob Hutchinson photo)

nose rays. Feeding rays will gobble up cut fish, clams, or squid. They are rarely hard to catch.

CARE, CLEANING, AND COOKING: While many Virginia anglers tag and release all they catch, sharks are excellent on the table. So are cownose rays, a fact that it took anglers a long time to accept. The smaller sharks, those of 100 pounds or less, are the best to eat. Large sharks are too big for the average fish box, though the smaller ones can be placed in boxes or ice chests and kept cool with plenty of ice. Cownose rays can be handled the same way. The larger sharks, if kept, can be watered down occasionally with sea water and handled as quickly as possible after reaching the dock. Large sharks are usually butchered and cut into steaks, but the smaller ones can be filleted. To fillet a cownose ray, first remove the two wings that contain the edible meat. Run the knife along the cartilage until a slab of meat is freed. Turn the wing over, and remove the other fillet. Repeat this process on the other wing. Finally, remove the skin from the four fillets by running the knife between the flesh and the skin. For *Charcoal Broiled Shark* the ingredients are 2 pounds of fresh shark meat, ¼ cup of melted butter or margarine, ¼ cup of lemon juice, ½ teaspoon of salt, ¾ teaspoon of paprika, and a dash of pepper. Cut the fish into serving size portions, and place on a well-greased grill. Combine the remaining ingredients and mix them well. Brush the fish with the sauce, and cook for 5 to 8 minutes approximately 4 inches from moderately hot coals. Baste with the sauce, turn the fish, baste, and cook for 5 more minutes. The fish is done when it can be flaked easily with a fork.

The Mackerels

The Boston, or Atlantic, mackerel kicks off the offshore fishing in Virginia when it arrives in an abundance in late March or early April. It isn't around for long, however, for the big schools of slashing bluefish are close on its heels to drive it north, to the delight of anglers along Maryland's coast. The Boston mackerel is a delightful little fish, fun to catch and tasty on the platter. The larger king mackerel arrives later, usually in June to add to the riches of the offshore fishing. Both the Boston and king mackerels travel in schools, with fish of the same general size often schooling together. These schools sometimes contain 1,000 or more fish. While the Boston mackerel moves into Vir-

Both king and Boston mackerel frequent Virginia waters. (© Zebco Consumer Division, Brunswick Corporation)

ginia waters and then on north, the waters off the North Carolina and Virginia coasts are considered the northern extreme of the king mackerel's range.

DESCRIPTION: The mackerels are slender, streamlined fish, and both have small finlets to the rear of the dorsal fins. The body of the king is a bit more slender than that of the Boston. The upper body of the Boston is a striking dark blue with irregular markings that run generally vertically down its upper sides. Its lower body is silver and free of markings. The slender body of the king mackerel is bright green or blue-green above and iridescent aluminum on the lower sides and belly. The king's deeply forked tail is an indication of its speed. Few ocean fish are faster than this mackerel. The average Boston mackerel caught off the Virginia coast will weigh 1 pound, but the fish sometimes grow to 6 or 7 pounds and stretches to 2 feet. The king is a larger mackerel that will average 5 pounds or more and can grow to over 50 pounds.

HABITAT: The mackerels are ocean fish of the open waters. They are offshore fish that approach the coast or move inshore in the spring. The king moves inshore with the Gulf Stream, and sometimes feeds along the edges of bays. The Boston frequents offshore bars.

SEASONS: The Boston or American mackerel moves into Virginia waters in late March or early April, and the peak of the fishing lasts just a few weeks, ending in the middle of May at the latest. The king comes later, usually with the start of the offshore fishing in June, and it remains in offshore waters into October.

GOOD WATER: While both mackerels are fish of the big ocean waters and spend most of their time offshore, both do move inshore at times. The Atlantic can be caught around inshore bars and reefs and even occasionally in the surf. Both fish are caught offshore in Virginia, with the Boston usually found only 5 to 7 miles out. Anglers normally go farther offshore for kings.

FISHING METHODS: Almost without exception, the mackerels in Virginia waters are caught by trolling. The first problem, of course, is to locate the fish. Boston mackerel can be located by diving birds or by slicks in the water indicating surface-feeding fish. The favorite lure for Boston mackerel is a plastic tube that resembles a worm. Red is the usual color. Flashing spoons and bright-feathered jigs are also good. It will also hit baits of various kinds, but most are taken on lures and by trolling. Trolling spoons or feathered jigs are also popular among those who fish for the king mackerel, a fish noted for its vicious strike and leaping ability. Leaps that clear the water by 10 feet are not unusual. The fish fight below the surface most of the time, however, making sizzling runs. A few anglers still-fish for them using live bait, but trolling is the most popular method. Wire leaders are essential to avoid losing lures and fish.

CARE, CLEANING, AND COOKING: The mackerel, Boston or king, should be iced as soon as caught, and since most fish are fairly small as ocean fish go, the average fish box or ice chest will accommodate them. For the very best taste, they should be cooked the day they are caught, but they can be frozen or even salted down—as the Boston is often handled commercially. The fish can be filleted or cleaned whole and steaked. To fillet make the cut just behind the gill covers to the backbone and then twist the knife and cut along the backbone to the tail. Flip the fillet over and remove the skin by running the knife forward between the flesh and the skin. Repeat the process on the other side. To clean whole, scale the fish if desired by working a knife or scaler against the scales and from the tail to the head. Actually, a better choice might be to steak the fish first and then remove the skin. In any event, open the fish by slitting the belly and removing the viscera, and use the tip of the knife to remove the blood from along the backbone. The mackerel is excellent filleted or steaked and broiled. For *Crispy Broiled Mackerel Steaks* the ingredients are 2 pounds of mackerel steaks, ½ cup of melted butter, ¼ cup of lemon juice, 1 teaspoon of salt, dash of paprika, 1 cup of crushed potato chips, ½ cup of crushed saltines, and lemon wedges. Place the steaks in a baking dish, and combine the butter, lemon juice, salt, and paprika. Pour the sauce over the fish, and marinate for 30 minutes. Turn the fish once in the process. Combine the crushed potato chips and the saltines. Remove the fish, but keep the sauce. Roll the fish in the crumb mixture, and place on a well-greased broiler pan. Drizzle the sauce evenly over the fish, and broil for approximately 5 minutes, or until brown, about 5 inches from the heat. Turn and broil for another 5 minutes or until the fish flakes easily with a fork. Serve with the lemon wedges.

The Wreckfish

Wreckfish does not designate a family of saltwater gamesters or a species. Instead it is an angling term referring to ocean fish that congregate around bottom structures, primarily old ship wrecks or artificial reefs. Virginia's briny waters hold an abundance of both. Sea bass and tautog are among the more popular of the wreckfish, but the colorful spadefish is growing in popularity. Other possibilites include amberjack, cod, flounder, porgy, and whiting. While the amberjack is not considered an edible fish, most of the others are among the best that the sea has to offer. Between them, the various wreckfish offer just about year-round

The tautog is one of many fine fish taken from old wrecked ships.

fishing in Virginia with the cod, and tautog active through the winter months.

DESCRIPTION: Generally, the wreckfish are not among the prettiest of the saltwater species, but beauty is a subjective quality, and the avid wreck angler can find beauty in even the dark and mottled sea bass. It is a fish that averages 1 pound or slightly over, has a single continuous dorsal fin with short spines, and is colored gray to almost black. The stockily built tautog is also dark, gray to almost black with some brown, and with irregular markings. It has sixteen dorsal spines. While it grows to over 20 pounds, the average Virginia fish is under 10. The stubby, deep-bodied spadefish could well be the most striking of the wreckfish, mostly because of the broad black bands that run vertically down its sides, all but circling its body. Against a silver body or background, they create a striking spectacle. These bands disappear quickly once the fish is killed. Spadefish average 4 to 6 pounds. A silvery body overlaid with blue and dusky fins edged with a pale yellow band also make the amberjack a handsome fish. It averages 10 to 15 pounds and is the largest of the wreck fish. The cod is a reasonably streamlined fish. The cod's color varies from brown to dark gray on its back to white on the belly. The edge of the tail of the cod is slightly convex, and it has three spineless dorsal fins, and single barbels below the chin. The cod will average 10 to 12 pounds. Both the porgy and the whiting are small fish, averaging 1 to 3 pounds, with the porgy the smaller. The porgy is a deep-bodied stubby fish, while the whiting is longer and more streamlined. The whiting also has a chin barbel. While the porgy is brownish on its back, the whiting is gray to black. The whiting is also a favorite of surf fishermen, though it is found around wrecks as well.

HABITAT: Although we are thinking of these fish primarily as wreckfish, they are also attracted to a wide variety of underwater objects, from bridge abutments to artificial reefs. Both the porgy and the whiting like sandy bottoms near the coast, while the sea bass and the tautog like rocks. The amberjack frequents offshore reefs.

SEASONS: Collectively, the wreckfish offer all-year fishing in Virginia, with the cod, and tautog the most popular winter species. The cod enters Virginia waters in December and remains until early March. There are two tautog seasons; the winter season hits its peak in December, with April and May being the top spring months. The sea-bass season is a long one, beginning in April and running into November. June is usually the peak month. Porgy, spadefish, and whiting are summer fish.

GOOD WATERS: Just about any wreck or artificial reef off the Virginia coast is likely to produce good fishing for most of the wreckfish. Sea bass are found near bottom structures well up the Chesapeake Bay and in some of the tidal rivers. Wrecks worth checking out include the *Cape Henry, Tiger,* and *Triangle* wrecks and the old concrete ships in the Chesapeake Bay. The islands of the Chesapeake Bay Bridge-Tunnel are also good. Other good spots include the V Buoy and the Plantation Light. The ocean waters off of Chincoteague offer good fishing for cod.

FISHING METHODS: Wreckfishing is a ripe area for head boats that anchor over the wrecks and allow the anglers aboard to bounce their baits off the bottom. There is nothing fancy or sophisticated about wreckfishing. Good baits include squid, crab, and even live bait such as balao, a favorite of amberjack anglers. Jigs and other artificial lures will also work. Cod fishermen like clams, but just about anything will interest this winter fish. Whiting like bloodworms, and flounder like live or dead minnows and strips of fish or shark belly. Spadefish often school near the surface above the wrecks, and when they do they can be caught on strips of jellyfish.

CARE, CLEANING, AND COOKING: Most of the wreckfish are excellent eating fish, among the best in salt water. They need the proper care from the hook to the pan, however, just as other fish do. Since most wreckfish are fairly small as saltwater fish go, they can be iced down in a fish box or an ice chest and kept cold and fresh until they are ready for cleaning.

Most of these fish are best filleted, a simple procedure that eliminates the need for scaling and gutting. To fillet the average wreckfish, place it on a flat surface, make a cut just behind the gills to the backbone, and then cut along the backbone to the tail. Leave a small piece of skin attached to the body, but flip the detached side over and work the knife between the skin and flesh back toward the head. This removes the skin. Repeat the process on the other side. To clean whole, remove scales, if they are present, by working a scaler or knife forward against the scales. Once the fish has been scaled, gut it by slitting along the belly and removing the viscera. Use the tip of the knife blade to remove the blood along the backbone. For *Sea Bass en Papillote* the ingredients are 2 pounds of sea-bass fillets, 1 medium green pepper sliced into rings, 1 medium onion sliced into rings, ¼ cup of melted butter or margarine, 2 tablespoons of lemon juice, 2 teaspoons of salt, 1 teaspoon of paprika, and a dash of pepper. Brush the fillets with half of the melted butter, and sprinkle with the seasonings. Position a plastic cooking bag into a baking pan and pour in the remaining butter, lemon juice, green pepper, and onion. Place the fillets in the bag on top of the vegetables. Close the bag, and puncture a few small holes according to the instructions with the bags. Bake for 20 to 25 minutes at 375° F. Slit the bag and serve, or arrange the fillets on a serving dish and garnish with cooked vegetables and fresh lemon wedges.

The Offshore Fish _____

Virginia's offshore fish include the mackerel, the sharks, and even the bluefish, as well as others discussed in previous chapters, but to the avid saltwater angler, offshore fishing means going far offshore near the edge of the continental shelf in the blue ocean waters. The offshore fish are not a family or a species, but rather a convenient grouping of fish that challenge anglers in those deep offshore waters. To many avid anglers of the briny waters, offshore fishing is the very epitome of angling, fresh or salt water. Nothing else can approach battling marlin, sailfish, and other popular saltwater species out there on that endless expanse of blue ocean water. Rarely is it inexpensive, though, by either private or charter boat. Here, we will forget the bluefish, the mackerel, and the shark and will give attention primarily to blue and white marlin, the real stars of the offshore waters. We won't overlook, however, the albacore, bonita, dolphin, sailfish, tuna, and wahoo. All contribute to the excitement and joy of Virginia's offshore fishing. Nowhere is the conservation ethic stronger than among offshore anglers who like to catch, tag, and release the fish they do battle with.

DESCRIPTION: White marlin outnumber blues ten to one in Virginia waters, but the blue marlin is a much larger fish and an unforgettable prize. The two fish are much alike in appearance. Together with the sailfish, they make up the billfish in Virginia. All have the long cylindrical spear, which is actually a prolongation of the upper jaw into a spear or sword. The upper sides of both marlins and the sailfish are vivid blue: dark on the blue marlin and sailfish, and greenish blue on the white marlin. The lower sides and belly of all three is light- or silver-colored. All also have vertical bands running from just behind the gills almost to the tail. The bands on the sailfish are formed by dots, while those of the marlins are solid, although lighter on the white marlin. The dorsal fin of the sailfish is much higher and saillike than that of the marlins. Size alone helps with the identification. The average sailfish will weigh about 30 to 35 pounds, with 60 pounds near the maximum. The white marlin is slightly larger, with an average weight of 30 to 50 pounds and the maximum near 100 pounds. The average blue marlin is a giant by comparison, 200 to 300 pounds, but growing to over 500. The false albacore, often called little tunny, is one of the smaller offshore fish, averaging about 10 pounds but growing to 20 or more. Its upper body is greenish or steel blue, shading to lighter tones toward its belly. Gray or yellowish bars run diagonally along its back and upper sides, and finlets follow both its anal and dorsal fins. Its body is watermelon shaped. Both the Atlantic and the oceanic bonita frequent Virginia waters. Both are full-bodied fish, though the Atlantic is the more slender of the two. On the Atlantic, dark blue bands run obliquely forward from its back to the middle of its sides. Its general color is light blue or silver. Finlets follow the anal and dorsal fins on both fish. The oceanic bonita is a silvery color, with tinges of brown or gold and dark brown lines that run horizontally along its body. The Atlantic, averaging 10 to 15 pounds, is the larger of the two bonita. The oceanic is a small fish that is usually less than two feet long and

The powerful blue marlin is one of the prizes of Virginia's offshore waters.

reaches a maximum weight of 20 pounds. Few fish are more colorful than the dolphin, or tastier on the platter. It is one fish that often goes into the fish box even when others are being tagged and released. Its color alone sets it apart, and no other means of identification are really needed. Though it may shift quickly from one color phase to another, there is usually a combination of blue, green, and yellow, covered with dark spots. Also distinctive are a long dorsal fin free of spines and a high, straight forehead. Its colorful body tapers rapidly from the front to a deeply forked tail. While the average fish may weigh only 5 pounds or so, the fish may grow to well over 60 pounds. Both bluefin and yellowfin tuna visit Virginia's offshore waters, but the bluefin is slightly the larger of the two. Both are watermelon shaped with finlets following both the anal and dorsal fins, and both have deeply forked tails. Both fish are dark blue on the back and upper sides, with the rest of the body being silver to white. The yellowfin's fins are yellowish, while those of the bluefin are more likely to be dusky with tinges of blue or green. The bluefin will average 20 to 40 pounds in Virginia waters, whereas the yellowfin is more likely to weigh in at 15 to 30 pounds. Both fish can top 100 pounds, however. Finally, there is the wahoo, a long, slender fish whose speed matches its build. It was seemingly built for speed. It's long, flat snout resembles that of a freshwater pike. Its back and upper sides are dark green or steel blue, with its lower sides being silvery or light green with some brown. Vertical bars ring its body from its head all the way to its tail. The average fish will weigh 15 to 20 pounds, but outsized fish may exceed 100 pounds.

HABITAT: All of the offshore fish generally follow the Gulf Stream north and south and are attracted to warm water. Most are pelagic, and they travel a lot—some in schools, such as the bonito, sailfish, and tuna. The marlin and wahoo are usually solitary fish, though the white marlin may school occasionally. The Atlantic bonito is usually near the surface, and the tuna often jumps a lot and creates surface disturbance as it moves in large schools.

SEASONS: June through October is the offshore fishing season in Virginia, a period when most of the more popular species are found off the Virginia coast.

GOOD WATER: The offshore fish are found along the continental shelf and over the first 40 to 60 miles of this underwater land of lumps and small hills. Bonito and tuna, however, may be found much closer to the coast. The Cigar, located approximately 60 miles southeast of Rudee Inlet, is one of the more popular fishing holes for both blue and white marlin.

FISHING METHODS: The offshore fish are taken by trolling from well-equipped charter boats or from private boats outfitted for the offshore waters. Most are equipped with outriggers that allow a party of four anglers to fish a pair of flatlines from the stern and an additional two from the outriggers. This is the typical marlin-fishing setup but is also used for most other offshore species. In fact, a single trip may produce dolphin and other species as well as marlin. The white marlin is far more abundant in Virginia waters than the blue, usually by a ratio of ten to one.

CARE, CLEANING, AND COOKING: The trend in fishing for marlin and sailfish is to catch, tag, and release. This is a growing conservation ethic. On the other hand, both marlin and sailfish are highly desirable as food fish, and injured fish are kept for table use. The dolphin, however, is the choice of most offshore anglers who want to take home some tasty fillets or steaks for the freezer. The tuna is equally desirable for table use. Most offshore boats are equipped with roomy fish boxes, and the fish kept can be iced down until they can be cleaned. Some anglers like to bleed tuna by cutting a small hole on the underside of the fish near the tail. It should be gutted and filleted or steaked as soon as possible and kept on ice until it can be frozen or prepared for the table. Tuna can be steaked by cutting vertically between the vertebrae. To fillet the fish, make two horizontal cuts, one along the backbone and the other midway down its body. This removes the meaty upper half of the body, the part best suited for table use. For *Tuna Steaks with Herbs* the ingredients are 4 pounds of ¾-inch tuna steaks, 1 tablespoon of grated onion, juice of 1 lemon, 6 teaspoons of melted butter, 1 teaspoon of salt, ¼ teaspoon of white pepper, ½ teaspoon of crumbled marjoram, 1 tablespoon of minced watercress or chives, and 2 tablespoons of minced parsley. Wipe the steaks with a damp cloth, and arrange them on a broiler rack. Mix all of the ingredients, pour them over the steak, and broil the steaks for 6 minutes on each side.

Other Saltwater Fish

Yes, there are other game fish in Virginia's waters, some very exciting ones such as the tarpon, and fine eating fish such as the sheepshead. Only their limited numbers keep them off of the popularity list. Others, such as the needlefish, pigfish, puffers, sea robin, and toadfish, are reasonably abundant, but small in size. They are of limited interest to most anglers. Most are edible, but several of the puffers are poisonous and should be avoided as food fish. Eels, the same kind discussed in chapter 19, "The Nongame Fish," are also found in salt water, but they too are of limited interest to anglers. Other saltwater fish may occasionally wander into Virginia waters, but the ones listed here are the major ones.

DESCRIPTION: The tarpon is by far the most exciting fish listed here. In fact, some anglers might object to it being listed in a catch-all chapter, but that is only because the great majority of Virginia anglers will never catch one in Virginia waters. It is an exciting leaping fish that is a joy to tangle with. Its body is long and slender and covered with large, thick scales. Its lower jaw extends forward of its upper one, and its body is silver with iridescent reflections. The tarpon will average 30 to 50 pounds in Virginia waters, but grows much larger. The sheepshead is a hand-shaped fish with a deep body and a concave tail. Vertical black bands run from its long dorsal fin to its belly. The fish averages 3 to 5 pounds, but grows much larger. The pigfish and the pinfish are deep-bodied, stubby fish like the sheepshead, with long dorsal fins and forked tails. The pig-fish has oblique lines on its upper body and horizontal ones along its lower body. Its color is blue and silver with touches of bronze. It is a small fish that may reach a foot in length, but rarely does. The pinfish is the true bream, the incorrect name often given freshwater bluegills. It is also called the sea robin. Its back and upper sides are olive green that turns bluish-silvery toward its belly. A large dark spot on its shoulder is very distinctive. It is a small fish that averages about 6 inches in length, but may reach 10. The needlefish, often called the sea lizard, is a long, skinny fish with prolonged jaws and needle-sharp teeth. Its color is silver, with some blue or green on the back. They may grow to 4 feet, but the average fish is much smaller. The toadfish is a brown, odd-looking crea-ture with mottled fins, a round tail, and a vicious bite. It is small, as is the puffer, a rough-skinned fish that can inflate its body when in danger. Both the toadfish and the puffer are small.

HABITAT: In Virginia the tarpon is found primarily in the shallow bays and inlets along the ocean side of the Eastern Shore. Virginia is the northern-most range of this normally tropical fish. Sheepshead are found around bottom obstructions and bridge abutments. Pigfish like rocky shoals and deep holes, whereas the pinfish is usually found around pilings in bays and inlets. Needlefish like warm water, and the puffer and toadfish like shallow water. The toadfish prefers muddy bottoms.

SEASONS: Tarpon move north with the Gulf Stream and are found in Vir-ginia from late June into September, with July and early August being the peak months. Sheepshead are found from May to October in Vir-ginia. Bream, needlefish, puffer, and toadfish are primarily summer fish.

GOOD WATER: The shallow bays and inlets along the ocean side of the East-ern Shore are the major fishing grounds of Virginia tarpon anglers. Sheepshead are found near many wrecks and other underwater obstruc-

Whiting are taken from the surf as well as from wrecks offshore.

tions in the mouth of the Chesapeake Bay. They also sometimes occur in the surf. The needlefish is often found near the surface in open water just about anywhere, but usually close to shore. The other fish are found in suitable habitat just about anywhere it occurs in Virginia waters.

FISHING METHODS: Tarpon, when they are spotted rolling on the surface, can be cast to and caught on a variety of spoons and other lures. Needlefish can also be caught on light spinning tackle with artificial lures, but the other fish listed are caught primarily by bottom fishing or fishing from bridges, docks, piers, or other platforms and from the surf.

CARE, CLEANING, AND COOKING: Tarpon are bony and generally considered inedible, but they are a fine game fish best played and released to fight again. That is the usual approach to tarpon fishing, though one may occasionally be kept for mounting. Puffers are best avoided as food when in doubt as to which of the species has been caught. Some, on the other hand, can be tasty. All of these fish are fairly small, and they can be kept alive in live wells or on stringers or placed on ice in an ice chest.

They can be scaled or skinned and cooked whole, or filleted, as is the croaker or spot. Any recipe appropriate for small saltwater fish such as the spot can be used for the sheepshead, pigfish, or pinfish. Needlefish can also be filleted and prepared in the same manner.

The anglers of few states are as blessed as are Virginians. The variety of opportunities is rich. At one extreme is the big blue marlin—500 pounds or more of pure dynamite 60 miles offshore in the blue Atlantic waters at the very edge of the continental shelf—and at the other is the tiny, but beautiful, brook trout up in a pristine mountain stream 5,000 feet above the ocean home of the marlin. Size alone does not make the difference. Mostly, it's a matter of individual angling tastes, and between those two extremes there is something for every fishing whim.

Appendixes

Index

APPENDIX A

Governmental Agencies

Virginia Department of Game and Inland Fisheries
4010 West Broad Street
P.O. Box 11104
Richmond, VA 23230–1104
Telephone 804-257-1000

Regional Offices

Route 1
Marion, VA 24354
Telephone 703-783-4860

209 East Cleveland Avenue
Vinton, VA 24179
Telephone 703-983-7704

1229 Cedar Court
Charlottesville, VA 22901
Telephone 804-296-4731

500 Hinton Avenue Chesapeake, VA 23323
Telephone 804-485-1126

U.S. Fish and Wildlife Service
5750 Charles City Circle
Richmond, VA 23231
Telephone 804-771-2481

Wildlife Refuges

Back Bay National Wildlife Refuge
4005 Sandpiper Road
Virginia Beach, VA 23456
Telephone 804-721-2412

Chincoteague National Wildlife Refuge
Box 62
Chincoteague, VA 23336
Telephone 804-336-6122

Great Dismal Swamp National Wildlife Refuge
Suffolk Post Office
Box 349
Suffolk, VA 23434
Telephone 804-986-3705

Presquile National Wildlife Refuge
P.O. Box 620
Hopewell, VA 23860
Telephone 804-458-7541

George Washington National Forest
Harrison Plaza
P.O. Box 233
Harrisonburg, VA 22801
Telephone 703-433-2491

Ranger District Offices

Deerfield Ranger District
2304 West Beverley Street
Staunton, VA 24401
Telephone 703-885-8028

Dry River Ranger District
112 North River Road
Bridgewater, VA 22812
Telephone 703-828-2591

James River Ranger District
313 South Monroe Avenue
Covington, VA 22426
Telephone 703-962-2214

Lee Ranger District
Route 1, Box 31A
Windsor Knit Road
Edinburg, VA 22824
Telephone 703-984-4101

Pedlar Ranger District
2424 Magnolia Avenue
Buena Vista, VA 24416
Telephone 703-261-6105

Warm Springs Ranger District
Route 2, Box 30
Hot Springs, VA 24445
Telephone 703-839-2521

Jefferson National Forest
USDA Forest Service
210 Franklin Road, S.W., Room 725
Roanoke, VA 24001
Telephone 703-982-6274

Ranger District Offices

Blacksburg Ranger District
Route 5, Box 15
Blacksburg, VA 24060
Telephone 703-552-4641

Clinch Ranger District
Route 3, Box 820
Wise, VA 24293
Telephone 703-328-2931

Glenwood Ranger District
Box 10
National Bridge Station, VA 24579
Telephone 703-291-2189

Mount Rogers National Recreational Area
Route 1, Box 303
Marion, VA 24354
Telephone 703-783-5196

New Castle Ranger District
State Route 615, Box 246
New Castle, VA 24127
Telephone 703-864-5195

Wythe Ranger District
1625 West Lee Highway
Wytheville, VA 24382
Telephone 703-228-5551

U.S. Army Corps of Engineers, Huntington District Office
502 8th Street Huntington, WV 25701-2070
Telephone 304-529-5395

John W. Flannagan Reservoir
Route 1, Box 268
Haysi, VA 24256
Telephone 703-835-9544

North Fork Pound Reservoir
Route 1, Box 369
Pound, VA 24279
Telephone 703-796-5775

U.S. Army Corps of Engineers, Norfolk District Office
803 Front Street
Norfolk, VA 23510-1096
Telephone 804-441-3500

> Gathright Dam and Lake Moomaw
> P.O. Box 432
> Covington, VA 24426
> Telephone 703-962-1138

U.S. Army Corps of Engineers, Wilmington District Office
P.O. Box 1890
Wilmington, NC 28402-1890
Telephone 919-343-4827

> John H. Kerr Reservoir and Dam
> Route 1, Box 76
> Boydton, VA 23917
> Telephone 804-738-6662

> Philpott Reservoir
> Route 6, Box 140
> Bassett, VA 24055
> Telephone 703-629-2703

Virginia Institute of Marine Science
Gloucester Point, VA 23062
Telephone 804-642-7000

Virginia Marine Resources Commission
2401 West Avenue
Newport News, VA 23607
Telephone 804-247-2200

Virginia Division of Parks and Recreation
1201 Washington Building, Capitol Square
Richmond, VA 23219
Telephone 804-786-2132

Virginia Division of Tourism
101 North 9th Street
Richmond, VA 23219
Telephone 804-786-4484

Virginia Saltwater Fishing Tournament
Suite 102 Hauser Building
968 South Oriole Drive
Virginia Beach, VA 23451
Telephone 804-428-4360

Shenandoah National Park
Luray, VA 22835
Telephone 703-999-2243

Blue Ridge Parkway
RR 3, Box 39D
Vinton, VA 24179
Telephone 703-982-6213

APPENDIX B

Conservation Organizations

Fly Fishers of Virginia, Inc.
P.O. Box 636
Richmond, VA 23205

Izaak Walton League of America
1800 North Kent Street
Suite 806
Arlington, VA 22209

Striper
P.O. Drawer 700
LaVergne, TN 37086

Tidewater Anglers Club
5204 West Lake Road
Virginia Beach, VA 23456

Trout Unlimited, Virginia Chapter
P.O. Box 7
Prince George, VA 23875

Virginia Anglers Club
P.O. Box 31494
Richmond, VA 23294

Virginia B.A.S.S. Federation
P.O. Box 511
Richmond, VA 23204

Virginia Beach Sharkers
P.O. Box 12025
Norfolk, VA 23502

The Virginia Coast Reserve
Brownsville
Nassawadox, VA 23413

Virginia Federation of Anglers
P.O. Box 735
Richmond, VA 23231

Virginia Wildlife Federation
4602 D West Grove Court
Virginia Beach, VA 23455

APPENDIX C

Government Publications

There is no charge for those titles for which no cost is specified.

Virginia Institute of Marine Science
Gloucester Point, VA 23062
Telephone 804-642-7164

Biology and Identification of Rays in the Chesapeake Bay.
Bottom-Dwelling Delicacy, the Flounder.
Chart of Fish Havens Off Cape Henry, Virginia. Cost $1.
The Chesapeake: A Boating Guide to Weather. Cost $1.
Chesapeake Bay Bluefish Recipes.
Cleaning and Preparing the Cownose Ray.
Don't Waste that Fish.
Handle With Care: Mid-Atlantic Marine Animals that Demand Your Respect.
   Cost $1.50.
Making the Most of Your Catch: The Bluefin Tuna.
The Marine Mammals of Virginia. Cost $1.
The Marine Resources Bulletin, a Quarterly Publication.
Mid-summer Treat: The Spot.
Nearshore Staple: The Croaker.
Offshore Delight: The Black Sea Bass.
Shark as Seafood.
Spring Resource: The American Shad.
Summer Bounty: The Bluefish.
Summer Special: The Seatrout.
Survey of Recreational Tuna and Marlin Fishing in the Mid-Atlantic.
Tide Graphs for Hampton Roads and Wachapreague.

Virginia Marine Resources Commission
P. O. Box 756
Newport News, VA 23607
Telephone 804-247-2200
Fishing in Virginia's Tidal Waters, Legal Sizes, Limits, Other Restrictions.

Virginia Saltwater Fishing Tournament
968 Oriole Drive, Suite 102
Virginia Beach, VA 23451
804-428-4360
Annual Virginia Saltwater Fishing Tournament.

Virginia Division of Tourism
101 North 9th Street
Richmond, VA 23219
Telephone 804-786-4484
Virginia Salt Water Sport Fishing.

Virginia Commission of Game and Inland Fisheries
4010 West Broad Street
P.O. Box 11104
Richmond, VA 23230-1104
Telephone 804-257-1000
Appomattox, James, New, Rappahannock, and Shenandoah River Canoe Guides.
Freshwater Fish.
Let's Go Freshwater Fishing in Virginia.
Virginia Fishing Regulations.
Virginia Official Highway Map, with boating access points and public fishing
    lakes on reverse side.
Virginia Wildlife. Monthly magazine, $7.50 per year.

APPENDIX D

Books on Fishing

The Art of Freshwater Fishing, by Dick Sternburg. Cy Decosse, Inc., 5900 Green Oak Drive, Minnetonka, MI 55343.

Baits, Rigs, and Tackle, by Vic Dunaway. Wickstrom Publishers, 2701 South Bayshore Drive, Suite 501, Miami, FL 33133.

Bass Fishing, by Bob Gooch. Tidewater Publishers, P.O. Box 456, Centreville, MD 21617.

The Care and Repair of Fishing Tackle, by Mel Marshall. Wincester Press, 220 Old New Brunswick Road, Piscataway, NJ 08854.

Cleaning and Cooking Fish, by Sylvia Bashline. Publication Arts, 5700 Green Circle Drive, Minnetonka, MI 55343.

Fish and Game Cooking, by Joan Cone. EPM Publications, Box 490, McLean, VA 22101.

Fishes of the Southeastern United States, by Charles S. Manock III and Duane Raver, Jr. North Carolina State University, Museum of Natural History, Raleigh, NC 27607.

Fishing Rigs for Fresh and Salt Water, Vlad Evenoff. Harper & Row Publishers, 10 East 53rd Street, New York, NY 10022.

Fly Fishing in Salt Water, by Lefty Kreh. Winchester Press, 220 Old New Brunswick Road, Piscataway, NJ 08854.

Largemouth Bass, by Don Oster. Cy DeCosse. Inc., 5900 Green Oak Drive, Minnetonka, MI 55343.

Muskie Mania, by Ron Schara. Henry Regnery Company, 180 North Michigan Avenue, Chicago, IL 60601.

Northern Pike Fishing, by Kit Berg. Dillion Pess, 500 South Third Avenue, Chicago, IL 55414.

Pan Fish, U.S.A., by Nick Sisley. Winchester Press, 220 Old New Brunswick Road, Piscataway, NJ 08854.

Practical Light-Tackle Fishing, by Mark Sosin. Doubleday & Company, Garden City, NY 11530.

The Scientific Angler, by Paul C. Johnson. Charles Scribner's Sons, 115 Fifth Avenue, New York, NY 10003.

Shad Fishing, by Boyd Pfeiffer. Crown Publishers, 419 Park Avenue South, New York, NY 10016.

Spinning for Trout, by Bob Gooch. Charles Scribner's sons, 115 Fifth Avenue, New York, NY 10003

Sportfishing for Sharks, by Frank Mundus and Bill Wisner. Macmillan Publishing Company, 866 Third Avenue, New York, NY 10022.

Sportsman's Guide to Game Fish, by Byron Dalrymple. Outdoor Life Book Club, P.O. Box 2000, Latham, NY 12111.

Walleye Fishing Today, by Tom Zenanko, Nystrom Publishing, Maple Grove, MI 55357.

The Ways of the Trout, by Leonard M. Wright, Jr. Winchester Press, 220 Old New Brunswick Road, Piscataway, NJ 08854.

World Record Game Fishes. International Game Fish Association. 3000 East Las Olas Boulevard, Fort Lauderdale, FL 33316-1616.

APPENDIX E

Maps of Value to Anglers

Maps Available from Alexandria Drafting Company, 6440 General Green Way, Alexandria, VA 22312, telephone 703-750-0510
Lake Anna
Back Bay Fishing Map
The Chesapeake Bay Map (36″ × 48″)
The Chesapeake Bay Map (24″ × 32″)
Chickahominy-Diascund Reservoirs
Chincoteague-Assateague Fishing and Recreation Map
Delaware Bay to Norfolk Canyon "Loran C"
Lake Gaston
James River Fishing Map
Kerr Reservoir
Lower Chesapeake Bay Fishing Map
Occoquan Reservoir
Potomac River Fishing Map
Rappahannock River Fishing Map
Smith Mountain Lake
Virginia Barrier Islands
Virginia Beach Fishing Map
York River Fishing Map

Maps Available from the Virginia Division of Mineral Resources, P.O. Box 3667, McCormick Road, Charlottesville, VA 22903, telephone 804-293-5121

State of Virginia Base Map, showing major streams and their tributaries.

U.S. Series Topographic Maps with scales of one inch to four miles. A set of 14 maps cover the state.

NOTE: Many of the fishing spots listed in chapters 6, 7, 8 and 9 are shown on the Alexandria Drafting Company maps.

Water Temperatures Preferred by Virginia Fish

Freshwater Fish

Largemouth bass	65 to 70 degrees
Smallmouth bass	65 to 67 degrees
Spotted bass	75 degrees
Bluegill	69 degrees
Green sunfish	87 degrees
Pumpkinseed	84 degrees
Rock bass	70 degrees
Other sunfish	60 degrees
Black crappie	70 degrees
White crappie	61 degrees
Brook trout	58 degrees
Brown trout	55 to 65 degrees
Rainbow trout	54 degrees
Chain pickerel	66 degrees
Muskellunge	63 degrees
Northern pike	63 degrees
Sauger	67 degrees
Walleye	67 degrees
Yellow perch	75 degrees
Striped bass	60 degrees
White bass	70 degrees
White perch	75 degrees
Brown bullhead	74 degrees
Channel catfish	80 to 85 degrees
Flathead catfish	84 to 88 degrees

American shad	66 degrees
Herring	54 degrees
Carp	84 degrees
Gar	92 degrees
Redhorse sucker	72 to 80 degrees
White sucker	72 degrees

Saltwater Fish

Albacore	64 degrees
Amberjack	65 degrees
Bonito	64 degrees
Croaker	86 degrees
Atlantic mackerel	46 degrees
Bluefin tuna	68 degrees
Bluefish	68 degrees
Blue marlin	68 degrees
Summer flounder	66 degrees
King mackerel	70 to 80 degrees
Red drum	71 degrees
Sailfish	79 degrees
Seatrout	72 degrees
Tarpon	76 degrees
Tautog	70 degrees
Wahoo	70 to 75 degrees
Weakfish	55 to 65 degrees
White marlin	70 to 80 degrees
Yellowfin tuna	72 degrees
Spot	80 to 90 degrees

APPENDIX G

Private Trout Waters Open to the Public for a Fee

Cedar Creek Valley Trout Farm State Route 600, Box 106 Maurertown, VA 22644 Shenandoah County Telephone 703-436-9395	Ponds
Cedar Spring Trout Farm Route 1, Box 296 Rural Retreat, VA 23468 Wythe County Telephone 703-686-4505	Ponds
Cripple Creek Trout Farm P.O. Box 723 Rural Retreat, VA 23468 Wythe County Telephone 703-686-4907	Ponds and stream
Graves Mountain Lodge Trout Pond Syria, VA 22743 Madison County Telephone 703-923-4231	Ponds

Montebello, Camping and Fishing   Ponds
Route 1, Box 3
Montebello, VA 24580
Nelson County
Telephone 703-377-2650

Orndorff's Rainbow Trout Farm   Ponds
Star Route
Maurertown, VA 22644
Shenandoah County
Telephone 703-436-3384

Freshwater Fishing Guides

Jim Abers P.O. Box 393 Boydton, VA 23917 Telephone 804-372-3557	Largemouth bass, striped bass, and other species in Buggs Island and Gaston lakes
Dan Beeber 202 Piedmont Avenue Colonial Heights, VA 23843 Telephone 804-590-2991	Largemouth bass, crappie, and other species in Lake Chesdin and Appomattox and James rivers
Blue Ridge Outfitters and Associates Route 1, Box 280 Covesville, VA 22931 Telephone 804-295-6589	Smallmouth bass and trout in James and other western rivers and streams
J. Wayne Dudley Route 2, Box 293A Vinton, VA 24179 Telephone 703-890-2641	Largemouth bass, striped bass, and other species in Philpott and Smith Mountain lakes
Danny H. Garrett Route 1, Box 33 Camelot Farms Hardy, VA 24101 Telephone 703-890-4331	Largemouth bass and striped bass in Buggs Island, Gaston, Philpott, and Smith Mountain lakes

Gene Hord
Route 3, Box 1382
Spotsylvania, VA 22553
Telephone 703-895-5608

Largemouth bass and
striped bass in Lake Anna

John R. Jones
Route 2, Box 309AA
Vinton, VA 24179
Telephone 703-890-2424

Largemouth bass and
striped bass in Smith
Mountain Lake

Bill Mathias
Route 1, Box 1025
Bumpass, VA 23024
Telephone 703-895-5114

Largemouth bass and
striped bass in Lake Anna,
Back Bay, the Rappahan-
nock and other rivers

Harry W. Murray
P.O. Box 156
Edinburg, VA 22824
Telephone 703-984-8126

Smallmouth bass and trout
in western Virginia streams

Tommy Lee Rogers
Route 2, Box 226A
Boydton, VA
Telephone 804-374-2244

Largemouth bass, striped
bass, crappie, and other
species in Buggs Island and
Gaston lakes

Dale Wilson
Smith Mountain Lake Guide Service
Route 2, Box 10
Huddleston, VA 24104
Telephone 703-297-5650

Largemouth and small-
mouth bass, striped bass,
crappies and other species
in Buggs Island, Gaston,
Leesville, and Smith Mountain lakes

Henry B. Wilson
Route 1, Box 263
Palmer Springs, VA 23957
Telephone 804-689-2811

Largemouth bass, striped
bass, and crappie in Buggs
Island and Gaston lakes

Charter Boats and Head Boats

Callao, Virginia

Captain John Klar   Telephone 804-529-6801
Pur Sand

Cape Charles, Virginia

Captain Ray Cardone   804-464-169
Miss Jennifer
Captain Charles Cook   804-331-1612
SST
Captain Bill Hamlin   804-331-2121
Anna D II
Captain Vernon Lewis   804-331-2058
El Pescadore
Captain Walter Lewis   804-331-2369
Nancy May
Captain Johnny Netherland   804-331-1013
Mako II
Captain Donald Stiles   804-336-5433
Elizabeth
Captain Monty Webb   804-331-3235
Quarter Note II

Chincoteague, Virginia

Captain John Abbaticchio   804-336-5722
Raider
Captain Arthur Birch   804-336-6584
Doris
Captain Billy Birch   804-336-5430
The Virginian
Captain Floyd Birch   804-336-6490
Regina S
Captain Donald Cherrix   804-336-6865
Betty J
Captain Norman Jester   804-336-6265
Roie Lee

Captain Lloyd Reed   Telephone 804-336-6669
Pinecove
Captain Walter Reed   804-336-5458
Eva K
Captain George Taylor   804-336-6374
Osprey

Cobbs Creek, Virginia

Captain Al Cothran   804-725-7510
Shutterbug
Captain John Willis   804-776-6790
Muriel Eileen

Coles Point, Virginia

Captain Roy Fagan   804-472-2903
Betty B

Deltaville, Virginia

Captain Buddy Allen   804-776-6694
Buddy Lee
Captain J. W. Blue   804-776-6283
Susan Carole
Captain Edmond Harrow   804-776-9661
Miss Ruth
Captain Walter Harrow   804-776-9656
Miss Nan
Captain Buck Hobeck   804-758-4036
Sweet Pea
Captain B. W. Miller   804-776-9885
Dawn II
Captain Howard McNamara   804-776-9786
Myrtle M
Captain Herbert Pinchefsky   804-358-8691
Pretty Lady
Captain Willie Q. Robinson   804-776-9684
Captain Q

Captain Edmond Ruark   Telephone 804-776-9394
Patty Lee II
Captain Bruce Walthall   804-776-9841
Snafu

Gloucester Point, Virginia

Captain Jimmy Payne   804-642-2786
Florence Marie

Greys Point, Virginia

Captain Dale Cook   804-758-2871
Michael C
Captain Oscar Fichett   804-758-2871
Sherwood
Captain William Glenn   804-758-2871
Bonita
Captain A. F. Henderson   804-758-2871
Modema
Captain John Holmes   804-758-2871
Miss Florence
Captain Edward Kidd   804-758-2871
Kathy
Captain John D. Miller   804-758-2871
John Boy
Captain Robert Miller   804-758-2871
Lee
Captain William T. Miller   804-758-2871
Wild Bill
Captain John Muse   804-758-2871
Ginger II
Captain Jim Thompson   804-758-2871
Locklies Lady
Captain James Thornton   804-758-2871
Miss Ruth
Captain Joseph Thornton   804-758-2871
Davea
Captain Ben Wormley   804-758-2871
Frances G

Hampton, Virginia

Captain Johnny Crabtree	Telephone 804-851-0511
After Five	
Captain Dee Johnson	804-877-2721
Reel Time	
Captain Lewis Wiley	804-723-0998
Miss Charlie	

Harryhogan Point, Virginia (Callao)

Captain Joe B. Moss	804-472-2358
SuBek	
Captain Robbie Robinson	804-529-7370
Fun	
Captain Robert Stoner	804-529-7370
Sweet Thing	
Captain Buddy Streat	804-529-7370
Dragon Fly	

Lewisetta, Virginia

Captain Herb Barnes	804-472-2486
Marnie	
Captain Warren Lowery	804-529-6276
Kathy L	
Captain Chuck Obier	804-529-6450
Miss Pam II	
Captain David Rowe	804-529-6725
Ken-Ma-Ray	
Captain Willie Thomas	804-529-7345
Willie B	
Captain Richard Woodward	804-472-3717
Playtime	

Little Creek, Virginia (Norfolk)

Captain P. T. Hodges	804-588-5401
Elmon	
Captain Charles Lovell	804-588-5401
The Screaming Eagle	

Captain Chuck Moltz   Telephone 804-588-5401
Gusto
Captain Harry Morgan   804-588-5401
Hustler, Jr.
Captain Paul Williams   804-480-2942
Grand Slam

Lynnhaven Inlet, Virginia (Virginia Beach)

Captain David Cassida   804-481-3513
Tammy Lynn
Captain Kevin Farley   804-481-7211
Big D
Captain Fred Keech   804-481-3513

Captain Alex Martin   804-481-7211
Capt. Alex
Captain H. B. Parker   804-481-7211
Kristen B
Captain Adrian Parks   804-481-3513
Klondike II
Captain Jim Rickman   804-481-3513
Cherokee
Captain Kevin Seldon   804-481-7211
Nancy Ann
Captain Charlie Ward   804-481-3513
Ballyhoo

Lottsburg, Virginia

Captain Frank Castle   804-262-2857
Meg C
Captain Maxwell Davis   804-333-3891
Cin-Cat
Captain Kelly Fisher   804-529-6645
Blurok

Oyster, Virginia

———————

Captain David Bell   Telephone 804-678-5498
Mary Page
Captain Jack Brady   804-331-2111
Little Bit
Captain Buster Hall   804-331-2044
Wanda-Fay

Poquoson, Virginia

———————

Captain Al Hartz   804-868-6821
Sandra

Quinby, Virginia

———————

Captain Archie Doughty, Jr.   804-442-6285
J-Mar
Captain Dorsey Fletcher   804-442-9738
Bobby
Captain Charles Roberts   804-442-7214
Timmy Kay

Reedville, Virginia

———————

Captain Roy Amburn   804-798-5183
Corsair
Captain Russ Burroughs   804-453-3525
Misty Blue
Captain Danny Crabbe   804-453-3251
Kit
Captain Rick DeVivi   804-453-7644
Skil Saw
Captain Wayne Hennage   804-493-8554
Challenger II
Captain Bill Jenkins   804-453-3513
Miss Cathy II
Captain Tabb Justis   804-776-9850
Captain Tabb

Captain Don L. Kuykendall   Telephone 804-580-7452
Don-El
Captain Wallace Lewis   804-453-5852
Hiawatha
Captain Don Markwith   804-224-7082
Midnight Sun
Captain Fred Maxwell   804-453-3491
Wahoo
Captain Walter Parkinson   804-224-0896
Big Dipper
Captain Fletcher Potts   804-453-4554
Mar-Chelle
Captain Ray Shepherd   804-462-7149
Southern Belle
Captain Otis Shook, Jr.   804-633-6045
Sherry Jerry
Captain Henry Smith   804-453-4474
Iona
Captain Danny Wadsworth   804-453-5325
Virginia Breeze
Captain Bob Warren   804-453-4639
Sunrise
Captain Richard Wood   804-222-8819
Sunchaser

Rudee Inlet, Virginia (Virginia Beach)

Captain Charles Alexander   804-464-2742
Poor Girl
Captain Albert Bonney   804-425-9253
Bros. Pride
Captain Billy Carroll   804-853-7361
Top Hook
Captain Chris Coverdale   804-428-1000
Abraxas
Captain Bob Cozzens   804-460-9443
Great Expectations
Captain Peter Dunthorne   804-425-9253
Hustler
Captain Tommy English   804-425-9253
Anxious

Captain Fred Feller   Telephone 804-425-9253
Sea Sport
Captain John Fleet   804-425-9253
Rhonda
Captain Don Griffin   804-484-3728
Kingfisher
Captain Richard Insley   804-425-9253
Red Fin IV
Captain Richard Insley   804-425-9253
Teaser
Captain Dennis Johnston   804-425-9253
Chelsea
Captain Linwood Martens   804-425-9253
Rainbow
Captain Mike Mayo   804-425-9253
Panacea
Captain Mike Merritt   804-428-6960
Ocean Atlantic
Captain Joe Monds   804-490-3581
Alibi
Captain Bill Moore   804-425-9253
Mel-O-Dee
Captain Andy Morris   804-425-9253
Bluewater
Captain Jeff Parks   804-425-9253
Miss Va. Beach
Captain Mike Peele   804-622-3624
Pinafore
Captain Rick Reid   804-460-3711
Iemanja
Captain Steve Richardson   804-425-9253
Smith Ltd.
Captain Jimmy Seeds   804-425-9253
Our Dream
Captain Marshall Smith   804-422-3499
Marsha Ann
Captain Wayne Smith   804-425-9253
Follow-The-Sun
Captain Milton Sykes   804-484-9334
Playmate
Captain Fred Tyler   804-425-6088
Four T's

Captain Joe West   Telephone 804-425-9253
Mar-Kim
Captain Don White   804-425-9253
Our Girl III

                                                       804-425-9253
Honey Bun
Captain David Wright   804-425-9253
High Hopes

Sanford, Virginia
——————————

Captain J. P. Cutler   804-824-5068
EC II

Wachapreague, Virginia
——————————

Captain Nat Atkinson   804-787-2105
Foxy Lady
Captain Bobby Cherrix   804-787-4576
Sea Fox
Captain Billy Colonna   804-787-4506
Cap'n Bill
Captain Tommy Colonna   804-787-4506
Sally Lee
Captain Gordon Eastlake   804-787-2105
Margo A
Captain Charlie Farlow   804-787-2105
Fern A
Captain Lawrence Jester, Jr.   804-787-2105
Nomad
Captain Zed Lewis   804-787-2105
Chips
Captain Frank McNeal   804-787-2334
Aqua-Gem
Captain Earl Parker   804-787-3341
Virnanjo
Captain Ray Parker   804-787-1040
Sea Bird
Captain Sam Parker   804-787-3070
Scorpio

Captain Greg Sutter *Rebel*	Telephone 804-787-2105
Captain Buddy Thornton *Lu-Lu*	804-787-2105
Captain Bobby Turner *Bonnie Sue*	804-787-2467
Captain Jimmy Wallace *Canyon Lady*	804-787-3272
Captain Kurt Wallace *Melissa D*	804-787-3272

Warsaw, Virginia

Captain William Garland *Hobo II*	804-333-4329

Fishing Piers

Chesapeake Bay Bridge-Tunnel

Sea Gull Fishing Pier	804-464-4641

Hampton, Virginia

Buckroe Beach Fishing Pier Resort Boulevard	804-851-9146
Grandview Fishing Pier South Bonita Drive	804-851-2811

Newport News, Virginia

James River Fishing Pier James River Bridge	804-247-0364

Norfolk, Virginia

Harrison Boat House and Fishing Pier   Telephone 804-587-9630
414 West Ocean Avenue
Ocean View Amusement Park Fishing   804-587-5276
Pier
Willoughby Bay Fishing Pier   804-588-2663

Virginia Beach, Virginia

Lynnhaven Inlet Fishing Pier   804-481-7071
Virginia Beach Fishing Pier   804-428-2333
15th and Ocean Front

Index